Social Work Ideals and Practice Realities

Social Work Ideals and Practice Realities

Edited by

Mark Lymbery and Sandra Butler

palgrave
macmillan

First published 2004 by
PALGRAVE MACMILLAN
Houndmills, Basingstoke, Hampshire RG21 6XS and 175 Fifth Avenue, New York, N.Y. 10010
Companies and representatives throughout the world

PALGRAVE MACMILLAN is the global academic imprint of the Palgrave Macmillan division of St. Martin's Press, LLC and of Palgrave Macmillan Ltd. Macmillan® is a registered trademark in the United States, United Kingdom and other countries. Palgrave is a registered trademark in the European Union and other countries.

ISBN 0–333–74976–6 paperback

This book is printed on paper suitable for recycling and made from fully managed and sustained forest sources.

A catalogue record for this book is available from the British Library.

10   9   8   7   6   5   4   3   2   1
13   12   11   10   09   08   07   06   05   04

Printed in China

Contents

List of Figures

Acknowledgements

We would like to thank all the contributors for their efforts in working on this group project. Their commitment to seeing the book to fruition was vital to our ability to shepherd it through to publication. Our thanks are also extended to Neil Fox and Tina Eadie for their support in the production of this book. Finally, we would like to acknowledge our appreciation to the inexhaustible patience shown by Catherine Gray.

Parts of Chapter 1 appeared first in Garrett, P. M. (2002) 'Social Work and the Just Society: Diversity, Difference and the Sequestration of Poverty', *Journal of Social Work*, 2, 2, 187–210; our thanks to the editor and to Sage Publications for permission to include this material. Chapter 2 was first published in modified form as Lymbery, M. (2001) 'Social Work at the Crossroads', *British Journal of Social Work*, 31, 3, 369–384; our thanks to the editors and to Oxford University Publications for permission to include this material. The main themes of Chapter 4 were first outlined in Badham, B. and Eadie, T. (2002) 'The voluntary sector and the state: a changing relationship', *Community Care*, 28 February–6 March, 34–36; our thanks to the editor and Reed Publishing for permission to include this material. Figure 6.2 in Chapter 6 was first published in Taylor, M., Hoyes, L., Lart, R. and Means, R. (1992) *User Empowerment in Community Care: Unravelling the Issues*, Studies in De-Centralisation and Quasi-Markets No. 11, SAUS Publications, University of Bristol, and is reproduced by permission of Policy Press. A version of Chapter 9 originally appeared as Canton, R. and Eadie, T. (2002) 'Practising in a Context of Ambivalence; The Challenge for Youth Justice Workers', *Youth Justice*, 2, 1, 14–26; our thanks to the editor and Russell House Publishing for permission to reproduce this article in an expanded form, and to the National Association for Youth Justice in whom copyright is vested.

List of Contributors

Bill Badham is now Development Officer for Active Involvement with the National Youth Agency, having been previously Programme Manager, Children in Communities, The Children's Society.

Peter Bates is a consultant working for the National Development Team.

Sandra Butler was Director of Social Work Studies in the Centre for Social Work, University of Nottingham until 2000.

Rob Canton is Principal Lecturer in Community and Criminal Justice at De Montfort University.

Marian Charles is Lecturer in Social Work in the Centre for Social Work, University of Nottingham.

Pam Cooke was Director of The Ann Craft Trust until 2001, and is now a freelance trainer and consultant.

Ann Davis is Professor of Social Work in the School of Social Policy and Social Work, University of Birmingham.

Tina Eadie is Senior Lecturer in Community and Criminal Justice at De Montfort University.

Rachael Ellis is a freelance trainer and consultant.

Paul Michael Garrett is Senior Lecturer in the School of Sociology and Social Policy, University of Nottingham.

Mark Lymbery is Senior Lecturer in Social Work in the Centre for Social Work, University of Nottingham.

Olive Stevenson is Emeritus Professor of Social Work Studies in the Centre for Social Work, University of Nottingham.

Jane Wilton is a manager in child care social work in Walsall Social Services Department.

Social Work Ideals and Practice Realities: An Introduction

Mark Lymbery and Sandra Butler

The basis of this book is that many social work practitioners and students in the United Kingdom experience a gap between the ideals that informed their entry into the profession – for example, a commitment to social justice and to making a difference in people's lives – and the realities of practice with which they are confronted. Practitioners are struggling to survive (let alone thrive) as they experience externally imposed changes to their work that move them away from their personal and professional values. The consequences of this are potentially shattering, as Jones (2001) has graphically depicted.

In the light of this, it is vital to give an account of how the goal of mere survival (which preoccupies many social workers, irrespective of setting) can be transformed into more constructive and empowering forms of practice. While social work is an inherently stressful occupation, it is the contention of this book that the main sources for discontent among practitioners are less to do with the nature of the job and much more concerned with the context within which it is carried out (Eadie and Lymbery, 2002). In taking full account of the social, political and organisational contexts of practice, the book aims to equip practitioners and students with the essential skills, knowledge and values of social work, enabling them to work effectively even within a climate that is perceived as hostile to many of these values. Our contention is that it remains possible for practitioners to respond

1

creatively and imaginatively to the problems that confront them. However, this is by no means easy. The public image of social work, while rarely good, has seldom been lower (Franklin, 1998); this contributes both to problems in recruitment and poor morale in practice. In addition, the conditions of practice have declined markedly (Balloch *et al.*, 1999; Jones, 2001), leading to a multiplier effect as far as increased stress and decreased job satisfaction are concerned. It scarcely needs to be said, but a dissatisfied and stressed social worker is unlikely to provide the best possible service for people in need.

Despite the book's recognition of this context, its tone seeks to be both realistic and optimistic. It is realistic in that it starts from an understanding of the genuine problems that confront social workers in practice. However, it is optimistic in that all contributors share a belief in the capacity of social work to make a positive difference to people's lives. The book contends that the balance between realism and optimism is a prerequisite for creative, engaged social work. In addition, it represents a considered argument in support of the maintenance and development of social work; in that sense it should be seen as a contribution to the active defence of professional social work practice (Munro, 2000; see also Harris *et al.*, 2000; Paylor *et al.*, 2000).

The context of practice

Social workers in the United Kingdom have experienced a period of great uncertainty for many years. While this changed in nature following the election of the 'new' Labour[1] government in 1997, along with its re-election in 2001, the sense of uncertainty did not disappear. The accession of a different government did herald significant changes to the system of welfare (usefully summarised by Savage and Atkinson, 2001), but other aspects of welfare policy – notably the continuing problems with the National Health Service (NHS) – have continued to take precedence over the interests of the personal social services. Indeed, many developments in social welfare provision that would previously have been categorised as 'social work' – largely located in the voluntary sector (see Jordan with Jordan, 2000) – have been presented as something entirely separate from the social work mainstream (Jordan, 2001; Garrett, 2002c; see also Butler and Drakeford, 2001).

---

[1] In this book the term 'new' Labour is used to denote the extent to which the policies of this government represent a discontinuity with past Labour administrations.

As a result, the role of social work within British society has become severely circumscribed, limited to a residual fulfilment of statutory functions (Jordan, 2001). Indeed, it has been suggested that not only is the term 'social work' rarely applied to the inclusive agenda of the Labour government, 'but when social work does emerge . . . it is almost always associated with the government in social authoritarian mode' (Butler and Drakeford, 2001: p. 14). This has forced social work into a narrow, reactive model, focused particularly on the limited role of assessing and managing risks (Jordan, 2001). The practice that remains is what Jones (1983, 2001) has defined as 'state social work'; from his analysis of the pressures and stresses that beset state social workers (Jones, 2001) it is clear that even this limited scope of work contains many difficulties for practitioners.

The uncertainty is compounded by the substantial organisational changes that have continued within social work. For example, the protracted process of local government reorganisation (LGR) had a major impact on both organisations and practitioners through the late 1990s (see Craig and Manthorpe, 1998). The ongoing establishment of unified care trusts will lead to the relocation of many social work functions – particularly, but not exclusively, in adult services – to the health service (Revans, 2001). The potential scale of this is enormous and could dwarf the upheaval generated by LGR (Millward, 2001). In addition, the joining together of health and social services at the organisational level is scarcely a partnership of equals, with continuing concerns regarding the power of health interests over social services (Bywaters and McLeod, 2001). Similarly, the establishment of youth offending teams (see Chapter 9 of this volume) following the implementation of the Crime and Disorder Act 1998, created an entirely new organisational structure – bringing together social workers, probation officers, police officers, among others – to deliver services to young offenders. Here, too, the distinctive contribution of social work can no longer be taken for granted.

The emphasis on the need for evidence-based practice in social care (see Sheldon and Chilvers, 2000) has also affected the context within which social workers operate. The core principle underpinning the development of evidence-based practice is simple: that practitioners and policy makers require the best quality of evidence in order to shape their interventions. This has been translated into the following proposition: 'Evidence-based social care is the conscientious, explicit and judicious use of current best evidence in making decisions regarding the welfare of those in need' (Sheldon and

Chilvers, 2000: p. 5). The essential tenets of this approach are hard to refute; as Sheldon (2001) has observed, few of us would wish to seek the services of doctors or dentists who had a limited idea of what actually worked in their practice! However, as Webb (2001) has demonstrated, the concept of evidence-based practice does need to be carefully examined. His critique is based on two related points – the extent to which evidence-based practice is based on positivist and empirical science, and the extent to which it represents an extension of technical rationality (see Blaug, 1995) into the social work field. Webb has suggested that both are antithetical to the essence of social work (but see Sheldon, 2001, for a witty rebuttal of Webb's argument). Indeed, following Schön (1987, 1991), commentators often emphasise that the professional decision making of social workers takes place where problems are inherently messy, confusing and not amenable to technical solutions (see, e.g., Parton, 2000; Taylor and White, 2000). However, it is tempting for organisations to construct their policies – and the practices that are required of social workers – *as if* the problems of human existence with which social workers grapple were capable of resolution through mechanistic, bureaucratised procedures. In addition, as Sanderson (2002) has observed, policy developments themselves are not always founded in evidence. As an example of this, the stampede to establish systems of intermediate care for older people (DoH, 2000b, 2001b) has been relatively little influenced by considerations of what actually works in this field.

Underpinning this range of organisational shifts is (yet another) review of the structure, purpose and function of social work education (DoH, 2000a). The last such paroxysm, which also took place in response to governmental concerns about the quality of practitioner produced from qualifying courses (Jones, C. 1996a), only occurred in the late 1980s. As Orme (2001) has indicated, the plethora of different organisations that will have a role in the planning, delivery and regulation of social work education is testimony to the fragmentation that characterises policy. In her view, the development of new, multidisciplinary organisations carries with it the danger that the unique character of social work could become subsumed into other categories of work.

The challenge for practitioners

Amid these contemporary debates about the direction of welfare and the organisational context of social work, it is all too easy for practitioners' achievements and daily realities to become submerged, with organisations constraining workers' creativity and freedom of expression (a theme that is further explored in Chapter 3). Successive governments have created huge pressure on social services organisations. While the general antipathy of the Conservatives to notions of public service has been replaced by the 'new' Labour predilection for regulation and performance, the outcome has been similar – organisations having to adjust to ever-increasing levels of external scrutiny. This has fostered an inherently defensive attitude by many organisations, constraining the activities of social work practitioners. The concept of 'defensive social work' was identified by Harris (1987); its basic proposition is that increased levels of external scrutiny and monitoring push social workers into making decisions more on the basis of what they can defend rather than what would be in a service user's best interests. The pressure on practitioners is to accept rather than challenge the limitations of policy because it is relatively easy to defend practice that follows the 'rules'. Being constrained to practise defensively has therefore caused social workers to feel powerless to act in ways that enhance the lives of those with whom they work (Jones, 2001). In addition, as the Victoria Climbié Inquiry makes distressingly clear, this can often mean that organisations devise and follow procedures that meet their own needs rather than the needs of the people for whom they were established to serve (Laming, 2003).

Needless to say, this experience does not accord with the values and ideals that most practitioners bring to social work. The pressure to conform to organisational requirements can severely compromise a social worker's ability to act in accordance with her/his cherished values. This book argues that it is essential for social workers to resist pressures to dilute the quality of their practice; however, it also recognises that practitioners need strategies that will help them to resist.

The book also concerns itself with the relationship between process and outcomes in social work, aiming both to legitimise good practice and to rebuild confidence within the profession. In that sense, it can be seen as part of the move to reclaim social work for the twenty-first century (see also Harris *et al.*, 2000; Paylor *et al.*, 2000; Parton and O'Byrne, 2000). The effect of all the political, social and organisational changes on social work has clearly been to erode its professional status (Munro, 2000). Indeed, the process skills of social workers have been devalued; as Marsh and Triseliotis (1996) have confirmed, many newly qualified practitioners experience problems with the stress on outcomes and the consequently reduced emphasis on the skills required for face to face work with service users. This book aims to help practitioners to integrate professional knowledge, skills and values within their practice through a reassertion of the importance of process within social work practice. The chapters in Part 2 examine how this can be achieved within the context and constraints of day by day activities.

The structure of the book

The book draws on three organising levels of analysis that will permeate the later chapters on social work practice. These are the *macro*, *mezzo* and *micro* levels (see Harris and Webb, 1987; May, 1991). The *macro* level refers to the broad social, economic and political factors that have impacted upon social work practice. The *mezzo* level refers to the organisational location of social work, and explores the way in which organisations have sought to manage their roles given the impact of social forces and government policies. The *micro* level focuses on the impact of both *macro* and *mezzo* analyses on direct social work practice. It is the contention of the book that social work practice can best be comprehended through an understanding of how the three levels interrelate. While the analysis on which the book depends is drawn from the authors' experiences within social work and social work education in England, the book should also be of relevance to readers elsewhere in the United Kingdom and beyond. Various authors (see, e.g., Rees, 1999; Lightman and Riches, 2000; Duncan and Worrall, 2000, in relation to Australia, Canada and New Zealand respectively) have pursued compatible lines of inquiry regarding the development of social work in these different countries. Indeed, the impact of globalisation on social work (charted in a special edition of the *European Journal of Social Work* in July 2000) has ensured that there is less variation between the experience of social work in different countries than once would have been the case, notwithstanding Pugh and Gould's warning (2000) of the danger of overemphasising these homogenising effects.

The book is divided into three parts. Part 1 presents the organising framework of the book through three chapters that explore in turn the *macro, mezzo* and *micro* dimensions noted above. In Chapter 1, Davis and Garrett reflect on the transformations that have shaped British society over the past two decades and their impact on the lives of those ordinary people who come into contact with social workers. They point out that while social work has a commitment to developing forms of practice that combat injustice, it is evident both that levels of inequality in society have increased and that social work has struggled to find a role in addressing issues such as social exclusion that are central to the Labour government's agenda for change.

The theme moves from the *macro* to the *mezzo* in Chapter 2, where Lymbery examines the various ways in which welfare organisations have adjusted to the pressures of social, economic and political change over recent years. He considers the growth of managerialism and bureaucratisation in social services organisations, and explores the extent to which this process is part of the de-professionalisation of social work. In reflecting on current policy developments he identifies alternative possible futures for social work – closer integration as part of formal multidisciplinary working arrangements, or fragmentation as the social work function is dispersed from unified social services departments (SSDs).

Chapter 3 draws attention to the *micro* level of analysis. Charles and Butler focus on the impact on social workers of the *macro* and *mezzo* level problems. They argue that processes of de-professionalisation have placed great pressures on practitioners, leading to a series of dilemmas that they face in attempting to integrate their values into daily practice realities. Utilising an analytical framework of control, influence and acceptance they explore the range of personal, professional and organisational devices that social workers can deploy to manage the complexities of their working lives.

Part 2 of the book includes six chapters that explore the effects of *macro* or *mezzo* themes on a particular area of social work practice. Each chapter utilises the analytical framework of Part 1 as a means of delineating the ways in which these aspects of social work have been affected by the social, political or organisational changes. From this basis, the various authors explore the potential of social workers to act positively and proactively, using a range of practice scenarios and examples that focus on the deployment of social work skills, knowledge and values. Therefore, all six chapters will link a *macro* or *mezzo* analysis to the *micro* level of practice. Chapters 4–6 explore the relationship between *macro* and *micro* themes, while Chapters 7–9 examine the interaction between *mezzo* and *micro* themes. All the chapters develop their themes through the use of practice scenarios, which illustrate the implications of their various arguments for social work practice.

In Chapter 4, Badham and Eadie explore the tensions inherent in the voluntary sector as it strives to 'hold on' to its cherished history while 'moving forward' to a new stage of development. They identify the risk to voluntary organisations in taking on activities that had hitherto been the province of the state, notably in the constraints that this places on the organisations' autonomy. However, they conclude that it is both possible and important for social workers in voluntary organisations to develop innovative and creative forms of practice. While there are threats to the sector arising out of closer links to government, they are clear that these can also present opportunities for development and growth. Chapter 4 is unique within the book in that it identifies the continuing place of social work within the voluntary sector, a consistent theme in the social work education provided at the University of Nottingham over the past decade (Anderson and Brady, 2002). This reflects a number of issues that characterise the sector within social welfare:

- It is important to remember that the genesis of social work in the United Kingdom was largely as a result of the pioneering work undertaking within the voluntary sector (see Chapter 2).
- Despite the gradual decline in the importance of the voluntary sector in the postwar period, from the 1980s there has been a resurgence of government interest in the sector. This has led to increasing numbers of social workers being employed within it.
- There is a vast range of social work activities carried out within the voluntary sector, encompassing a wide spectrum from individual work to collective forms of community action.
- As a result of these three points, we believe that the experiences of working as a social worker within voluntary organisations need to be separately analysed and addressed.

As testimony to the range of areas within which the voluntary sector is engaged, Chapter 4 addresses a variety of different practice scenarios. As Badham and Eadie demonstrate, the model that is advanced in the chapter can be used to analyse a wide range of practice settings.

Chapters 5–7 are linked by their focus on issues related to the development of social work with adults. For example, in Chapter 5 Bates and Butler explore a key issue in mental health work, notably the need to ensure that service users are empowered to have more control over their own lives. They start from a recognition that traditional psychiatric day services have failed to promote community inclusion effectively, leaving users of mental health services excluded from much of ordinary life. They conclude that the development of Community Connections programmes can help to draw users of mental health services back into the mainstream of society, while also providing a means to deploy the knowledge, skills and values of social work.

In Chapter 6, Cooke and Ellis turn their attention to issues relating to people with learning disabilities – their abuse and exploitation, protection and empowerment. Whereas the *macro* level explores how society treats learning disabled people, the *micro* level is concerned with individuals' feelings about their place in the community and the consequent implications for social work practice. Throughout the chapter, Cooke and Ellis examine the extent to which effective social work practice can simultaneously open up choices for people with learning disabilities, while ensuring that they are protected from abuse and exploitation.

In the first of the chapters exploring the *mezzo/micro* relationship, Lymbery in Chapter 7 charts the impact of community care policy on social work practice with older people. In examining the development of care management, he focuses on the extent to which the practice of social workers has become dominated by organisational and managerial priorities. While accepting the prevalence of managerialist thinking within this area of work, he also identifies ways in which social workers can reclaim the centrality of social work knowledge, skills and values in their practice. He concludes by arguing that practitioners can foster empowering social work with older people, despite these constraints, by their concern for the whole person in their social world.

Chapter 8 is the first of two chapters that examine issues related to social work with children and young people. Here Charles and Wilton explore the difficulties in managing the tension between ideal child care social work practice and the practice realities of bureaucratisation and proceduralisation. They demonstrate how essentially bureaucratic devices – in this case the assessment and action records from the *Looking After Children: Good Parenting, Good Outcomes* materials (DoH, 1995a) – can act as a vehicle for reflective practice in the hands of creative practitioners. They argue that the life chances and opportunities of children 'looked after' are enhanced through the establishment of satisfying relationships in which context child-centred, empowering work can then be undertaken.

In Chapter 9, Canton and Eadie explore the ambivalence that characterises policy towards young offenders, notably the tension between the desire to help and the need to be seen to punish. They

focus on the challenges for practitioners arising out of this ambivalence, paying particular attention to the organisational context in
which youth justice tasks are undertaken. They suggest that the
current managerialist ethos risks constraining reflective practice by
attempting, on the pretext of consistency, to prescribe both the what
and how of practice. However, through an examination of the need
for professional discretion in working with a young offender, they
demonstrate the knowledge, skills and values required in balancing
the tension between the prescriptions of the organisation and the
exercise of judgement in decision making.

Part 3 of the book consists of a single chapter. In Chapter 10,
Stevenson has the opportunity to shift attention from the here and
now – legitimately the concern of the remainder of the book – to
survey the prospects for social work in the future. Through deployment of the *macro/mezzo/micro* levels of analysis, she draws out core
themes with which social work must engage. In arguing for the maintenance of social work as an essential element of a co-ordinated
response to social problems, she suggests that there needs to be a
fresh consideration of the balance between the exercise of professional judgement and responsibility and the need for organisational
accountability.

Note on the production of the book

A core feature of this book is that all contributors have been closely
associated with the Centre for Social Work at the University of Nottingham; the material in the book has been largely generated from
the research and teaching activities of these people. Charles, Garrett
and Lymbery are currently core members of staff within the Centre,
where Stevenson is Emeritus Professor of Social Work, and where
Butler was formerly Director of Social Work Studies. Eadie moved
from the centre for social work to De Montfort University in 2003,
Wilton was formerly a tutorial assistant in the Centre, while Badham
maintained a long involvement with the MA/DipSW programme as
a member of its Programme Management Committee. Both Cooke
and Ellis were formerly employed by the Ann Craft Trust, which is
located within the Centre. Davis was an external examiner for the
MA/DipSW course, while both Bates and Canton were employed in
local social work agencies and contributed to the programmes from
these perspectives. This has ensured a genuine unity of approach
between contributors, who shared a vision of what the book is trying
to achieve.

Part I

1

Progressive Practice for Tough Times: Social Work, Poverty and Division in the Twenty-first Century

Ann Davis and Paul Michael Garrett

Introduction

> Poverty affects your self-esteem, your confidence, things like that, basically. You feel powerless . . . because you can't do a lot of things, you can't live up to the expectations that people have (Young person quoted in Beresford *et al.*, 1999: p. 90).

Social workers are faced daily with contested accounts of inequality and oppression from personal, cultural and institutional sources. Service users' desolate, angry and resilient testimonies about their lives collide with, and often contradict, official accounts of the kinds of people who use social services and why. Social workers' responses to perceptions of the failure, 'abnormality' or moral deficit of those accessing welfare services lie at the core of their practice. In mediating between the marginalised and the mainstream, practitioners find themselves negotiating with a divisive and unequal social order, and in so doing, need to orientate themselves to the power dynamics permeating British society (McDonald and Coleman, 1999).

This chapter, in providing the *macro* context for the book, examines the transformations that have shaped Britain over the past two decades, their impact on the lives of people who use social work services, and the challenges this creates for social workers. It begins by looking at social work's attempts to evolve frameworks for practice that are – at least rhetorically – informed by critiques of societal injustice (see also Hawkins *et al.*, 2001). Next, the discussion explores the more recent preoccupation with notions of difference and diversity. These ideas are then contextualised by reference to significant economic, political and cultural changes, their effects on the social construction of diversity, difference and division, and on the delivery of welfare.

The impact on the lives of those who have borne the costs of social and economic change is considered. The intensification of inequality has impacted upon the ways in which poverty and social exclusion affect those with the least power. Increases in social divisions have frayed the fabric of social life with dire consequences for many disadvantaged communities, groups and individuals. The events of 9/11 have also led to an increase in marginalisation and racism for many minority groups in Britain and elsewhere in Europe (Mann, 2001; see also 'Union leader sees racism in the "politics of fear"', *The Observer*, 23 February 2003). In this situation, the scope for, and possibility of, working for a more harmonious and inclusive society has looked precarious. In assessing the consequences of these changes for social work, the chapter highlights issues about its purpose and direction, raising some of the key dilemmas, contradictions and challenges that social workers face in practising in complex and hazardous social contexts. The chapter concludes by discussing the ways in which social workers can develop a more socially progressive practice.

Power, diversity, difference and division

In developing ways of working with service users that take account of the oppression and inequality they experience in their daily lives, social work continues to develop ideas and strategies associated with anti-discriminatory (Thompson, 2001), anti-racist (Dominelli, 1997; Williams, 1999) and anti-oppressive practice (Dalrymple and Burke, 1995; McDonald and Coleman, 1999; Dominelli, 1997). These paradigms are historically rooted in the professional value base (Forsythe, 1995) and in endeavours to engage with notions of power, diversity, difference and division. Nevertheless, social work, both institutionally and theoretically, did not evolve its 'critical' strategies in a social and economic vacuum. These formulations also reflect the longstanding struggles throughout Western civil and industrialised societies of a variety of social movements (Harman, 1988). These struggles include those for workers' rights and industrial democracy (Meiksins Wood, 1995) and the battle for women's equality (Segal, 1987). The fight for racial equality in the metropolitan centres and for national self-determination for 'subordinate' nations confronted by imperialism and neocolonialism (Dooley, 1998; Cohen *et al.*, 2002) has also been significant. More recently welfare service users' movements in Britain that are confronting oppression in relation to disability (Oliver, 1984; Campbell and Oliver, 1996) and mental health system 'survivors' (Rogers and Pilgrim, 1989; Sayce, 2000; Barnes and Bowl, 2001) have made their contribution to both theory and practice in this area.

However, the belief that social work can engage with issues of power and oppression and be part of a wider emancipatory project (Leonard, 1997) is vulnerable to critique in terms of both the lived experiences of users of social services, and social theory. In the late 1970s and the early 1980s, for example, a range of 'radical' texts identified social work as part of the capitalist state's 'ideological apparatus' – using Althusser's (1971) terminology (see, e.g., Simpkin, 1983; Jones 1983). These insightful and stimulating contributions were, however, perhaps too economically reductionist and insufficiently attentive to structural discrimination and oppression also rooted in patriarchy (Butler and Wintram, 1991) and racism (Dominelli, 1997). In addition, they paid limited attention to the realities of social workers' practice and the organisational context within which they worked. In part, this stemmed from an inadequate understanding of the power held by social workers. As Harris (1997: p. 33) points out, 'social work has always contained . . . strands of both liberation and constraint'. He argues that 'a certain ambiguity of focus [is] proper and inevitable, if uncomfortable for its practitioners, charged as they are with working with the dispossessed in an unfair system'. It is essential for social workers to comprehend the impact of power relations, as it is the exercise of power that structures society, shaping the social processes that influence our lives. Power is embedded in political processes as well as in personal encounters (Harris, 1997); a focus on its distribution and use in society directs attention to those groups which have the resources and influence to control others economically, ideologically and coercively.

In this respect, social work can be seen as one facet of what Foucault (1977) termed 'disciplinary power', which he associated with the evolution of the 'psy professions' (psychology, psychiatry, criminology) and the spread of new discourses and technologies of treatment and surveillance (see also Donzelot, 1979; Cohen, 1985; Rose, 1985). The locating of social work within the matrix of the 'disciplinary society' was highly influential within the social work academy in the 1980s and the early 1990s (see, e.g., Rojek, 1986; Webb and McBeath, 1989; Parton, 1991; Rodger, 1991). During the 1990s, however, the related social theory of postmodernism has superseded this particular theoretical perspective (see McBeath and Webb, 1991; Howe, 1994; Parton, 1994; Parton and Marshall, 1998). Social work's postmodernist turn has, however, had little impact on practitioners, and has been subjected to a number of cogent critiques from within (Peile and McCouat, 1997; Smith and White, 1997; Ferguson and Lavalette, 1999; Williams 1999).

In understanding the dynamics of power relations, social workers necessarily have to interrogate the meaning of diversity, difference and division. Williams (1996: p. 70), fusing feminist and postmodernist ideas, has offered an interesting conceptualisation of these terms (see also Ferguson and Lavalette, 1999). For her, *diversity* refers to 'difference claimed upon a shared collective experience which is specific and not necessarily associated with a subordinated or unequal subject position', for example, 'a shared language, nationality, regional origin, age, generation, sexual identity, marital status, physical condition and so on'. *Difference* refers to 'a situation where a shared collective experience/identity – say, around or combining gender, ethnicity, sexuality, religion, disability – forms the basis for resistance against the positioning of that identity as subordinate'. *Division*, meanwhile, means the 'translation of the expression of a shared experience into a form of domination. This is where a dominant subject position – for example, being white, British, heterosexual, a man – forms an identity which protects a privileged position'. None of these categories are fixed, or closed, and movement can take place from one category to another.

If this formulation is accepted as an adequate explanatory framework, it can be argued that social work's more progressive professional aspiration should centre on the celebration of diversity, the acknowledgement of difference and a commitment to fight division. Indeed, as Dominelli (1998) has argued, an application of the notion of diversity has the potential to challenge the basis of existing power relationships as well as the ways in which dominant groups define the position of others. It is therefore essential to the framework of anti-oppressive social work practice in contemporary Britain.

A willingness to wrestle with diversity and difference, even if only, at times, in a rhetorical way, informed the debates in the late 1980s, regarding social work education and training. (see Jones, C., 1996a, 1996b; Gledhill, 1989; Humphries, 1997; Patel, 1999). These debates, which were focused on the Central Council for Education and Training in Social Work (CCETSW) requirements for competence in social work practice, led to damaging charges of 'political correctness' being levelled at social work by politicians and the media (see Hopton, 1997, Campbell, 1998; Philpot, 1999). In part the exchanges reflected the determination of the New Right to 'close down' those spaces that provided for progressive debate and for a social work practice informed by a concern to combat structural inequalities. These attacks also evidenced a more generalised backlash against some of the gains made, for example, by feminism since the late 1960s (see Faludi, 1992; Phillips, 1997).

Ironically, these social work ruminations on power and difference – and its attempts to change institutional practices – received some validation with the publication of the Inquiry into the racist murder of Stephen Lawrence (MacPherson, 1999). In particular, the use of the term 'institutional racism' to capture the ways in which professional practice within the police and other state agencies, were shaped by assumptions and stereotyping, explicitly or implicitly endorsed by organisational cultures, echoed CCETSW's references to 'endemic racism' in late-1980s social work education literature (CCETSW, 1991).

While social work has made efforts to respond constructively to the realities of discrimination and oppression, its success has been limited. For example:

- It has made a patchy response to the challenges of 'race' and racism (Dominelli, 1997; Singh 1997).
- It has frequently gone no further than a sentimental fixation with the 'social aerosol' of empowerment (Ward and Mullender, 1991; Baistow, 1994/5; Humphries, 1996a).
- It has continued to make assumptions about white homogeneity and failed to interrogate white ethnicity (Roediger, 1994). This, for example, has been evidenced by the lack of understanding of anti-Irish racism and the failure, within the mainstream discourse, to integrate an Irish dimension into anti-discriminatory theory and practice (see Garrett 2000a, 2000b, 2000c, 2002a, 2003).

- Related to this, it has all too often lacked critical perspectives that encompass the users of social services (Dominelli, 1999).
- It has paid scant attention to social class (Jones, 1997, 1998).
- It has failed to respond adequately to mass poverty (Becker, 1997; Jones and Novak, 1999).

While some of these challenges facing social work are explored in the latter part of the chapter, we must first establish the nature of the transformations that have divided Britain and account for their origins. This historical landscape has played a substantial role in limiting social workers' practice when confronted by the constraints on choice, direction and the possibilities of life for the least powerful in society. There are several factors that have contributed to the economic, political and social change experienced within Britain since the 1980s. We focus, in the next section on some of these key economic and political factors that have impacted at a macro level on social work practice.

The 'market society': economic transformations

From the 1960s onwards, the United Kingdom experienced a marked contraction of its manufacturing base, more so than most comparable industrialised countries. In 1960, 36% of the UK population was employed in manufacturing; by the late 1990s this figure was 15% (HM Treasury, 1997). Worldwide changes to labour processes and the general culture of work (see Taylor, 1999) heralded, for some, a shift from a Fordist to a post-Fordist organisation of production (see Sivanandan, 1990; Amin, 1994; Taylor, 1999). Worldwide recessions in 1986 and in 1991 also contributed significantly to new patterns of employment. At their height, official estimates of those unemployed in the United Kingdom reached over three million, but this was experienced differentially by men and women. The labour market became characterised by an expansion of semiprofessional and professional jobs, the contraction of semi- and unskilled work and a sharp reduction in male full-time work.

The proportion of men who were low paid doubled between the early 1970s and the late 1990s (Walker with Howard, 2000). Associated with this has been the growth in the service sector, low paid, female and part-time working and 'casualisation'. These developments can also be viewed alongside 'globalisation' (Hall, 1991; Sivanandan, 1998/99; Bauman, 1999), and its apparently inexorable progress towards increased marketisation, privatisation and fragmentation of services. Consequently, a growing minority of citizens have 'lost out' because of the contracting, insecure, unregulated and low paid job market for unskilled workers. These changes systematically disadvantaged particular groups – including young people, older workers, those from minority ethnic groups and those adults whose ill health and disability have placed them at a disadvantage in the evolving and fragmented conditions of the labour market (Dean and Melrose, 1999; Walker with Howard, 2000). As Pratt highlights in her considerations of the position of the labour market position of Britain's minority ethnic groups, factors such as 'concentration in areas of high unemployment, youth, and lack of sufficient human capital or educational qualifications' have all contributed to the marked disadvantage of these groups in the labour market (Pratt, 2002: p. 95). Alongside this, note has to be taken of the fact that over one half of the nine million people of working age in Britain who have some form of disability are in paid employment.

The emergent forms of employment, particularly in service industries, have provided increased opportunities for women to enter paid work – albeit often on a part-time basis. This 'feminisation' of the labour market has had a significant impact on patterns of employment, with the proportion of women in paid work increasing from 43% in 1951 to 69% in 1998. Women now comprise 35% of full time employees and 88% of part time employees (Hakim, 1993; Callender, 1996). These changes are not evenly experienced, however; women from minority ethnic groups experience higher levels of unemployment than women in the population as a whole (Pratt, 2002). Tensions have developed in the workplace as well as in households, communities and wider society as a result of women's increased activity in paid employment, particularly in debates about the break up of the traditional family and the related diversification of family formation and structure (Millar, 1998; Office for National Statistics, 1998).

Government responses to this transforming labour market have included an attempt to curb pressures on resultant rising social security expenditure. The 1980s and the 1990s saw the collapse of the insurance base of unemployment benefit as well as cuts in benefit levels, the promotion of private forms of insurance, attempts to target benefits on those most in need through increasingly stringent means testing and the tightening of eligibility criteria for state assistance in cash and kind. Throughout this period, however, there was a steady expansion in expenditure on social security rising by 109% during

1973 to 1995. This reflected, in the main, the growth in people who were unemployed and lone parents claiming benefits (Evans, 1998; Walker with Howard, 2000).

A Joseph Rowntree Foundation inquiry, mapping patterns of income and wealth distribution in Britain in the 1980s and the 1990s, indicated that during the 1980s the poorest 30% of the population had been excluded from sharing in economic growth (Hills, 1995). Between 1979 and 1994 real incomes (after housing costs) of those in the poorest tenth of the population fell by 13%, the average rose by 40%, while the richest found their incomes rising by 63% (Oppenheim, 1997). A combination of changes in fiscal and welfare policy together with economic restructuring and demographic shifts over two decades have succeeded in substantially increasing the incomes of the richest in British society, with no evidence of wealth 'trickling down' to benefit the poorest. Between 1994–95 and 1999–2000, overall income inequality continued to increase (DSS, 2001).

Income inequality has grown faster in the United Kingdom since the 1980s than in any other industrialised country except New Zealand (Barclay, 1995: p. 14). Currently, around one in four of the population of Britain (just over 14 million people) live on income below half of the national average (DSS, 2001) and 4.3 million children live in households with less than half of the average income. This means that 34% of children (compared with 10% in 1979) live in poverty, a figure higher than in any other European Union country (Dean and Melrose, 1999; DSS, 2001). Among the poorest fifth of Britain's population there is a disproportionate representation of people from minority ethnic groups as well as women, children and older people (Amin and Oppenheim, 1992; Glendinning and Millar, 1992; Hills, 1995; Hickman and Walter, 1997; Pratt, 2002). These widening divisions and inequalities over the past two decades need to be understood as part of the continuing economic, social and cultural changes that have reshaped the contours of British society. In effect, there has been an undermining of many of the assumptions embedded in the postwar consensus about the role and remit of the Welfare State (Hill, 1993). For example, the attempts to restrain public expenditure in the face of growing social needs have had overwhelmingly negative consequences on the lives and environments of the poorest in society.

The transforming, fractured and divided socioeconomic landscape of Britain has, over the past two decades, compromised social cohesion and promoted social injustice (Craig, 2002). This has ensured that those who have the least experience deteriorating housing conditions (Modood *et al.*, 1997; Hills, 1998; Murie, 1998), poor educational experiences (Cohen *et al.*, 1992; Smith and Noble, 1995; Smith *et al.*, 1996) and ill health and disability (Townsend and Davidson, 1982; Walker and Walker, 1997; DoH, 1998b; Rainford *et al.*, 2000).

The economic changes that have transformed Britain have delivered little in the way of new opportunities and resources to its poorest citizens. The limited and fragmented responses received from public services have been delivered with messages about the stigmatised, dependent and inferior status of state welfare recipients. As Wilkinson (1996) has argued, the consequences of this are not just confined to those in greatest poverty. Growing inequality and the weakening of social cohesion reduces the quality of life in general, while increasing divisions reduce the capacity of any society to work towards common ends and to secure social justice for all.

'Thatcherism', of course, played a major part in shaping the political and welfare arenas in Britain in the 1980s. Thatcherism (Hall and Jacques, 1983, 1989) was a project characterised by a drive to erode the welfare state and to (re)privatise key parts of public services. It contained elements of economic neoliberalism and social neoconservatism (Gamble, 1994), associated with an increasingly coercive and authoritarian state (Scraton, 1987a; Hillyard and Percy-Smith, 1988; Hillyard, 1993). This was evident in the criminalisation of much trade union activity, as well as in other rhetorical and legislative interventions aimed at pathologising and marginalising a range of diverse groups (Gilroy, 1987; Scraton, 1987b). Indeed, the popular appeal and political reach of Thatcherism was, in part, rooted in this hegemonic strategy.

Walker and Walker's (1997, 1998) analysis of successive Conservative governments' approaches to welfare policy during 1979–97 identifies five related themes:

- The drive to cut public expenditure on social welfare.
- The need, through state subsidy, to privatise and extend market principles to areas of welfare provision.
- Attempts to replace universal social security benefits with selective means-tested benefits.
- Reduction of taxation to provide incentives and stimulate the growth in private and voluntary welfare provision.
- The centralisation of resource control in social welfare combined with the decentralisation of operational responsibility.

Underlying these themes were three assumptions. First, that the welfare state creates 'dependency' in those individuals using public welfare services; this has been constructed as economically and morally undermining for the individuals involved, as well as for society in general. Second, non-state forms of welfare – the family, self-help groups, private and non-government organisations – have been promoted as superior to state welfare provision, to be encouraged as major forms of welfare assistance. Finally, in order to sustain a culture of 'enterprise' in Britain, it has been argued that it is necessary to reward those with the highest incomes so that over time the fruits of enterprise will 'trickle down' (Walker and Walker, 1997). The working through of these assumptions and their associated policies had a major impact on those sections of the population, already identified, who found themselves increasingly marginalised from the mainstream in relation to stable employment opportunities and improving living standards.

'New' Labour and neoliberalism

It is sometimes easy to forget that Tony Blair came into office in 1997 with a commitment to addressing inequality and poverty in Britain (see, e.g., Piachaud and Sutherland, 2001). Furthermore, the election of his 'new' Labour administration was viewed by many as a time for hope in that the defeated Conservative Party – the architect of so many divisive social policies – was left in political disarray, while Blair appeared to have a mandate for a programme of social and economic reconstruction. Indeed, the language used in official documents connected to the ideas of user choice, equality, citizenship and empowerment that were part of progressive social work discourses in the 1990s. But there was, at the same time, a continuing privatisation of welfare, promotion of managerialism in social work organisations and removal of people from public welfare services. Blair's account of the direction of this programme spoke of moving from 'a welfare state that primarily provides passive support to one that provides active support to help people become independent' (Blair, 2000). To deliver on this agenda modernisation programmes were launched throughout the public services together with a range of initiatives designed to address inequality, poverty and social exclusion – among which were the Social Exclusion Unit, Health Action Zones, Education Action Zones, Sure Start, New Deal for Communities, New Deal for Employment schemes.

The ethos and priorities of the first two 'new' Labour administrations in reconstructing welfare services, heavily influenced by the former Clinton administration (Garrett, 2002b), have also echoed those of the Thatcher and Major governments of the 1980s and the early 1990s (Hall, 1994; Pilger, 1995; Jordan with Jordan, 2000; Craig, 2002). 'New' Labour's continued ideological and material investment in the superiority of a 'market society' is fundamental to this approach. The 'market society' is associated with 'a more general cultural . . . process which works to naturalize the generalized extension of market competition, and therefore market provision, into many different spheres of life as a kind of modern-day common sense – a measure of the spokesperson's "realistic" grasp of the modern world' (Taylor, 1999: p. 53). Highlighting the significance of such ideas is not, moreover, a retreat into abstraction because the 'market society' continues to shape, and destroy the lives of those who require social services.

'New' Labour's 'conservative modernity' (Hall, 1994: p. 26) can, at best, be associated with a tentative wish to 'lightly' regulate the market and to leave private capital to do whatever it will (Coates, 1996). Indeed, the shallowness and timidity of the 'new' Labour vision is, as Sivanandan (1998/99: p. 10) observes, reflected in its deployment of the term 'partnership' – a word frequently used in the discourse of social work – which appears to be applied as a loose synonym for privatisation (Glendinning *et al.*, 2002). Equally troubling for those working with some of the poorest and most socially marginalised has been the fact that single parents, disabled people, asylum seekers and refugees are the groups which have had to face benefit cuts (see, e.g., Smith, 1999). Coupled to this has been 'new' Labour's verbal attacks directed at, for example, 'addicts and winos' (see also Bullock *et al.*, 2001). The authoritarian and populist cast of social policy has been reflected in an array of measures, rhetorically directed at individual and community 'empowerment', that have resulted in the creation of a welter of enforcing top down bureaucracies, concerned with remoralising the poorest families and communities (see George, 1998; Garrett, 1999a; Jordan with Jordan, 2000; Craig and Taylor, 2002).

Significantly, given our concerns here, the resources and organisational structures for delivering 'new' Labour welfare agendas have been largely positioned outside mainstream social work agencies (see, e.g., Garrett, 2002c). Blair's government, with a stated mission to address social inequality and exclusion, has chosen not to re-engage the community work roots of social work practice in their enterprise. Indeed references to social work as a source of positive change by politicians and civil servants have visibly diminished. Despite the introduction of a new social work degree, 'social care' is the preferred term with social work being used 'for activities that are largely narrow and negative, concerning with rationing and risk assessment' (Jordan, 2001: p. 527; see also Jordan with Jordan, 2000).

Placed, as they are, on the margins of initiatives to combat poverty, social workers appear sceptical about the aims of 'new' Labour in combating 'social exclusion' perceiving them as a attempt by middle-class people 'to impose middle class solutions on people who do not want them' (Chadda, 1998: p. 1). Alongside fresh investments in modernising and New Deal agendas, the Blair administrations have continued, as did their Conservative predecessors, to exhort citizens to take 'active' responsibility for their own lives, and look to sources outside of public welfare to meet their needs and those of their dependants.

The cumulative effect of all these trends, within a context of 'globalisation', has been viewed by a number of commentators as deleterious for social work. Dominelli and Hoogvelt (1996) have specifically linked globalisation to changes in social work practice, contending that a shift to technocratic competencies is an inevitable consequence of the global dominance of markets. At the same time, notions of identity and difference are constructed within a framework of shifting and fluid geographical boundaries (see Bauman, 1999). In the national context, the debate about whether the establishment of devolved administrations in Scotland and Wales represents a 'breakup' of the United Kingdom is a reflection of these processes, as is the establishment of the Northern Ireland Assembly. Events such as these not only have material consequences, they also impact on key themes, such as diversity, difference and division, which, as we have observed, are associated with anti-oppressive social work theory. In seeking to address how these can be pursued it is important to listen to the accounts of those who have 'lost out' as a result of the transformations we have witnessed over the last twenty years (see also Alibhai-Brown, 2000).

'Differentness'; the human costs of inequality and division

> I was a walking zombie, outside a brave smile telling everyone I was fine, inside I was dead, numb – I couldn't sleep without pills. I couldn't get up

without pills. I didn't know the time of day or day of the week. I remember going down to the social one day, my sister had been nagging me to do it. I got to the door and turned round. I couldn't face the questions (34-year-old woman, with two children and a partner in prison, quoted in Davis, 1992: p. 79).

Much research conducted in the 1990s contains moving accounts of the impact of poverty on the lives of individuals and communities (see, e.g., Davis, 1992; Cohen *et al.*, 1992; Beresford and Turner, 1997; Beresford *et al.*, 1999; Dean and Melrose, 1999). These provide a powerful counterbalance to neoliberal and government claims about a growing and disaffected 'underclass', intent on using their 'welfare dependency' to construct deviant and destructive lifestyles, and subvert mainstream moral values (Murray, 1990). The voices of people who have shouldered the burden of growing inequality and social division testify to the hardship, undermining of physical and mental wellbeing, shortening of lives and constraints on aspirations and opportunities which face those managing their lives on the margins of society.

Walker's (1994) investigation of social assistance, which focused on the experiences of those living on state benefits in the early 1980s, provides a detailed description of the energy that benefit claimants devote to daily survival. She pointed out that only 12% of the 400 or so claimants she interviewed said that they were managing well on benefit level incomes. Most described themselves as doing no more than 'getting by' or 'getting into difficulties' with no spare resources to reserve for future planning and emergencies. She concluded:

> Claimants generally aspire not to continental holidays, nor a car, but merely to be able to choose the kind of food they would like; meat, fresh fruit and vegetables, to keep warm and pay their bills without worry, to give their children the same things that their friends have, and not to panic when they have to pay for the school trip or buy a packet of soap powder. *Most of all, claimants want dignity and that means being full members of the society in which they live* (Walker, 1994: pp. 78–9; emphasis added)

Morris' (1993) study of three groups of unemployed workers and their households in northeast England in the late 1980s and Kempson's (1996) work on low income families – employed and unemployed – in Britain in the early 1990s reached similar conclusions. The aspirations and lifestyles of these citizens did not fit the pattern of a deviant and dangerous 'underclass'. Hopes to acquire jobs, decent homes and an income that would cover the bills were the dominant concerns of those interviewed in these studies. As Kempson (1996: p. 163) notes, 'social and economic changes that have benefited the majority of the population . . . have made life more difficult for the growing minority', placing even modest aspirations out of their reach. Her detailed scrutiny of the managing styles of households on incomes below half the national average pointed to the resilience and resourcefulness that goes into making ends meet.

Managing the thin line between surviving and 'going under' takes a tremendous mental and physical toll. Poor people, whose accounts of their lives reveal the energy, strength and ingenuity, required to survive. Anxiety, fatigue, boredom, anger, depression and desperation are among the feelings that colour the hard work of surviving (Beresford *et al.*, 1999). People are all too aware of the costs that are exacted from them in terms of their mental and physical well-being as well as their personal and social relationships. Yet, as Holman (1993), Kempson (1996) and others (Kempson *et al.*, 1994) have pointed out, the predominant view among people living in poverty is that they must strive against these odds to try and secure 'ordinary' and 'decent' lives for themselves and those for whom they have responsibilities.

The gap between this goal of an 'ordinary life' and the experience of poverty and social exclusion shapes people's perceptions of themselves and what is possible for their families. As Middleton *et al.* (1994: p. 150) comment in their study of families in poverty:

> Poorer parents attempt to teach their children about the limitations of the family budget from an early age . . . Yet it is equally apparent that many parents must be unable to meet the financial demands which participation involves, however skilfully they juggle resources or however great their sacrifices. Their children begin to experience the reality of their 'differentness' at an early age. Parents try to teach them not to ask, and the children begin to learn how to go without.

This experience of the 'differentness' which inequality and poverty constructs echoes across many studies which have drawn on service users' perceptions of their lives. Barham and Hayward (1991) researched the experiences of 24 people with a diagnosis of schizophrenia claiming welfare benefits and living mostly in 'hard to let' public housing. In this study users of mental health services talked about their feelings of marginalisation, lack of social networks and the limits placed on their social lives and aspirations. These consequences – often interpreted by professionals as symptoms of mental illness – are understood in a fundamentally different way by those receiving services. It is poverty, combined with a diagnosis of schizophrenia, which were the major forces shaping their self-perceptions and views about their futures. As Henry, an unemployed man in his late thirties, living in a ground-floor flat of a rundown council estate, explained:

> With schizophrenia, you are not living, you are existing. There is not a lot of future for you but you come to terms with the illness . . . I am labelled for the rest of my life . . . I think schizophrenia will always make me a second class citizen. I go for an interview for a job and anxiety builds up . . . I haven't got a future. It's just a matter of waiting for old age and death (Barham and Hayward, 1991: p. 98).

Experiences of poverty and powerlessness combine with the differences that are socially attached to such experiences as illness, disability, 'race' and ethnicity, sexuality, gender and age to amplify and shape the divisions within society, conceptualised earlier by Williams (1996). For example, Millar (1996) has discussed the impact of poverty on women, while Amin and Oppenheim (1992) and Pratt (2002) have highlighted how ethnicity and poverty are interrelated. In numerous publications, Walker has insisted that deprivation and poverty are disproportionately experienced by older people (see, e.g., Walker, 1993). Similarly, Oliver and Sapey (1999) note that poverty is a major problem for many people with disabilities, while Davis and Hill (2000) demonstrate how this is also experienced by people with mental health problems. Being affected by these structural inequalities, people develop negative views about their place in the social order, how they are perceived and valued by others. Deprivation influences the way people think about the world and their ability, or otherwise, to control their lives. It also plays a significant part in the relationships formed with others, thereby contributing to social exclusion.

The user-centred literature provides painful testimony of the ways in which contact with state welfare services can create a sense of stigmatised low worth and a lack of self-respect intensifying the original difficulties which users experience. In Beresford *et al.*'s study (1999), poor people repeatedly referred to the stigma attached to being poor, and described how this infused their relationships with others including the staff of welfare agencies. Such voices are a reminder to practitioners of the work that needs to be directed at acknowledging and challenging the messages that poor people receive about themselves when they have contact with 'the welfare' and when they hear and read media accounts about welfare recipients. These contribute powerfully to a devalued and excluded sense of self in a society that has become increasingly focused on achievement through paid employment, the market and independence from collective state provision.

Challenges for social work in the twenty-first century

The growth in inequality, and the resultant increase in social divisions, raises substantial practice and policy dilemmas for social workers and their employing agencies. Social workers deliver services that have increasingly become 'programmes for the poor' (Becker, 1997: p. 160). As Schorr (1992: p. 8) observed, 'the most striking characteristics that clients of social services have in common are poverty and deprivation. Often this is not mentioned . . . Still everyone in the business knows it'. The impact of poverty continues to underpin a range of social work concerns. In the late 1980s, for example, Bebbington and Miles (1989) found that 20% of children becoming 'looked after' were from families in receipt of Income Support. Freeman and Lockhart's research suggests that, in some areas, 75% of children entering the 'looked after' systems are from families relying on benefit (in Becker, 1997: p. 111). More generally, 'nine out of ten users of social services are claiming benefits and the majority are on means-tested benefits reserved for the poorest' (Becker, 1997: p. 88). Many of those in receipt of benefits – and *not* in receipt of benefits – have also been trapped in debt (Ford, 1991).

Specific benefit policy changes have also had an impact on the users of social services. Particularly prominent here was the scrapping of 'single payments' (Cohen and Tarpey, 1988) and the introduction of the Social Fund under the Social Security Act 1986 (Stewart and Stewart, 1986; Craig, 1989). Central government constraints on welfare expenditure in the face of increasing poverty and deprivation have resulted in cuts in the financial assistance made available by SSDs. This has been managed by the introduction of increasingly stringent 'classifications of needs', used to ration access to services and resources (see also Hillyard and Percy Smith, 1988; Jordan with Jordan, 2000).

Perhaps there is some recognition from social work bodies of the need to challenge this policy and practice context. Social workers in training were required by CCETSW, their accrediting professional body until 2002, to demonstrate competence in assisting 'people to have control of and improve the quality of their lives' and be 'committed to reducing and preventing hardship and disadvantage for children, adults, families and groups' as well as intervening 'in the lives of people whose life chances may have been adversely affected by poverty, ill health, discrimination and/or disability' (CCETSW, 1991: p. 18). The General Social Care Council (GSCC), which replaced CCETSW in 2002 as a regulator of professional education and practice, has issued a code of practice for social care staff that states that social care workers must 'protect the rights and promote the interests of service users and carers' (GSCC, 2002). In outlining what this involves the GSCC mentions the following:

- 'Respecting, and where appropriate, promoting the individual views and wishes of both service users and carers';
- 'Supporting service users' rights to control their lives and make informed choices about the services they receive';
- 'Promoting equal opportunities for service users and carers';
- 'Respecting diversity and different cultures and values'.

In seriously pursuing these aspirations, social workers have to develop their practice in the face of political, professional and organisational environments that have systematically denied the impact of structural adversity and the resulting issues of social justice (Becker, 1997; Jordan, 2001; Cohen *et al.*, 2002). However, there has been little evidence in the social work literature during this period to suggest that alternatives are possible (Walker and Walker, 1998; Jones, 1998; Garrett, 2002d). If social workers choose to explore the possibility of developing challenging stances within the current policy and organisational environment then they need to look beyond the individual 'case' experiences which comprise their workloads. They must engage in a consideration of how the economic, social and political forces that have shaped British society over the last two decades have impacted generally as well as particularly on the lives of those using social work services.

More generally, however, social workers have been expected to respond to the damaging consequences of the deepening divisions in British society by 'targeting' what is available on those deemed to be at most risk while also meeting the standards set by central government for service delivery (DoH, 1998a). This process is seen at its most regulatory and restrictive in relation to community care (Langan, 2000). The personalised forms of investigation and intervention, which are the hallmark of social work, increase its potential to become a prime means for determining the allocation of not only scarce welfare resources, but also blame to the poorest in society. Internalising feelings of 'failure', poor people in contact with social work services risk becoming labelled as the 'losers' and 'scroungers' portrayed by government and the media as a drain on, if not a danger to, society (Bullock *et al.*, 2001). Traditional social work has often colluded with the notion that the problem of poverty is a consequence of the *behaviour* of those who are poor, rather than of structural economic inequalities (Jones, 1997). Furthermore, as Becker (1997) points out, there is little evidence that social workers and their departments are doing anything substantial about the impact of poverty.

Constructing progressive social work and 'democratic professionalism'

The dilemma for social work is deceptively simple; how can a more 'progressive' form of practice be developed within the 'conventional' (Mullaly, 1997) understandings of social work dominant in Britain? Social workers are exhorted to demonstrate through their practice that society is concerned to protect those unable to participate fully as citizens. Simultaneously, as we have observed, they find themselves enforcing targeted, residual and controlling responses to those deemed to have failed to act as 'responsible' and 'self-sufficient' citizens.

Simply embracing the concepts of 'diversity' and 'difference' is hollow if unaccompanied by an understanding that the creation of inequality and division is a direct consequence of economic and state processes. Social workers seeking to develop progressive practice responses sensitive to service users' needs as shaped by dimensions of structural inequality must, therefore, operate at two interrelated levels. This type of work could be achieved in four key ways:

- *Networking and campaigning against poverty.* Since social workers deal with the consequences of poverty more than any other professional group (Davies, 1995), they are uniquely placed both to publicise its effects and to develop creative responses (see also, however, Dean, 2001; Patterson, 2001).
- *Emphasising the importance of welfare rights within social work.* Since income deficiencies are core social work problems (see

Bateman, 1999) social workers must be committed to providing welfare rights advice and/or referring to specialist agencies.

- *Undertaking and facilitating critically focused research on the impact of poverty.* Such research, carried out collaboratively with users of services, has the potential to produce professionally and politically useful and accessible 'snapshots' and locally based audits (see, e.g., Barnes *et al.*, 1999).
- *Working with those living with the impact of poverty.* As Beresford and Croft (in Becker, 1997: p. 164) note, there is a strong case for this on 'philosophical, practical and political grounds'. They assert that 'it makes possible more relevant, effective and participatory analysis and research', resulting in more successful and appropriate campaign methods and results.

However, it is insufficient for social workers simply to intervene structurally – a central weakness in the prescriptions of much 'radical' literature of the 1970s and the 1980s (see Jones, 1983; Simpkin, 1983). In short, social workers must simultaneously operate at structural and individual levels, since *macro* intervention on its own is unhelpful to an individual facing immediate problems (Cohen, 1975; see also Davis, 1991). In grappling with this problem, Cohen suggested that social workers should identify goals to govern their individual work, alongside objectives to impact upon wider social inequalities. At the core of a social work that is directed at challenging rather than accommodating to the status quo must also be a set of values embracing social justice. In recognising the oppressive forces that construct difference so as to create division, and which ignore diversity, these values can help to sustain the capacity for practitioners to enable marginalised citizens to develop alternative, creative responses to their difficulties, building on their capacities and skills.

Perhaps, it is unsurprising that only a minority of practitioners have sought to challenge the status quo, given the ambiguity of the social work role. However, there is evidence that some have succeeded in delivering valued alternatives to the traditional mainstream. In a study of disabled people's experiences of being assessed for community care services, some specialist social work teams were identified as practising in ways that were not constrained by the rigid risk and resource driven guidelines of their departments. These social workers shared values based on the social model of disability and were supported by managers convinced that assessments should be the basis for a collaborative response to users' own agendas, drawing on resources outside as well as inside their agencies. Their ways of relating to service users, as well as their assessments, were also highly valued by those in contact with them (Davis *et al.*, 1997). Holman (1993) and Lister (1998) have similarly highlighted the success of practitioners who have drawn on poor people's expertise and resources. This work has stressed the importance of working closely with families through supporting and engaging with neighbourhood groups. For example, listening and learning from group members' accounts of engaging with welfare organisations becomes a prime means of developing new responses, promoting 'inclusion', and expressing belief in co-operation and mutuality. All of this is vital if, as Holman (1998: p. 71) indicates, income, wealth and power are to be redistributed.

Social workers must therefore understand and embrace issues of power, diversity and difference in ways that work *for* rather than *against* the capacities of service users to strive for increased control and direction over their lives. This involves practising to facilitate integration rather than the exclusionary control that serves to perpetuate social division. In moving in this direction, social workers need to recognise the varied and interrelated forms of inequality faced by service users. New ways of thinking about, and working with, these changing patterns of inequality and exclusion will emerge where social workers are actively reflecting on the relationship between the individual and the structural. This is essential in combating the widespread acceptance of individualistic explanations of social problems, and in developing a practice that can work with individual agendas for change, informed by structural understandings (Davis, 1991).

Mindful of Hugman's (1998a) view, we can maintain that collectivities, such as Black, Irish, gay and lesbian and women's groups, representing interests wider than social work, can promote change and creativity in welfare practice. While recognising the difficulties of establishing such approaches in current political and organisational climates, Hugman argues that they still have the potential to provide a vital external reference point for those striving to intervene in ways that challenge prevailing practice and political orthodoxies (see also Leonard, 1997; Healy, 2000). In confronting power relations and 'social exclusion', Hugman (1998a) also makes a case for the development of a democratic professionalism in social work to counter market consumerism. He emphasises the importance of developing openness in order to increase service users' awareness of the range of options available as well as defining what is non-negotiable in welfare encounters. This approach, he argues, opens up the possibility of creating a critical and reflexive professionalism where social work skills and knowledge are rendered more accessible to service users (see also Lymbery, 2001).

Conclusion

In this chapter, we have attempted to deconstruct some of the strands of structural inequalities and divisions woven into the recent history of British economic and social policies. In offering a critique, we have emphasised that notions of diversity and difference are rendered meaningless if they are not grounded in a recognition of mass poverty and its relationship to social class, racism, sexism, heterosexism, ageism and disablism. The 'sequestration of poverty' (Garrett, 2002d) from social work has been challenged and we have endeavoured to provide a combination of collective and individual practice agendas, which can translate into meaningful, localised activity at the *mezzo* and *micro* levels. These activities and ideas might help to reconnect social work with more enlightened forms of practice and emancipatory politics.

More fundamentally, of course, embracing issues of power, diversity and difference in ways that contest oppression poses a challenge to mainstream social work practice and theory. This is because we seek recognition of the contradiction between the 'core' social work values of care and compassion and the current emphasis on assessment, rationing and welfare enforcement. In short, social workers must address the tensions generated by increasing inequality and division by seeking to widen the possibilities for inclusion and participation of those citizens bearing the brunt of social change and neoliberalism. The next chapter, in shifting the focus to the *mezzo* level, introduces the organisational imperatives that have constrained social workers in achieving their emancipatory ideals, and deepens the discussion about the paradoxes inherent in contemporary social work practice.

2

Responding to Crisis: The Changing Nature of Welfare Organisations

Mark Lymbery

Introduction

The purpose of this chapter is to chart the organisational changes that have affected social work within Britain. While the chapter concentrates particularly on the experiences of welfare organisations within England and Wales, the political, economic and social context within which these changes have taken place is applicable to the rest of the United Kingdom, as are the organisational responses that are described. The focus of the chapter is at the *mezzo* level, although there are also short summaries of issues that derive from the *macro* analysis of Chapter 1, since these contribute to a fuller understanding of this chapter in its own right.

Since social work practice cannot properly be analysed without considering the settings within which it is located (Howe, 1991), the chapter starts by summarising the development of social work within its organisational framework from the late nineteenth century to the present day. It then demonstrates that a range of economic, political and social factors have affected social services organisations in recent years. The extent to which the subsequent organisational changes have altered the conception of social work's professional status is then considered. The chapter concludes by reflecting on the ways in which the discretion and autonomy of social workers could be enhanced, and the reasons why this might improve the quality of social work received by service users and carers.

The development of social welfare organisations

Most British histories of social work trace it to three sources, the Charity Organisation Society (COS), the Settlement movement and some of the work of staff employed under the Poor Law (Young and Ashton, 1956; Woodroofe, 1962; Seed, 1973; Crowther, 1981; Jordan, 1984). A distinction can be observed between the growth of social work within the voluntary sector and the development of the administrative apparatus of the Poor Law. The voluntary sector's purpose was to help people avoid destitution, whereas state's role was to provide residual support for those who were already destitute (Lewis, 1995). Both sectors held similar views concerning how help was to be constructed, and the moral dangers inherent in providing generous levels of assistance. Care by the family was a crucial underpinning of the work of voluntary organisations and the state, and stress was laid on the stigmatised nature of a family in receipt of charity. The parallel involvement of the family, voluntary organisations and the state is evidence that the concept of a mixed economy of welfare should not be considered as a modern invention (Lewis, 1995).

As its name implies, the COS was created to co-ordinate charitable effort; the origin of social work lies in the recognition that the effective organisation of charity required a systematic methodology to carry it out (Cooper, 1983). Assessment was the necessary precursor to decisions about service provision; the assessment process started from home visits and resulted in the production of a written report which was the basis for further action (Woodroofe, 1962). Decisions were then made regarding the 'eligibility' of the individual or family to receive assistance. The possible actions following the assessment were numerous, including the distribution of money as well as the provision of less tangible 'support'. The amount of assistance depended on what was judged to be sufficient to achieve a regeneration of the family (Young and Ashton, 1956; Woodroofe, 1962). Those people defined as 'undeserving' would be denied the assistance of the COS, and would be required to seek assistance through the Poor Law. (Forsythe and Jordan (2002) point out that this 'discriminatory moralism' continues to be a feature of contemporary social work.) State-provided services under the Poor Law were both residual and minimal, pitched at a level that would discourage people from voluntarily having recourse to its services (Crowther, 1981; Jordan, 1984).

Within the voluntary sector, professionalising tendencies can be identified through the development of education for social work, with training courses being established in Liverpool and Birmingham universities, and the School of Sociology and Social Economics in London between 1900 and 1910 (Woodroofe, 1962; Crowther, 1981). This was at the instigation of voluntary organisations, which accepted that successful interventions required both skills development and understanding of the circumstances from which their clients came. At the School of Sociology and Social Economics (which was later incorporated into the London School of Economics), courses were also offered for Poor Law officers, with other universities also taking on that responsibility soon thereafter (Crowther, 1981). At the same time, social work was gradually being introduced within state settings, notably in hospitals and in the courts with the development of the probation service. This pattern of incremental modification continued until the Second World War.

The immediate postwar years saw considerable organisational change. The commitment of the incoming Labour government in 1945 was to improve the welfare of all, following the hardship of war and the preceding economic instability. The Beveridge Report (Beveridge, 1942) provided the conceptual means to achieve this task, and heralded the development of what became known as the 'welfare state': the establishment of universal benefits as a safety net for all combined with the conviction that it was better to organise welfare within the state rather than the voluntary sector (Hill, 1993; Midwinter, 1994). While the main focus of welfare policy was on areas other than the personal social services – particularly health and social security – legislation was passed that created the modern organisational framework for social work. One aspect of this was the 1948 National Assistance Act, which finally ended the Poor Law. This process had begun in 1929 with the passage of the Local Government Act, which gave local government the responsibility for meeting the welfare needs of older and 'handicapped' (*sic.*) people. The relieving officers became local government employees, and were renamed public assistance officers; as Crowther (1981: p. 153) has it, they can be seen as among 'the ancestors of today's social workers'.

The second area of development was in respect of child care. The Children Act 1948 was passed following the report of the Curtis

Committee, which was established following the death of a child in foster care. The report identified major problems in co-ordinating child care services; a recommendation of the committee, enacted in the subsequent legislation, was that children's departments should be created in local government, under the management of a designated children's officer, in order to clarify responsibilities and accountability for child care. This gave a boost to social work, which was the core occupational discipline in the children's departments; indeed, the 'missionary zeal' (Jordan, 1984) of the new child care officers ensured that work with children became the dominant strand of social work.

The growth of state social work in the immediate postwar period was slow and uneven. There was a gradual process of unification through the 1950s and the 1960s, helped by the establishment of generic training programmes and professional journals (Younghusband, 1978). This process was assisted by the work of the Seebohm Committee, which was established in the mid-1960s to report on the most appropriate structure for social services in England and Wales. The committee recognised that there were problems with existing structures, which can be summarised as follows:

- Inadequacies in the amount and range of service provision, and its uneven distribution between authorities.
- Deficiencies in the quality of those services.
- Poor co-ordination between organisations and uncertainty about which should be approached for assistance.
- Insufficient adaptability to respond quickly to changing needs. (Hallett, 1982)

Social work interests seized the opportunity offered through the Seebohm Committee with alacrity, had a particular impact on the committee's deliberations and were instrumental in the subsequent creation of unified social services departments (SSDs) (Cooper, 1983; Hill, 1993). In many ways, this was a propitious time for social work, with an expansion in the numbers of qualifying training courses as SSDs clamoured for more staff. At the same time there was the establishment of a single professional association for all social workers within the United Kingdom (Payne, 2002). Within SSDs, despite the teething problems of reorganisation (Satyamurti, 1981), there was a spirit of optimism in the potential for social work to contribute to a more just and equal society (Bamford, 1990).

This process also confirmed the ascendancy of the statutory sector and marked the continued decline in influence of the voluntary sector. The growth of state-provided welfare services had a direct impact on its role and structure (Deakin, 1995); many voluntary organisations reduced the scale of their work in the early part of the twentieth century, while others experienced financial difficulties and became more dependent on the state for subsidies (Lewis, 1995). As a result, the voluntary sector moved from being the first point of contact if a family was in difficulty to more of a supplementary service.

The period of optimism within state social work was not long lasting. Public expenditure reduced dramatically from the mid-1970s, resulting in a change of emphasis within the operations of local government. In addition, the political climate for social work and other public services was to undergo a sea change through the 1980s. This affected both the financial settlements and the general ideological circumstances within which SSDs worked. The following section will identify the key aspects of this.

The economic and political context of social work

Chapter 1 outlines key developments in British economic and social policy in recent years. It is not the intention of this chapter to repeat these arguments, but rather to outline the effect that the changes have had on the organisational context of social work. The 30 years from the end of the Second World War to the mid-1970s is traditionally treated as being consensual (Hill, 1993; Midwinter, 1994), with the main political parties broadly agreeing the goals of policy, but arguing over the best means of achieving them. By the 1980s, a range of economic and political factors had served to break this consensus.

The initial economic warnings came in the 1960s, with a steady decline in Britain's industrial performance. The consequences of this were evident in the growth of unemployment, leading to increases in both public expenditure and taxation (George and Miller, 1994a). Matters were aggravated by the worldwide recession in the mid-1970s. The economic crisis had a strong effect on social policy – curtailing the vigorous expansion in public expenditure that had contributed to the growth of the welfare state. This was most evident in 1976, when the Labour government was forced to seek a loan from the International Monetary Fund, the terms of which required the government to pursue deflationary policies and cut public expenditure (Hill, 1993). This did not sit comfortably with a party that had sought to rebuild relations with the trade unions on the assumption that public expenditure would be maintained as a necessary safety net in troubled times (O'Brien and Penna, 1998). In fact, the Labour government was forced to instigate several years of wage restraint, which created fissures between the Labour administration and unions, directly contributing to its defeat in the 1979 general election.

The election of the Conservative Party – and their subsequent 18 years in power – provided ample time for their economic and social policies to become embedded in the fabric of the nation. In the early years of Conservative rule, the ideology of the New Right was a dominant force. As Gamble (1994) has it, the New Right drew on a combination of neoliberal economic ideas and neoconservative views about the role of the state. The basis of economic neoliberalism stemmed from the intellectual case for the benefits of capitalism. It was argued that the social-democratic principles that had underpinned postwar social policy were economically damaging. For neoliberals, the damage was attributed to two core factors. First, that the intervention of the state was said to harm the free operation of the market, deemed to be the most appropriate way to ensure growth. Second, that state intervention in the economy was held to curtail individual freedom expressed in both economic and moral terms (O'Brien and Penna, 1998).

Particular characteristics of neoliberal thought on the role of welfare can be identified. On the economic side, the welfare state is seen as problematic for four key reasons:

- It interferes with the workings of the market, by reducing both the rewards for success and the punishment for failure (George and Wilding, 1994).
- The levels of taxation required to finance the welfare state create a disincentive to enterprising individuals (George and Wilding, 1994).
- It creates an economic burden, both in respect of the direct costs of providing welfare, and in the 'unproductive' fact that a large element of the workforce are employed in welfare services (Midwinter, 1994).
- It has been inefficiently managed, and is therefore economically wasteful (Hill, 1993; George and Wilding, 1994).

The impact of neoliberal thought was evident in the policies of successive Conservative governments, which introduced a range of 'New

Right' policies into welfare as a direct consequence of the above analysis. Although a 'new' Labour government was elected in 1997, it initially pledged to work within the spending parameters which it inherited. While there have been rhetorical shifts in relation to welfare, the economic stringency introduced by previous administrations has remained substantially unaltered (Johnson, 2001), although alleviated by the budgetary plans announced by the Chancellor of the Exchequer in 2002. This means that the following factors, initially thought to be characteristic of Conservative governments (Hill, 1993; George and Miller, 1994b; George and Wilding, 1994) have been perpetuated by the 'new' Labour government:

- A commitment to the control of the overall cost of welfare.
- A preference for selectivist over universalist principles in welfare.
- The replacement of public sector approaches to welfare problems with market solutions.
- A commitment to institutional reforms within traditional welfare state organisations.

The 'new' Labour government has responded to the legacy of the Conservatives by extending the reforms in some areas and modifying them in others. A striking feature of the administration has been the absence of a traditional socialist ideology – indeed, as Powell (2000) has it, welfare is organised on a pragmatic sense of what works rather than any ideological commitment or consistency. This is reinforced by a strongly populist, socially authoritarian slant to policy (Jordan with Jordan, 2000; Powell, 2000; Butler and Drakeford, 2001). In respect of social services, this has led to the consolidation and extension of patterns established by the Conservatives (Jordan, 2001), with the establishment of the Best Value regime a case in point (see pp. 49–50 for more detail about Best Value).

At the *mezzo* level, these changes have had an impact in numerous ways. Welfare budgets have failed to keep pace with need, causing cuts in the range and levels of service provided. The application of market principles has led to a process where traditional bureaucratic mechanisms for distributing welfare have been replaced by competitive structures, with a consequent change in the role of voluntary and private organisations. The increasing power of the Audit Commission has also been a significant factor, as welfare organisations have been forced to accept the discipline of the 'three Es' – economy, efficiency and effectiveness – and hence to become more fiscally accountable to the centre (Power, 1997). As a consequence of this, mechanisms of audit – first introduced by the Conservatives as part of the development of the new public management (Power, 1997) – have proliferated within the welfare state (Clarke *et al.*, 2000). Langan (2000) has placed this within the context of a 'drive for accountability', which she has argued is the distinctive feature of the 'new' Labour approach to social services.

These changes did not arise in a political vacuum, but are closely linked to ideas that gained particular currency in the 1980s and beyond. For example, the organisation of social services was subject to increasing criticism through the 1970s and after. Large SSDs were criticised as being unresponsive and over-bureaucratised, and caricatured as 'Seebohm factories'. Those on the political left excoriated social work for exercising coercive and controlling powers over a small section of the population (Jones, 1983); despite the universalist rhetoric within the Seebohm Report, a selectivist focus had quickly become apparent. In addition, the voices of people who had traditionally been excluded from much decision making about welfare, even though they were disproportionately likely to receive services, began to be heard more loudly (Taylor, 1993; Thompson, 2002). While the analysis from the left was influential – particularly within social work education – it was the critique from the political right that had a greater impact on its delivery.

Another core element of New Right policy was privatisation, which rested on two linked contentions:

- That services could be provided more efficiently and economically outside the local authority.
- That the transfer of services into the private sector would reduce the cost of welfare and curb the organisational power of unions and staff.

While privatisation of social care services through compulsory competitive tendering was not required, the application of the Best Value policy to large areas of social services activity has generated comparable effects (Powell, 2000; Johnson, 2001). The intention of much social services policy though the 1990s – particularly in community care – was to introduce competition into social care through the separation between 'purchasing' and 'providing' (DoH, 1989). This represented a shift for SSDs away from their roles as direct

providers of care services towards a model where they act as com-
missioners/purchasers to ensure that services are available from
sources which may be outside the SSD. These features of what has
been described as 'the enabling state' (Taylor, 2000) have been perpetuated by the two 'new' Labour administrations.

The outcome of these changes was the creation of a social care
market, more accurately defined by Le Grand and Bartlett (1993) as
a 'quasi-market'. The role of the SSD is to manage the market and
develop new forms of contractual relationships between itself
and service providers. It is presumed that this arrangement will
promote competition and hence improve quality and drive down cost,
while increasing the level of choice available to the service user. In
organisational terms this has had vast implications for social work (see
Chapters 7–9).

These changes have had a major impact on the nature of the social
work role. In community care, it has been suggested that the development of care management represents a deprofessionalising of the
social work task, and hence an unattractive future for social workers
(Lymbery, 1998a). In practice with children and families, Hood
(1997) has argued that the purchaser/provider separation represents
a fragmentation of the social work process, with a chasm having
opened up between purchasers with decision-making powers on the
one hand and providers with most knowledge of the service user but
limited powers on the other.

The creation of a social care market *also* has had implications for
voluntary sector organisations, as it accelerated a shift from financial
support being given through grant aid to relationships based on contracts (Gann, 1996). However, as Lewis (1996) has observed, the introduction of contracting raised difficult questions about the purposes,
aims and objectives of the voluntary sector. Some organisations perceived contracting as requiring that they must act as the purchasers
dictate, which may be in conflict with the history and mission of that
organisation (see Lewis, 1995, in respect of the Family Welfare
Association). The adoption of a contract culture has had an effect on
the campaigning role of voluntary organisations, which is less likely
to be funded under contract. While the development of the 'Voluntary Sector Compact' was meant to ensure the continued independence of the voluntary sector in its dealings with government,
particularly in respect of its ability to influence and shape policy
rather than just respond to it, there remain concerns about the extent
to which this campaigning independence can be maintained

(Osborne and McLaughlin, 2002). Therefore the requirement to provide services under contract may reduce the range and scope of what can be offered by the voluntary sector within social welfare.

The neoconservative perspective on welfare insists that the development of state services has reduced the moral authority of the family and the ability of the community to provide for its own. Typically, welfare services are seen as either interfering or insufficiently controlling, according to circumstance. For example, social workers in child protection have to steer a difficult middle ground between too much or too little intervention, and are likely to be castigated for their failures to know which path to follow at any given time. In respect of community care, the ideological direction of policy has refocused attention on the family and the informal network of care. Dalley (1996) has argued that the prevailing individualist understanding of the concept of caring has obstructed the development of a more collective approach, and placed considerable stress on those people involved in the provision of informal care.

The development of the concept of consumerism, particularly evident in community care, is another aspect of policy that bears the imprint of New Right ideology. As far as public services are concerned, it is felt that they will 'become more accountable when they are made to respond directly to the choices of individual consumers rather than to the pleas of service providers' (Ransom and Stewart, 1994: p. 14), hence being more responsive to consumer needs. However, this concept of consumerism in welfare is problematic on two counts:

- That 'the language of consumerism cannot encompass the scope of public action' (Ransom and Stewart, 1994: p. 19), and that concepts of citizenship are more appropriate for determining public services.
- That the range of functions of public organisations – particularly when controlling, coercing, rationing or balancing competing needs and demands – indicate that they have a wider duty than simply meeting consumer demand.

Within community care, the term 'empowerment' was used by the Conservative government to describe the purpose of its policy (DoH/SSI, 1991b). However, as Means *et al.* (1994) point out, when used in this sense empowerment is not about enabling people to exercise their rights as citizens but their power as consumers. This ignores the structural limits placed on this power by a range of societal factors – poverty, education, gender, disability, race, etc.

With its gradual implementation of the 'modernisation agenda' (DoH, 1998a) the 'new' Labour government has effected significant change on the social care landscape. For example, the Care Standards Act 2000 saw the establishment of a new national body for the registration and inspection of a range of care services – moving this responsibility out of local authorities and health authorities, where it had rested since the Registered Homes Act 1984. Simultaneously, the Care Standards Act created the General Social Care Council, which sees its role as being the guardian of standards for the social care workforce, aiming to increase the protection of service users, their carers and the general public. The General Social Care Council is to operate in three core areas (GSCC, 2002):

- agreeing and issuing codes of practice;
- setting up a register of social care workers and dealing with matters of conduct by those people registered;
- regulating and supporting social work education and training.

The Care Standards Act 2000 also saw the establishment of the Social Care Institute for Excellence (SCIE), whose role is defined as the promotion of 'quality and consistency of social care practice and provision through the creation and dissemination of best practice guidelines in social care' (SCIE, 2002). In particular, SCIE – which has been established on the same model as the National Institute for Clinical Excellence (NICE) in the health service – has a particular role in the dissemination of evidence about what is effective in social care. Taken together, these changes represent a major development in the infrastructure that supports the delivery of social care.

In addition, the organisational frameworks within which social care is delivered have also been subjected to change. There has been a particular emphasis on the benefits of inter-professional arrangements, as witnessed by the creation of Youth Offending Teams (see Chapter 9). Changed patterns of inter-professional working are highlighted in the NHS Plan (DoH, 2000b), which identifies the government's wish to establish a new relationship between health and social care that 'will bring about a radical redesign of the whole care system' (DoH, 2000b: p. 71). The proposals to establish unified care trusts as an extension from primary care trusts are particularly significant in this respect, as they are envisaged as providing for 'even closer integration of health and social services' (DoH, 2000b: p. 73), and would be established as single bodies to commission and deliver primary and community health and social care. Although the desirability of establishing care trusts through voluntary arrangements is emphasised, there is also a more coercive edge. For example, if effective partnerships cannot be developed voluntarily, the government reserves the right to *impose* integrated arrangements through the establishment of care trusts (see para. 7.11). While the services affected by these changes largely concern adults, similar tendencies exist in other areas of social work – particularly in respect of child protection. Indeed, one of the issues particularly exposed by the Victoria Climbié Inquiry (Laming, 2003) was the apparent inability of different agencies to work together effectively. Although Laming rejected the establishment of a National Child Protection Agency (Laming, 2003: p. 6), he made stringent criticisms of the effectiveness of all the public services that were concerned with the protection of Victoria Climbié. Clearly, major structural change within child care services generally cannot be ruled out in the future.

In summary, the cumulative effect of this has led to a significant reorientation within social work. No longer can there be assumptions about local government providing a safe and supportive environment for the practice of social workers. An increasing volume of social work takes place outside SSDs – in the health service as well as voluntary, not-for-profit and private organisations, with the role of the state changing markedly in its focus. As will be clear later in this chapter, the implications of this for the professional development of social work in Britain are considerable.

Social changes and their impact on social work organisations

The most significant social changes to have affected social work are discussed in depth in Chapter 1. This section concentrates on those elements that have particularly affected social work organisations. It also discusses how the development of new social movements has created tensions within the occupation. Two general societal changes need to be acknowledged:

- The increased level of inequality in recent years (Walker and Walker, 1997; see also Chapter 1). A disappointing failure of the 'new' Labour government has been its inability to reduce the levels of social inequality that it inherited from the

Conservatives (Jones and Novak, 1999). The level of poverty experienced by people in receipt of social services has increased, exacerbating other social problems which people experience.

- Demographic changes which mean that there is a much higher percentage of older people than previously (Tinker, 1997), with a particular growth in the numbers living into very old age. This has marked a sharp increase in the 'dependency ratio' (Finch, 1990), that is the numbers of people who are 'dependent' – older people, children, people with disabilities – are an increasing percentage of the population. There have also been fundamental changes in the structure and formation of families, under the impact of factors such as increasing divorce and remarriage, the break-up of the family as an economic unit and geographical distance between family members (Finch, 1990). As Johnson (2001) has observed out, the family remains a core concept in 'new' Labour approaches to welfare, in part as a recognition of the above.

A combination of the two has increased the demand for services at a time when economic pressures have forced a reduction in expenditure. Social workers have to balance needs and resources, and their departments have to manage budgets that are not equal to the demands on them. As will be argued in the following section, this has led to a defensive form of practice.

The growth of 'new social movements' has been a feature of society recent years (see Byrne, 1997). Taylor (1993) has identified challenges to social work coming from the women's movement, Black people, gays and lesbians, and disabled people (see also Thompson, 2002). Although these challenges have come from groups with restricted access to power and resources, especially in relation to the service providing organisations with whom they work (Croft and Beresford, 1998), they questioned the very nature of social work practice, and led to a crisis of confidence in the 1980s. This was a period of much soul-searching, reflected in the first versions of the rules and regulations for the Diploma in Social Work (DipSW) (CCETSW, 1989, 1991), which contained strong statements about the need for social work to combat injustice and discrimination. As Jones (1996) reports, this brought social work into direct conflict with the government of the day, resulting in substantial amendments to the rules and regulations for the DipSW (CCETSW, 1995) to reflect a more conformist vision. The requirements for the new award in social work (to replace the DipSW), which were announced in 2002 (DoH, 2002a), have continued this process as they focus on the practical knowledge that social workers require to the exclusion of the role of social work in combating social injustice (Lymbery, 2003a).

Social work's position was also weakened by its increasingly poor public image from the 1970s onwards. Practitioners were subject to increased levels of scrutiny, most evidently in child protection where their apparent failings were criticised in a series of public enquiries. More generally, social workers struggled within a popular culture where they were caricatured (in often mutually exclusive ways) as 'saints, simpletons, scapegoats and scoundrels', in Golding's (1991: p. 90) arresting phrase. The fact that social work did not enjoy a secure status in the public eye meant that it was particularly vulnerable to ideological assault.

The practice of social work has become increasingly difficult as a result of all the above changes. Essentially, it has been caught between three conflicting tensions:

- Economically, its place in the public sector has ensured a constant pressure to reduce costs, and do more for less.
- The political climate has proved to be increasingly unsympathetic to social work.
- Groups of service users have become more assertive in their demands.

The combination of these factors has led to a period of crisis, with both social services organisations and social workers re-evaluating their role and function. The 'new' Labour government's 'modernisation agenda' can be seen as a response to the perceived failings of social services organisations (DoH, 1998a) and as a means whereby the declining public confidence in social services can be addressed. However, the unremitting pace of change is creating its own problems for organisations.

The organisational response

The purpose of this section is to identify ways in which social welfare organisations have responded to the pressures on them. As Harris (2002) graphically illustrates, the world of social work has been changed immeasurably by the pressures that have been outlined. Organisations have had to operate in circumstances where a critical consensus has been reached on their failings – what Langan (2000) has identified as a 'discourse of failure'. This section will argue that the 'new managerialism' has become centrally important within social welfare organisations as they have tried to respond to this criticism. While the impact of managerialism was initially associated with the introduction of the new public management (Hood, 1991) under successive Conservative governments in many ways it has been intensified under Labour (Clarke *et al.*, 2000). Although the worst excesses of this have been felt within SSDs, its impact within voluntary organisations is also charted.

The roots of managerialism are in the belief that effective management can resolve a range of social, economic and political problems (Pollitt, 1993). However, this does not sufficiently explain its nature as an ideology, its connections with the political philosophy of the New Right, and the ways in which managerialist thought has contributed to a consensus regarding problem definition and resolution within welfare agencies. Clarke (1998) has suggested that an understanding of managerialism depends on two key perspectives. He accepts that it has made an active contribution to the restructuring of the welfare state, and hence acted in the interests of the New Right reformers. However, he adds a crucial second point, that the people who have promoted managerialism have been pursuing their own separate and distinct interests. This perspective helps to explain the apparent collusion of managers, noted by other writers (see Farnham and Horton, 1996: p. 269), and the persistence of managerialism into the Labour years. In addition, as Langan (2000) has argued, the precise form of managerialism within social services has shifted in accordance with the preoccupations of the Labour government, particularly in relation to the primacy of performance measurement (see also Watson, 2002).

Clarke (1998) has provided a detailed analysis of the ways in which managers have sought to handle their role, and bring about the organisational transformation that they believe to be necessary. The managerialist strategy has included the following elements:

- Controlling bureau-professional power within organisations by subjecting them to new forms of regulation through centralised processes of financial control and methods of evaluation, as well as the increased power of the consumer.
- Recruiting organisations to processes of self-discipline characterised by the internalised acceptance of performance targets and financial limits, among other mechanisms.

These processes have had specific consequences for social work practice within SSDs. The first of these concerns financial management, a particular feature of community care policy and practice (see Chapter 7 for more on this theme). SSDs recognise that budgets are incapable of meeting need within their locality and budgetary constraints have both encouraged closer scrutiny of social workers' decision making and heralded the widespread introduction of various means of rationing expenditure. Examples of this include the use of quotas for admission into residential and nursing homes; cash limits for complex care packages, and so on. While the above examples relate to social work with adults, similar themes can be identified in relation to child care, notably the overemphasis on child protection and the limited development of preventative work and family support (Stevenson, 1996).

The second theme refers to the increased level of bureaucratisation within SSDs, graphically illustrated by two papers that chart the extent to which social work practice has become dominated by bureaucratic, managerially defined responses. Howe (1992) has argued that the proliferation of guidelines in the wake of the Children Act 1989 has contributed to an increased sense that social work practice is dominated less by the exercise of professional discretion and judgement than it is by the need to follow rules. Sturges (1996) has identified the development of an 'administrative model' of care management, with the core aspects of this model including routinised ways of working, large caseloads, and completion of numerous complex forms. While it would be a caricature to suppose that all social work practice is governed by such requirements, Howe and Sturges together make a strong case that bureaucratisation within social work has increased. An inevitable consequence of this growth has been the development of ever more detailed procedures for every aspect of social work. There are positive reasons for this, notably the need to ensure that members of staff know what is required of them when implementing a new policy. Equally, there is some benefit to be had from knowing that the type of service offered will be consistent. However, procedures exist not only to ensure good practice but also to ensure that the organisation has a basis through which it can control its members. As Howe (1992: p. 497) has pointed out, this transforms the role of managers from 'casework consultants' to 'designers of surveillance systems', a shift which serves the managerialist project.

In many ways, the introduction of the Best Value regime (DETR, 1998) has served to intensify these developments. The ostensible purpose of Best Value is to ensure that local authorities establish arrangements to secure continuous improvement in the way in which its functions are exercised. The key means of doing this are by measuring the performance of such authorities against a set of performance indicators and by requiring that authorities set up Best Value reviews to assess its performance in all its functions. Although Best Value was trailed as representing a decisive break with the past, continuities can be observed between it and the mechanisms it replaced. For example, it is defined as being the 'duty to deliver services to clear standards – covering both cost and quality – by the most *effective, economic* and *efficient* means available' (DETR, 1998: para. 7.2, p. 64 – emphasis added). This language clearly derives from the Audit Commission, and it is usually financial matters that dominate Best Value reviews (Boyne, 2000). In this respect, it represents an extension of the power of audit within society at large, and local government in particular (Power, 1997). While there are many contradictions within the policy (Geddes and Martin, 2000), it does represent an increase of the control that central government can exert over local government. To the extent that it places considerable emphasis on performance management it also fits comfortably within the managerialist climate that was inherited from the Conservatives (Sanderson, 2001). That this is to be a continuing priority is evident in the *Draft Circular on Best Value and Performance Improvement* (ODPM, 2002).

Although the above changes have been particularly significant within SSDs, the voluntary sector has also been affected. For example, voluntary organisations had to accommodate to the demands that accompanied contracting; Taylor and Lewis (1997) identified four specific areas of concern about this:

- The tightening up of financial agreements, with terms largely dictated by the funder.
- Competition in the marketplace.
- The shift from a more general form of grant aid to the purchase of specified services under contract.
- The knock-on effects of restricted public expenditure on the voluntary sector.

These changes mirror those in the public sector, and have forced voluntary organisations to review their systems; this has led to increased managerialism as one means of coming to grips with the problems these changes have engendered. Although some writers have noted that the threat of contracting to the foundations of the voluntary sector may be exaggerated (Batsleer and Paton, 1997), others have warned that its consequences may be critical. For example, Taylor *et al.* (1995) have argued that the pressures of organising and funding community care may tend to reduce the variety and diversity of services which characterise the voluntary sector, and which are essential to the full development of responses to community care needs.

In summary, therefore, it can be seen that all social welfare organisations have responded in similar ways to the pressures that have been placed upon them. As I have indicated, the development of new managerialism has contained an ideological dimension, while simultaneously using the self-interest of many managers who have ensured its perpetuation. It has served to justify ever-greater levels of control of the content of practice which front-line social workers experience (Harris, 1998). In the light of this, the following section will explore the affect of the organisational climate on the professional status of social workers.

Professionalism in social work

The above factors have had a considerable impact on social work as a profession. This section addresses the ways in which their impact can be analysed. The analytical starting point is in the general critique of professionalism (Wilding, 1982), which led to an 'anti-professional' movement within social work (Simpkin, 1983) with many social workers actively opposed to the supposedly 'elitist' concept of professionalism. In addition, as a 'state-mediated' profession (Johnson, 1972) social work was vulnerable to political assault as part of the New Right's reforming project. Larson (1977) has argued that professions engage in the process of organising a market for their services and thereby take on a collective process whereby the status and prestige of the occupation – and individual members – can be enhanced. She termed this activity the 'professional project', and argued that this level of analysis can be applied to a number of occupations.

The development of the social work profession contains several moments when it has been able to claim a clear, agreed and recognised role. These tend to coincide with those periods when the sense of mission in social work was at its strongest – in the late nineteenth century, the immediate postwar period, and at the time of the

Seebohm reorganisation (Lymbery, 2001). The creation of unified
SSDs following the Seebohm Report marks the high water mark of the
social work 'professional project'; the period since then can be seen
as a retreat from the professional possibilities that were opened up.

There are a number of ways in which this can be interpreted. First,
and most obviously, the change in the nature of the state, and the
neoliberal recasting of welfare, has affected the way in which it has
chosen to interpret its mediating role. The New Right did not hold
with the ideal that social work could be used as a unifying force within
society, but imposed on it a more coercive and restrictive role, thereby
denying it a full measure of professional autonomy. Similarly, the
political left did not acknowledge that social workers possessed
unique skills and qualities that would differentiate them from ordinary people, and were resistant to the label of professional. This
placed social work in a double bind; in order to justify claims for professional status, it had to claim a particular monopoly of skill and juris-
diction, which the state was reluctant to grant. However, in order to
communicate better with the people it served, social work sought
to present its work in terms which could readily be understood, and
therefore appeared to be something for which neither special skills,
knowledge nor vocabulary was required – hence denying itself professional status (see Wilensky, 1964: p. 148).

The effects of bureaucratisation and proceduralism have further
weakened social work's claims to professional status, as they have
affected what Jamous and Peloille (1970) termed the 'technicality/
indeterminacy' ratio. They claim that professions must be able to
maintain a balance between technical aspects of the work (translated
into rules and procedures), and indeterminate areas that require the
exercise of professional judgement. The balance between the two elements is critical; Sheppard (1995a) has argued that it has fundamentally shifted within social work with adults in the context of
community care, and it is clear that Howe (1992) would take a similar
view in relation to social work and child abuse.

In addition, another core effect of managerialism has been a
breakdown of the mutually supportive relationship between organisation and profession (Larson, 1977). This has upset the balance
of power between practitioners, administrators, and teacher/
researchers which Freidson (1986; see also Howe, 1991) argues is
central to the maintenance and development of a profession. It
is managers who are the dominant voices within social work, and managerialism which has created a new ideological hegemony; managers

now define and control the nature of the professionals' work (Howe, 1986; Harris, 1998), and have instituted the process of bureaucratisation noted earlier. This has shifted the balance of the technicality/indeterminacy ratio, and weakened the ability of social workers to exercise professional judgement.

This can be viewed, in Abbott's (1988) terms, as a jurisdictional dispute over the nature of social work. Managers have borrowed from the general ideology of professionalism, created their own separate professional identity by emphasising the particular skills of management, and used this to justify an increase in their own organisational power. The consequences for professional practice are critical, as many of the most cherished aspects of social work – notably the search for meaning to help explain the lives of service users – become less relevant.

The morale of social workers within SSDs is observably poor (Jones, 2001). The changes in political rhetoric that have characterised 'new' Labour have failed to lead to an enhanced role for the profession. Indeed, social work appears to be absent from many of the welfare initiatives that have been set in train (Jordan with Jordan, 2000). There is a clear problem in recruitment, with social work remaining unattractive to new entrants. In some ways, voluntary organisations are the beneficiaries of the crisis within statutory SSDs, as they seem to represent an environment where the more traditional role and skills of social workers are welcome. However, as we have seen, managerialism has also affected many such organisations, so that the actual levels of professional discretion may be less than expected.

In summary, therefore, a number of factors have contributed to a fundamental challenge to the professional status of social work. The extent to which this constitutes a process of deprofessionalisation (Hugman, 1998b) is unresolved. While this chapter has charted numerous tendencies that contribute to a reduction of the professional scope of social work, there are indications from elsewhere that there remains the potential to revive the professional future of social work practice. Indeed, this volume can be seen as contributing to this process.

The future for social work in welfare organisations

This section focuses on the prospects for social work within the changed organisational structures. While the pressures on the occupation are undoubtedly serious, a bleak future is not the only possible outcome. There are elements in the nature of social work that may help to ensure its continuance, and provide ways for practitioners to resist the continued erosion of their autonomy and discretion.

The first point to note is that the White Paper *Modernising Social Services* (DoH, 1998a) does offer a commitment to the strengthening of social care services – although social work as a distinct profession is often subsumed under the more general terminology deployed. Significantly, the GSCC is intended as a means of improving the quality of the social care workforce, while also raising public confidence in the services that they carry out (DoH, 1998a: pp. 84–95). This may be the dawning of a (belated) recognition that the managerialist dominance of professions has generated consequences that are both bad for the profession and for the people it serves. For example, if professionals are made to be reactive and passive then damage is done to the sense of service that must motivate them if high-quality work is to be generated (Foster and Wilding, 2000). Also, there is little evidence that highly managerialised welfare actually provides a better service than it used to do when professionally dominated. Certainly, at the micro-level of social work interaction, the retention of some discretion in decision making is vital to enable the needs of service users to be addressed sensitively.

It is also important to remember that SSDs were first created in response to anxiety about the fragmented nature of service provision, and the fact that a range of different bodies were involved in people's lives in an overlapping and relatively uncoordinated fashion. This pattern of service did not sufficiently focus attention on the individual, family, group or community, leading to a partial and inadequate response to need. This is a problem which extends outside the world of social work, as there have been calls for different professions and organisations to work more closely together, in recognition of the degree of overlap between their tasks (Leathard, 1994; Owens *et al.*, 1995). In the future it is increasingly likely that social workers will be employed in many different organisational frameworks, with a particular emphasis on multi-professional work. This already happens in Youth Offending Teams (see Chapter 9 of this book) and is certain to increase as more care trusts are established as the NHS Plan unfolds (DoH, 1997, 2000b).

This presents an alternative, and potentially more positive vision for the future of social welfare, where the emphasis is on the integration of different organisations and professions in recognition of their shared interests. Indeed, Clarke and Glendinning (2002) have argued that the creation of a partnership focus within public policy is a distinctive move away from both hierarchical and market forms of organisation. There have been many examples where this has been actively developed, with a greater or lesser impact on organisational forms. In child care, the need for closer co-operation underpinned the creation of Area Child Protection Committees, although these have left the form of the participating organisations relatively unchanged. However, in the fields of, for example, mental health and learning disability there has been a pooling of staff from different occupational backgrounds and organisations into unified teams that focus on broader needs. Here, social workers function alongside doctors, nurses, occupational and other remedial therapists, and so on; although the pitfalls of this sort of working have been well identified in the literature on inter-professional work (Dingwall, 1982; Dalley, 1989), its potential is considerable (Hudson, 2002; Herod and Lymbery, 2002). Although many of the features of managerialism also exist in other organisations (Pollitt, 1993), the social work profession should be open to the possibilities that such developments may reveal.

In addition, the attempt to control social work practice by managerial decree is problematic. Much of what has been said about managerialism – notably the impact of increased bureaucratisation – affects the form of social work rather than its content. If, as Davies (1994) indicates, the uniqueness of social work is displayed as much in *how* work is carried out as in *what* is actually done, then there is space to transfer control back to individual practitioners. Much social work practice, particularly that of field workers, is unobserved by managers, who are therefore heavily reliant on what is reported to them by practitioners (Pithouse, 1998). This places some measure of power with social workers as it points to the existence of limits to effective managerial authority.

This analysis is linked to the concept of 'street-level bureaucracy' developed by Lipsky (1980), who contends that the nature of managerial control in welfare organisations is such that practitioners have considerable licence to reinterpret agency policies in their face-to-face work. Therefore, while managers can regulate the formal aspects of work, and the climate within which it is undertaken, they have more difficulty in governing what social workers actually do in direct contact with service users. Lipsky's analysis represents an important reminder that there are limitations to the effectiveness of top-down management, characteristic of the new managerialism. In summary, therefore, it can be seen that there are numerous ways in which managerialist dominance can be challenged by social workers. The development of empowering, reflective social practice cannot be achieved by the imposition of such structures, and it is vital for social workers to identify ways in which they can be combated.

Conclusion

It appears certain that the present organisational arrangements for British social work will alter. Two apparently contradictory developments can be observed. On the one hand, there is likely to be the establishment of increased levels of formal multidisciplinary working, where the social worker will operate alongside other professions. While issues of professional power and status always impact upon multiprofessional working, this represents an opportunity for social work to consolidate its position and would point to a more integrated future. Indeed, the continued rhetorical commitment to notions of 'partnership' supports this development (see Glendinning *et al.*, 2002).

On the other hand, there is a continued drive to separate the assessment of need from the provision of services, a direct legacy of *Caring for People* (DoH, 1989). The development of purchaser/ provider relations has meant an increased role for both the private and voluntary sectors – a move that has massively changed the pattern of provision of residential and home care, for example. The impact of this on the voluntary sector needs to be viewed with caution, as the campaigning focus of voluntary action may be overtaken by the increasing requirement to provide services under contract (see Chapter 4). The growth of care-for-profit presents numerous problems which have already become apparent, notably the dispersed nature of the care industry leading to problems of quality, and the conception of service user as consumer, the limitations of which have already been pointed out. The overall impact of this has been to fragment the pattern of service delivery.

This chapter has identified the forces that have impacted upon social welfare organisations in recent years, and has pointed to the alternative futures of fragmentation and integration that appear to be possible. In either case, it is important for social work to be able to redefine its core roles and tasks so that it is able to survive a move into different organisational locations. A renewal of its sense of purpose is urgently required, so that the value of social work to society can be maximised.

3

Social Workers' Management of Organisational Change

Marian Charles and Sandra Butler

Introduction

Given the effect of neoliberal policies on social work, alongside the burgeoning of managerialism and the implementation of 'modernisation' measures under 'new' Labour (DoH, 1998a, 1998b, 2000a), what scope is there for practitioner-led approaches to organisational change? Drawing on the emergent critiques of chapters 1 and 2, and applying the analysis from the *macro/mezzo* levels, this chapter engages with some of the *micro* dilemmas confronting social workers in bridging the gap between their ideals and practice realities. Although the chapter is framed within the context of policy and practice within Britain – specifically England – we believe that the analysis can be applied elsewhere. The concept of the reflective practitioner (Schön, 1991) on which the chapter is based has broad validity within different welfare regimes and across different professional disciplines.

After considering the impact of de-professionalisation, we present two models conceptualising practitioners' responses to organisational life, namely the reflection-in-action (Schön, 1991) process and the accommodation cycle (Summit, 1983; Morrison, 1996). A framework, consisting of spheres of control, influence and acceptance, is then utilised. Within this framework, the practice implications of these models, and the ways in which workers manoeuvre between them, can be understood. For each sphere, we delineate examples of personal, professional and organisational devices employed by social workers to maintain their assertiveness and personal boundaries alongside their management of organisational change. Fundamental to this is an examination of organisational power relationships coupled with the nature of authority underpinning workers' realms of influence over decision making. We reflect on areas of policy, practice and organisational culture over which workers have limited influence and hence, out of necessity, need to accept.

Our aim is to move away from scapegoating practitioners towards viewing them as initiators of change. Prominence is given to strategies through which workers are empowered rather than demoralised by constant organisational upheaval. The chapter postulates that the devaluing of emotional elements of practice needs to be set alongside an increasing emphasis on indirect and mechanistic social care planning. In response to this, the chapter outlines ways of challenging those organisational practices fundamentally at odds with social work values.

Impact of de-professionalisation

As outlined in Chapter 2, during the past thirty years there has been an increasing crisis of confidence and legitimacy in the professions (Schön, 1991), fuelled by critiques of their power base, the negative consequences of their solutions to public problems and their claims for expertise (Foster and Wilding, 2000). There is scepticism about the professional effectiveness of social work, while contemporary practitioners have been engulfed by the constant desire of senior managers to reorganise and rationalise in the wake of central government policies and resource constraints (Schorr, 1992; Statham, 1996). This has left many social workers exhausted and cynical about their employing agencies' motives.

Ironically, reorganisations often maintain the cultural stability and predictability of organisational life, creating a smokescreen around the need for meaningful change impacting positively on service provision. Schön (1991) argues that the professions are now confronted by an unprecedented requirement for adaptability, given that practice situations are inherently complex and uncertain, necessitating constantly evolving knowledge, values and skills. He believes that professional knowledge, as it has been traditionally constructed, is mismatched to the changing character of organisational and practice indeterminacy. Parton (1998, 2000) contends that uncertainty and ambiguity lie at the heart of social work, and always have done.

This tension is exemplified in social work's de-professionalisation, an undercurrent in the managerialism, proceduralisation and bureaucratisation discussed in Chapter 2. On a *micro* level, the impact of de-professionalisation is epitomised by the following issues:

- There is a pull between professional ethics involving 'respect for persons' (BASW, 1996) and organisational efficiency drives. Senior managers have adopted new ways of managerialist thinking that lead to conflict, as staff see the effect of reductions in services, or ill-thought-out changes, on disadvantaged groups with the least power and the most needs. Simultaneously, social workers are thwarted from making connections between their own and users' experiences.

- Social work has a contested and fluctuating knowledge base (Payne, 2001), hallmarked by competing professional paradigms. The continual reshaping of social work's role has demanded usable, pluralistic knowledge, with social workers producing multiple, shifting views of their practice (Schön, 1991). Awash with uncertainty, practitioners find it difficult to articulate the relationship between theory and practice (Schön, 1987; Parton, 2000).

- As social work is under more pressure to be cost-effective, organisational cultures have accommodated increased levels of work set against decreased professional responsibility. Collings and Murray (1996) attribute social work stress to difficulties in reaching workload targets coupled with expanding administration.

- An increase in organisational calls for mechanistic responses has constrained professional discretion (Lymbery, 1998a). Organisational frameworks operate *as if* practice issues are resolvable in a calculative, probablistic manner (Parton, 1998), thereby missing opportunities for valuing creative professional judgements.

- A lack of devolved decision making to social workers is juxtaposed with pressures on first line managers to respond to unique practice situations under stressful conditions and with limited space for analysis. Paradoxically, workers develop a siege mentality, a process of alienation in which 'us and them' becomes a way of understanding manager–worker interactions. Practitioners come to believe that the managers are out of touch with the intricate realities of their experiences (see Jones, 2001).

- The quest for certainty and risk elimination has pushed social workers towards practice dominated by 'risk management' (Kemshall and Pritchard, 1996; Parsloe, 1999) where the quality of work is judged against criteria of prioritising, assessing, monitoring and reducing risk (Parton *et al.*, 1997). 'Risk' has become the yardstick against which scarce resources are targeted, vulnerable groups protected and social workers rendered accountable (Parton, 1996b).
- The drive for 'technical rationality' applies knowledge to instrumental decisions (Schön, 1991) while avoiding any recognition of the emotional threads of practice. The distressing content of social work, and the resonances this has in workers' lives, becomes sanitised and defined out (Blaug, 1995).
- Patriarchal, heterosexist, disablist and racist control in agencies is promulgated through a hierarchy of competition; amid unprecedented levels of change, some managers demonstrate an extraordinary need to colonise other workers' thoughts and statements. The acceptance, let alone validation, of difference and diversity is excluded in this frame of reference.
- The relentlessness of practice and ethical conflicts within bureaucratised and insensitive organisations leave many social workers demoralised and propelled into defining themselves as victims – epitomised by defensiveness, routinised responses and reactive, rather than proactive, approaches to practice (Harris, 1987; Hill, 1990).

These factors have had a marked effect on job satisfaction. Balloch *et al.*'s (1999) survey revealed considerable dissatisfaction among social workers arising out of the emphasis on financial management as opposed to professional expertise, the devaluing of practice skills, cutbacks in support and supervision, and the lack of social work, as opposed to management, career opportunities. Empirical studies demonstrate that social work is a highly stressful occupation (Gibson *et al.*, 1989; Jones *et al.*, 1991; Bennett *et al.*, 1993; Collings and Murray, 1996; Balloch *et al.*, 1999). Agencies have failed to meet their dual responsibility to respond to users' needs while supporting frontline staff (Audit Commission/The National Assembly for Wales and SSI, 2000).

Given the current economic and political climate, it is hard for workers to remain psychologically intact when employed by a welfare organisation. Thompson *et al.*'s (1996) study points to the organisational culture as the key to understanding the dynamics of workplace stress. It is to this that we shall now turn.

The social work accommodation cycle

How do social workers manage this de-professionalisation, communicated and sustained through the organisational culture? To address this question, we concentrate on the extent to which workers either accommodate to, or take reflective action in respect of, organisational imperatives. This section examines the former. Organisations operate dispersed or integrated patterns of shared meaning supported by norms and rituals that influence agencies' abilities to handle change (Morgan, 1997). While all workers accommodate to these dynamics, the means and degree of accommodation varies. We focus on groups of practitioners facing discrimination as their experiences illustrate graphically what is at stake.

Beginning with patterns of shared meaning, masculinist workplace ideologies define organisational 'credibility' and 'competence' in terms of the dual elements of heroism/'being strong' and maintenance of secrecy. This presents a double bind; one option for social workers is to deal with this through the accommodation cycle (depicted in Figure 3.1), which builds on the work of Morrison (1996), and Summit (1983). The model helps to explain how workers become trapped in unsatisfactory forms of existence. Under patriarchy, the myth of heroism/'being strong' is perpetuated; 'fortitude' and 'courage' are valued qualities. This macho culture places additional burdens on women, as the 'superwoman' image is presented as a role model for female professionals (Langan and Day, 1992). For example, the myth of the strong African-Caribbean woman practitioner or user has seeped into organisational culture, echoing beliefs that she can shoulder whatever responsibilities the agency deems appropriate.

Secrecy, however, operates through workers denying the effects of organisational life on themselves. This, in turn, feeds the trappings of contemporary managerialism. A social worker may avoid disclosing the emotional aspects of practice as covert agency stances restrict the opportunities and permission to do so. This detachment has unconscious as well as bureaucratic significance. Empathy and intuition become marginalised, the assumption being that emotions are unworthy of informing decisions in the same way as the intellect. Consequently, workers' needs, fears and aspirations are ignored. In addition, complex oppressive processes imbued with secrecy prevent

Figure 3.1 Professional accommodation cycle. Development of Morrison (1996), and Summit (1983)

certain practitioners from realising their full employment potential, while many white able-bodied men are promoted beyond their capabilities (Itzin and Newman, 1995; Shaw and Perrons, 1995; Davidson, 1997; Halford and Leonard, 2001).

The double bind of heroism and secrecy is highlighted in the following example. A first line manager is held accountable for the deployment of restricted resources, burdening her/him with policy and practice uncertainties. Consequently, s/he may exude heroism by telling senior managers just enough to assuage their unease, thereby shrouding her/his management task in secrecy. This illustrates Morgan's (1997) metaphor of organisations as political systems, where surface manifestations of power are not be confused with deep power structures. In this scenario, the power play enacted by the various layers of management is underpinned by structural dynamics, where the tactics employed are congruent with organisational agendas and explain why difficulties are ignored until times of crises or unavoidable exposure. Using a sticking plaster approach, the underlying processes are left intact.

Heroism and secrecy, being influenced by these external, interactional and internal aspects, may precipitate a sense of helplessness, ignoring of problems, or blinkered thinking, although these are only healthy responses to an unhealthy environment (Summit, 1983). If practitioners' needs for personal and professional development remain unmet, they act out of self-protection to deal with perceived threats. Anxious not to feed into stereotypes, workers become sucked into the masculinist principle of never revealing their vulnerabilities because the agency resents helplessness. Morgan (1997) demonstrates how workers become enmeshed in 'cognitive traps' where false assumptions, taken-for-granted beliefs and unquestioning ways of operating combine to create a self-contained cultural view shaping and constricting organisational actions, allowing problems to be ignored. When a dominant organisational view emerges and uses a range of communication patterns to reinforce this, other interpretations exist only in the shadows. An unwillingness amongst those with normative power to recognise different, but equally valid, perceptions and definitions of reality results in blinkered thinking.

In response to these patterns, workers professionally accommodate, that is, suppress their feelings as ways of managing uncertainty and unpredictability. Heroism and secrecy, continually threatening workers' psychological integrity, are turned into seemingly normal occurrences. Psychic survival is gained at the expense of distorted perceptions of external and emotional reality. In examining conflict management, Morgan (1997) characterises accommodation as submission and compliance whereby workers continually attempt to satisfy others' concerns. Despite the ensuing tensions, practitioners try ever harder to hide their physical and emotional suffering. Secrecy and helplessness are reinforced in renewed attacks on workers' professional autonomy. A sense of entrapment occurs in response to the paradoxical injunction that emotional expression is 'unprofessional' while maintenance of a dishonest position is 'coping'.

Delayed or unconvincing disclosure of stress and emotions or any self-doubt about levels of competence, credibility and commitment may precipitate sickness, aggression or resignation, leaving the underlying double bind intact. In revealing these unconscious processes operating within agency structures, the overrationalisation of organisational life allows no room for emotional expression (Morgan, 1997). Anger may be ridiculed or pathologised, emotional stress treated with a few days leave, and a subversive act with increasing forms of control. Finally, retraction occurs. Faced with disbelief or avoidance, workers harbour feelings of abandonment and fears of being written off as incompetent and consequently withdraw the disclosure. Secrecy and heroism resume, thus completing the accommodation cycle. Crucially, this way of operating is then passed onto, and mirrored in, practitioners' interactions with service users.

Contemporary social workers, therefore, face a predicament. They start with an ideal picture of what they hope to achieve, but quickly find that the requirements of the job appear to leave little time for reflection. How long is it possible to maintain this image? Newly qualified workers, looking for role models, are disappointed and confused by what they see. Feelings of letting others down, of betraying radical causes, become another burden of responsibility for those experienced workers trying to conceptualise their own actions. The cumulative effect of this on self-respect and integrity are enormous. Faced with increasing workloads and the rapidly changing nature of practice, 'deskilled' practitioners must employ reflective processes in order to hold onto any sense of professional autonomy.

Reflection-in-action

Modifying these stress levels involves considerable structural and ideological shifts. However, through reflective practice social workers can perceive themselves as initiators rather than as victims of organisational change (Schön, 1987, 1991; Fuller and Petch, 1995). In the model depicted in Figure 3.2, meeting the challenges of contemporary social work requires creativity and improvisation (England, 1986; Siporin, 1988; Goldstein, 1990; Lymbery, 2003a).

Schön (1991) describes a process of reflection-in-action, mirroring Kolb's (1984) experiential learning cycle, as a legitimate form of professional knowing. Experienced practitioners are not so much atheoretical as they are practical, concrete and intuitive (Martinez-Brawley and Mendez-Bonito Zorita, 1998), developing practice wisdom along the way (Sheppard, 1995b). This involves the ability to think in action. Schön emphasises that:

> . . . [in] professional practice, there is a hard high ground where practitioners can make use of research based theory and technique and there is a swampy lowland, where situations are confusing 'messes' incapable of technical solution . . . (Schön, 1991: p. 42).

Faced with the uncertainty and instability of practice, social workers develop the ability to explore and reflect on what is happening in a specific situation as it unfolds. This is *experiential* knowledge where sensing, feeling and intuitive dimensions are developed

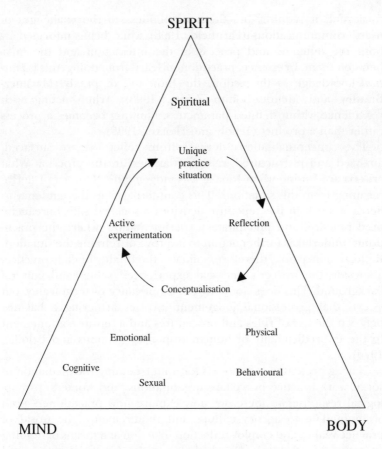

Figure 3.2 Holistic framework of social workers' reflection-in-action. Development of Schön (1991) and Kolb's (1984) experiential learning cycle

at the point of encounter (Heron, 1996; Reason and Bradbury, 2000). Simultaneously, practitioners draw on *propositional* knowledge (derived from theories through the conceptualisation of experience over time) and interactions with other service users to advise them of necessary action. Nevertheless, even when workers consciously use theories or practice models, they remain dependent on the fusion of judgement, performance and intuition. Often, intuitive knowing cannot easily be described because it operates on a more spiritual and emotional level. Such reflection-in-action is the antithesis of the rigid application of mechanistic procedures and techniques. To be successful, it requires practitioner openness to the challenges of users' communications (Farnfield, 1998) while being informed by both the outcome and process of the interaction and the links between them. In essence, practitioners learn from doing; this is *practical* knowledge *in* the action, the 'how to', or praxis (Martinez-Brawley and Mendez-Bonito Zorita, 1998). When acting with confidence within defined parameters, knowing becomes a process rather than a product (Yelloly and Henkel, 1995).

The conceptualisations derived from reflection are surfaced, analysed and restructured, raising awareness in the process: 'What criteria am I using when I make this judgement?' 'How can I derive meaning from this situation?' This counterbalances the tendency to become stuck in the repetitive activities associated with bureaucratised practice, and precipitates experimentation, where the practitioner undertakes further action to improve or reframe the situation. Reflection-in-action, therefore, validates the fluidity of daily practice, alongside the worker's personal experiences, values and cultural background. This does not deny the significance of technicality, but asserts that professional judgement involves achieving a balance between the use of rules and procedures and a sensitive attunement to the unpredictability of human responses (Jamous and Peloille, 1970).

Having presented two models for understanding the mediation of social work practice by welfare organisations, and workers' psychological responses to these, we now explore how practitioners both accommodate to agency culture and requirements, the world of practice reality, and employ reflection-in-action as a means of holding onto social work ideals. Caught between dominant definitions and their own intuitive knowledge, workers evolve balancing strategies to bridge the gap. Some strategies involve adaptation of dominant meanings (minimisation, denial, avoidance) while others constitute an explicit challenge and restore workers' threatened sense of professional integrity. Using a framework of *control, influence and acceptance* (Figure 3.3), we examine a number of personal, professional and organisational devices employed to manage this ideal-practice reality tension.

While the impact of organisational change is enormous, it offers greater scope for creativity and self-determination than frequently assumed (Parton, 1996a). Social workers can exert considerable personal, professional and organisational control within their working lives. Ways of 'beating the system' are unearthed through exploiting

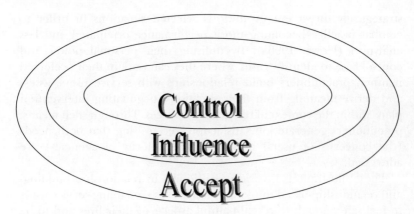

Figure 3.3 Framework of control, influence and acceptance in social workers' management of the ideals/practice reality tension

the tension between bureaucratic requirements and the dictates of professional integrity.

Personal devices

Despite organisational upheaval, timescales and legislative constraints, practitioners retain personal responsibility for organising their workloads. They have degrees of control over how their time is allocated and to where their energies are directed, offering freedom to work creatively while holding onto professional discretion (Pithouse, 1998). Take, for example, the duty worker constrained by strict eligibility criteria for services. Rather than regarding this as evidence of the erosion of professional judgement, the reflective practitioner views this as a vehicle for purposeful, in-depth activity requiring essential social work skills. The nature of the response to the user's initial contact is largely within practitioner control. S/he 'sets the stage for assessment and determines the scope of the exploration and the information necessary to collect for judicious intervention' (Meyer, 1993: p. 17). This is achieved through counselling techniques, interpersonal skills plus an extensive knowledge of available resources. The user experiences a well-structured interview with clarity of purpose, undertaken by a practitioner who displays good listening skills, avoids jumping to conclusions and is honest about potential solutions and available choices. Alternatively, workers may strategically direct energy towards selected situations in order to combat practice becoming more performance orientated and less analytical (Howe, 1996a). By utilising their personal power and control base to identify 'cases' where they can work in their preferred manner, practitioners build relationships with service users, assess and derive meaning from their situations, negotiating intervention plans within the context of restricted resources. Through such means, practitioners generate job satisfaction, recognising that both needs (the concerns of users) and risks (the priority of agencies) are addressed.

These illustrations involve practitioners in relationship building, and relationship-based thinking (Howe, 1998), enabling service users to feel safe enough to reveal painful aspects of their lives and to be supported in facing change. Such activities impact powerfully on workers. Reflection enables practitioners to become aware of the personal effects of these experiences, and to recognise how emotional avoidance reduces their efficiency (Hawkins and Shohet, 2000), promoting personal stress. Alert to agency denial of emotionality, practitioners assume responsibility for maintaining their emotional balance, choosing when, how and with whom to share the intensity of and anxiety about the demands made upon them. Hence, emotional expression may be excluded from formal supervisory agendas, as workers opt to take comfort from trusted colleagues with whom it is reciprocally permissible to allow vulnerability to surface. Liberated from continually holding down pain, workers are able to battle consistently with the distressing situations that constitute their daily labour.

Practitioners accommodating to the prevailing agency culture may elect to follow the 'secrecy' road, choosing not to share and/or ignoring their feelings. This results in behaviour designed to reduce the uneasiness stemming from 'emotional proximity and mutual influence' (Jordan, 1990: p. 87). Workers take frequent spells of sick leave (Jones, 2001). They may choose to see people in the office rather than at home, thereby avoiding any identification with aspects of users' lives beyond agency or social work help. They avoid team meetings, where increased flexibility, co-operation, and informal sharing of others' work, with its potential for stress exposure, may be expected.

Some devices have a negative impact. Practitioners engulfed by masculinist modes of operation may lose belief in their ability to sustain personal control. Through minimisation, they lose the power to recognise and reflect on the impact of events, censoring their thoughts and denying the extent of workplace and societal oppression. Existing in a world of cognitive dissonance, their statements and actions contradict their thoughts and impulses. Any courage and commitment to challenging oppression diminishes. Control is exercised by 'closing down', with a loss of attunement to colleagues' and users' pain and distress. Consequently, social work assessments become based on factual evidence alone. Individuals are processed: sufficient criteria points may be scored to ensure a residential placement for an older person, but without due consideration of the inherent personal losses in such a move or of any separation experiences in the practitioner's life (see Chapter 7).

Alternatively, to maintain personal control, workers may 'try harder', a misguided notion aligned to the accommodation cycle's heroic behaviour (see Figure 3.1). Since many women workers never acquire the recognition deserved, one 'solution' is to do more of the same in the hope of gaining some approval. This situation often ends in resentment when perpetual giving fails to reap the personal rewards anticipated.

Professional devices

In the current technocratic climate, reflective practitioners are required to perform a balancing act between their need to exercise professional judgement and the agency's wish for routinised responses. (This is a core element of chapters 7–9.) First, to maintain this equilibrium, practitioners need to draw on their sources of professional power, including control of knowledge in the 'high ground'. Skilful utilisation of contemporary research, selecting and evaluating alternative approaches and highlighting the efficacy of particular outcomes, commands the attention necessary to induce preferred courses of action. For example, using research findings to illustrate how the lack of available support to non-abusing carers affects their ability to help their children (Farmer and Owen, 1995) can become the key to unlocking scarce resources.

Second, reflective practitioners achieve professional control through selecting working methods capable of demonstrating changes in users' lives. The growth in demand for cognitive-behavioural techniques (Raynor *et al.*, 1994; McGuire, 1995), with their potential to address complex relationships between thoughts and behaviour, is not accidental, particularly given their apparent effectiveness (Macdonald and Sheldon, 1992) and their consequent attractiveness within the climate of 'evidence-based practice' (Sheldon and Chilvers, 2000). Acting as a palliative device in keeping with agency expectations for measuring professional 'competence' through observable behavioural outputs, such methods are deployed to build up track records of 'getting things done'. An established reputation enables workers to introduce additional practices addressing social, environmental and structural dimensions, allowing effective intervention in respect of not only the immediate problem, but also users' general welfare and well-being. Workers move from the limitations imposed by a single theoretical perspective towards a more holistic approach. Developments such as behavioural management programmes for parents experiencing difficulties with their children indicate the attraction of such combined methods with both measurable outcomes and supportive, welfare approaches (Charles *et al.*, 1996).

Third, the desire to hold onto interpersonal, therapeutic and nurturing aspects of social work may direct reflective practitioners towards specialised roles. Allsopp (1995) suggests that child protection workers, constantly investigating child abuse allegations, achieve a high degree of job satisfaction. This relates to control over discrete tasks, for which certain skills, such as the sensitive interviewing of children, require development to a high level of competence. Alternatively, reflective practitioners pursue career paths within settings, often located within the voluntary sector, which encourage in depth explanations of situations and where their supportive, therapeutic and interpersonal skills are valued (Butler and Charles, 1996).

The quality of supervision affects job satisfaction. Social workers are critical of the value of supervision received; although they acknowledge the work pressures confronting supervisors, they also harbour resentment about the non-delivery of appropriate support. In Menzies' (1970) eloquent terms, supervision is characteristically low on personal relatedness issues and high on checking out correct task completion. Reflective practitioners grasp this reality and instigate the fourth element: taking charge of supervisory agendas and accepting that their needs are unlikely to be fully met by one individual. To acquire what they want they seek out specialist workers with consultancy functions to explore dimensions untouched within formal supervision. Colleagues with similar needs/interests are approached to establish peer supervision and mentoring arrangements. With an emphasis on equal power relations, these mechanisms ensure that practitioners are afforded opportunities to discuss ideas and ethical and practice dilemmas. In contrast, workers trapped within agency systems lessen the priority allocated to supervision, frequently cancelling sessions in order to cope with fresh crises. In so doing, supervision's role as a mechanism for interrupting the downward spiral of energy drain is ignored, thereby exacerbating rigid, defensive practice and leaving routinised responses unchecked.

Agency quests for certainty through risk management, especially in child welfare and mental health areas, are a central feature of practitioners' roles. Inevitably, this has led to the evolution of checklists and guides (see Magura *et al.*, 1987; Sheppard, 1990; Waterhouse and Carnie, 1992) in an attempt both to improve practice and develop 'foolproof' methods of assessing 'high risk' situations. Yet the knowledge base for distinguishing levels of risk is hotly disputed; in reality, strict adherence to guidance generates confusion as well as illumination (Munro, 1998a). Workers anxious to satisfy procedural requirements gather a wealth of information yet are uncertain as to how to interpret it, ultimately producing superficial risk assessments. In contrast, reflective practitioners sift the facts amassed within a range of theoretical frameworks, identify their interrelationships, weight the significance of potential associative factors and acknowledge the impossibility of risk elimination. They consider users' overall welfare, demonstrate the need for services and resources while avoiding individuals being unnecessarily subjected to compulsive procedures.

The strategies outlined in this section have illuminated how practitioners utilise or avoid professional control as a means of straddling the ideal-reality gap. This theme is pursued through exposition of some available organisational devices.

Organisational devices

How can there be multiple sources of power operating in welfare agencies and yet many feelings of powerlessness? Within bureaucratic structures, workers bemoan their powerless position yet, in reality, exert considerable control over agency activities. Important power sources within organisations lie in:

- self presentation;
- resource management;
- the ability to manipulate uncertain situations, information control and communication channels.

First, reflective practitioners contemplate their own self image. In current efficiency drives, being punctual, having a desk free of clutter or producing well-written, concise reports all exude positive messages about organisational skills and professional credibility. This image contributes to individual control over workloads, as refusing additional work or inappropriate tasks is then perceived within an overall picture of someone who appreciates agency requirements and whose organisational and time management skills are beyond question.

Second, image building links to the contemporary emphasis on social workers as 'human resources'. In exerting control over their professional development, those who have sought a niche conducive to their practice preferences cultivate scarce skills, becoming invaluable resources upon whom the agency depends. Witness, for instance, the burgeoning of child sexual abuse units offering a range of therapeutic services and staffed by those with a wealth of knowledge and expertise. In enjoying considerable power, do they share the learning derived from their specialised work – for example, advising practitioners about the potential for sexual re-abuse during contact visits (Foulds *et al.*, 1996) – or seek to increase their control by retaining their knowledge and gaining 'expert' status?

Third, reflective practitioners relish the uncertainties inherent in working in 'the swamp', using these to increase their organisational power. Control is elicited by coping with ambivalence and manipulating uncertain situations, with a view to ensuring their actual or imagined continuation (Morgan, 1997). Hence, risky situations carry on being 'risky', thus preventing the withdrawal of supportive or preventative services. Fourth, all workers demonstrate control over information flow in and out of the agency, although the manner in which this is exhibited varies. Reflective practitioners draw on their knowledge and expertise to legitimate their activities, whereas a rigid, unquestioning adherence to procedures validates the 'accommodating' approach to information control. The former provide users with optimum information about available services and resources so as to maximise their available choices. However, these reflective practitioners also act as gatekeepers, judiciously filtering incoming information to 'beat the system' and advance their own or users' ends. 'Accommodating' workers, however, shape information solely to satisfy agency concerns, deciding on versions of reality that are 'fit for purpose' and mask users' unhappiness with services. Research has revealed how workers exaggerated the number of carers leaving the fostering system at their own request rather than highlighting their dissatisfaction with family placement services (Triseliotis *et al.*, 1998). Ignoring or denying such problems defends 'accommodating' workers against examining their competence in offering carers' emotional support whilst allowing the agency to perceive both the worker as coping and the system as satisfactory.

Welfare agencies perpetuate their stereotyped attitudes and discriminatory behaviour towards their workforce through manipulation of our fifth power source, communication channels. Language acts as a powerful tool to caricature and dismiss subordinate groups, and to promulgate managerialism. Communication patterns between men and women are well documented (Spender, 1985; Graddol and Swann, 1989). Men encode behaviours in language to which women are not privy, so they have to choose between challenging or ignoring statements, or accepting explanations at face value. Commonly used phrases and images lead not only to misinformation about, and misrepresentation of, women's realities, but also, ironically, to subordinate groups' internalisation of the dominant agency culture. To retain control of their working lives, some women learn to use male language in the hope of allaying criticism and achieving a modicum of power. Here, blinkered thinking is characterised by a code of acceptable behaviour where women become 'surrogate men'.

'Accommodating' practitioners achieve a sense of control in the wake of these power sources, adopting the language, routines and standardised practices prescribed by agency policies. Maintaining boundaries through strict adherence to work schedules, they respond to the workplace's emotional intensity by bureaucratising difficulties. Compartmentalising tasks in this way dissipates the emotional overtones of a given situation, denying workers ownership over their practice experiences, with a concomitant loss of initiative and decision-making powers. Hierarchical positions become entrenched with the opinions of those perceived to be superior assuming dominance, leaving practitioners unheard (Reder *et al.*, 1993). Consequently, the service offered to users tackles the immediate, surface situation with scant regard for the structural dynamics affecting individuals' lives (Howe, 1996a).

Organisational control mechanisms, and workers' responses to these, are complex and multilayered, necessitating a myriad of accommodating and reflective strategies. This situation applies equally to personal, professional and organisational influence, to which we now turn.

Influence

Akin to the 'control' analysis, workers rarely admit to having 'influence' over organisational culture, citing numerous constraints, limited options for action and environmental requirements as justification. How can social workers influence a complex social welfare agency where only a fraction of its activity is under their direct control? While agency contexts confront practitioners with contradictory prescriptions for behaviour, social workers do influence organisational practices in the following ways.

Personal devices

First, reflective practitioners make choices about the extent to which they operate from a position of honesty. If dishonest with themselves, how can workers be sincere with users, colleagues and allies? In any given moment, workers choose to think positively or negatively. Those with the ability to reframe workplace situations affirmatively can work purposefully with their personal power. They recognise the energising effects of venting rather than internalising anger about agency policies and practices, but consider the appropriate timing, circumstances and politics of expressing emotion.

Second, workers, with clarity of perspective and purpose, retain their belief systems despite the weight of the organisational culture. They find methods to reinforce anti-oppressive perspectives. Under the organisational system of dominant-subordinate realities, minority groups learn to straddle a range of cultural views, while the dominant group encroaches upon others' space, devouring alternative explanations. Those who resist develop a reputation for being 'a thorn in the side', but workers at ease with their personal and political belief systems maintain a sense of irony, locating agency decisions and actions within a structural context.

Third, reflective workers who monitor and nurture the emotional atmosphere of social work teams are influential in germinating fresh initiatives. This expressive, maintenance function in teamwork is concerned with the extent to which members inspire one another, provide mutual feedback on performance, and attend to interpersonal well-being (Payne, 2000a). These qualities are traditionally undervalued; nevertheless, instrumental interpretations of teamwork miss the point. Without attendance to the emotional temperature of practice, the workplace is a sterile environment producing highly circumscribed work. Equally important is the display of leadership skills by team members. The motivation for leading from within springs from several sources:

- habitual challenges to formal authority;
- desire to be in league with those in power;
- need to bolster the formal leadership;
- commitment to the team's aims;
- fear of the existing leadership's incompetence in meeting them.

'Leadership' evokes an image of a charismatic individual who brings out the best in others and operates as a role model, but whose qualities are deemed to be unattainable by those with whom s/he works. Reflective leadership skills, however, are interwoven with a humanistic style of operating where feedback from team colleagues is welcomed and encouraged.

Professional devices

First, reflective practitioners identity agency vulnerability (see Chapter 8) and use this to influence organisational agendas and decisions. Appreciating the interplay between experiential/emotional knowing and research based/theoretical knowledge, such practitioners seize opportunities to present coherent arguments underpinned by sound professional knowledge in order to pinpoint dangerous agency practices. By appealing to the organisation's unwillingness to display its weaknesses, such action ensures that senior managers know where the ultimate responsibility lies. Second, gaining credibility through high standards of professional presentation carries considerable influence in circumstances where social work is perceived to be of lower status than the established professions of law and medicine. Here, the authority held by the worker is intertwined with her/his communicative power (Clegg, 1989) – for example, the significance of this has been amply demonstrated in research that focuses on the interaction between social workers and health professionals (see Lymbery and Millward, 2001). Across all of these situations, the practitioner works with and through the boundaries of professional discretion and organisational accountability (see Chapter 9 for an example of this in relation to work with young offenders).

Our third strand, social workers' evaluation of their own practice, links to the extension and maintenance of a professional knowledge base. This critical awareness can focus on the quality of practice, rather than work quantity, drawing on personal values and commitments (Shaw and Shaw, 1997) and offering a balanced picture of the strengths and weaknesses in a given instance. Sheppard (1995b) suggests that this facilitates imaginative responses, which, in combination with the uncertainty of the situations to be worked with, limit 'the extent to which routinization can characterise practice' (p. 289). This is also circumvented by grounding practice in users' evaluations of social work, which offer a consistent message: the quality of the relationship is all important (Thoburn *et al.*, 1995), and has a positive or negative impact on users' self-esteem, self-efficacy and sense of autonomy (Howe, 1998). Users appreciate helping relationships where they feel valued and respected by honest and accessible professionals, who are prepared to provide regular information exchanges and involve them in decision making processes (Brown, 1986; DoH, 1995b; Wilson, 1995; Morris, 1998a, 1998b). For practitioners, critical awareness means challenging the devaluing experiences endured by users and incorporating avenues for their self-validation (Brown and Smith, 1992a). With users' perspectives given due prominence and through evaluation processes, reflective practitioners maximise aspects of their role to increase their manoeuvrability. Care managers operating within a purchasing framework, for instance, may highlight shortfalls in resource provision through their assessments, thereby recording and monitoring how and why community care policies are not being implemented.

Fourth, reflective practitioners stick to the 'rules', but exploit them to their own and users' advantage. Budget allocations for Section 17 payments (Children Act 1989, Section 17(6)) are notoriously small and generally flanked by tight procedural access, although payments are made in a wide range of circumstances (Aldgate and Tunstill, 1995). In such circumstances, approaches to managers, known for their empathy and understanding of the nuances in child welfare or recognised for accepting sound arguments in areas alien to their own sphere of professional practice, are within practitioners' orb of influence.

Finally, due to elements of indeterminacy in reflection-in-action, practitioners demonstrate adaptability in broadening their communication base and negotiating skills to extend their flexibility and scope in managing people within the organisation as well as interprofessionally. This involves networking around specific areas of knowledge building and awareness of how other agencies influence their own professional development. The reflective process involves disseminating evidence of good practice, innovative projects, or user evaluations of services. Forming alliances with users to bring about change is integral to this, occurring successfully in the learning disabilities and mental health fields. Practice is not compartmentalised, users' experiences are not fragmented; rather, the mission is to present a rounded, collaborative picture.

We have illustrated how professional influence, carried out reflectively, captures the essence of good quality social work, rooted in responsiveness to users' hopes and fears. Complex and difficult judgements emerge from checking out and evaluating, while listening to the inner intuitive voice. Nevertheless, professional influence, drawing on inductive as opposed to deductive processes, is always mediated by organisational power dynamics, our next focus.

Organisational devices

For reflective practitioners, influencing organisational practices and cultures necessitates clear understanding of how hierarchical power operates. Effective agency adaptation presents 'an organisational predicament' (Schön, 1991) as it disrupts the constancies of organisational life. Oppressive organisations utilise a system of 'face-fitting' where privileges are granted to those in the dominant group, while disadvantaged groups are excluded. This ensures rejection of feminism, Black perspectives and any radical practice. Dominant agency members use their position to modify or protect organisational policy-making structures. Hence, any conversation about anti-oppressive practice negotiates, controls or triggers emotional responses in the interests of organisational goals. Reflective practitioners, therefore, carve out areas over which they have organisational influence, largely at the *micro* level, whilst recognising the impact of the *macro* and *mezzo* on organisational behaviour. By being self-critical and adaptive, they increase their capacity to contribute to organisational change, while representing a danger to bureaucratic stability.

The most significant form of organisational influence derives from collective action. Union participation, lobbying of groups with a professional agenda or special interest, all has a momentum greater than the sum of their parts. Similarly, reflective workers from disadvantaged groups often create their own support structures and systems within organisations that are preoccupied with ensuring their own survival. Nevertheless, using support mechanisms effectively to influence the organisation needs careful thinking through. Part of the control system is to isolate practitioners from each other. Managers may discourage the forging of connections through worker-initiated support groups on the grounds that these are ineffectual, creating unhealthy relationships and unrealisable expectations among users. In such an environment, it is expected that practitioners' allegiances are with management, not with disadvantaged colleagues or users. Hierarchical structures only tolerate alternative networks if the overall power structure remains *in situ*. Any intimation of real power shifts is met with resistance and control, attempting to colonise change so that it fits the bureaucratic image. Given such opposition, the desire for solidarity can encourage co-operative ways of working in order to take a stand against agency oppression. Workers can use others' advice and feedback systematically, so as to assess the viability of courses of action and regain their sense of balance. Without these reference points, they lose their sense of timing and perspective on events, not knowing when to confront or let incidents pass. Talking through personal and political dynamics of specific incidents is affirming, addressing the implicit signals of discrimination alongside taken-for-granted segmentation of tasks and roles. Problematic situations are defined structurally rather than personally, leaving workers better equipped to develop a holistic interpretation of agency activity and power differentials.

'Accommodating' workers often say they are 'playing the game' until they occupy positions of real influence. Assimilation is employed in an attempt to blend in with organisational culture. For reasons of self-protection, practitioners may choose to agree superficially with dominant views and avoid challenging statements or practices they find offensive. Such behaviour reduces the incidence of overt conflict and gains the approval of at least some colleagues. Alternatively, workers may identify a potential link between agency and anti-discriminatory/anti-oppressive goals, but recognise differences in interpretation typifying the gulf between the perspectives. The use of dilution tactics indicates that managers believe they share the same language as disadvantaged workers, without recognising the paradoxes. This approach reduces political challenges to a common denominator, involving, for instance, the reframing of feminist/Black ideology in ways palatable to a white male audience.

Acceptance

Acceptance conjures up images of uncritical absorption of organisational policies and practices by workers ready to absorb whatever the agency throws at them. As a concept and *modus operandi*, acceptance is riddled with derogatory connotations as the polemic surrounding social work's role as a change agent increases. While social workers engage in change inducing activities, there is an underlying subtext that users should accept their lot, however intolerable. The 'acceptance' we wish to promote is significantly different in nature; we perceive this as a conscious process in which workers respond affirmatively, agreeing or conceding to limitations imposed by particular practices or organisational scenarios. This vision involves the use of constructive emotional, cognitive and physical energies, with potentially liberating effects and outcomes. Ironically, the ability to accept these restrictions is highly dependent upon the capacity to be reflective across the personal, professional and organisational domains. We consider how underdeveloped reflective skills expose practitioners to the organisational treadmill and the deluge of ever growing demands to 'put up and shut up'.

Personal devices

Reflective practitioners monitor the effects on themselves of the professional accommodation cycle, identifying its potential to erode professional discretion and practice ideals. The recognition of how easily 'accommodation' takes hold encourages workers to build checks and balances into their working environment, thereby ensuring that signs of secrecy, blinkered thinking and withdrawal are nipped in the bud. Central to this is seizing personal responsibility for health maintenance. Holistic health hinges on energetic balance in the material, emotional and spiritual spheres. If practitioners hold a restrictive view of health simply as a series of symptoms, accommodating patterns are more likely to flourish. The dominant cultural drive for the suppression of emotionality as *the* acceptable normative standard creates expectations that 'coping' is preoccupied with physical not psychological existence. This creates a paradoxical injunction; while the organisation separates itself from emotional awareness, workers face the despondency generated through practice while simultaneously avoiding the splitting of their emotional and physical selves. The permanently exhausted practitioner, complaining of lethargy and tiredness yet struggling through the daily grind, has accommodated by ignoring the connection between her/his physical presentation and absorption of the emotional pressures inherent in the work.

Conversely, a practitioner with a holistic conceptualisation of health appears different from the worker portrayed above. S/he has learnt to accept the importance of 'being' in the present. Having reflected on past lessons, and not worrying unduly about the future, s/he creates an inner, sustaining calmness, enabling her/him to rise above the turmoil of professional life. The reflective practitioner, with a strong sense of well-being, is heavily motivated by her/his inner life. This creates a protective shield warding off the confusion of practice and organisational messes.

This stance frees practitioners to be at ease with themselves, which in turn fosters an ability to check when personal agendas spill out inappropriately. Acceptance of self and those aspects requiring change and development avoids defensiveness and the insecurities generated by the search for approval. This sense of security is fed by a strong awareness of the significance of personal background, emotional baggage, cultural/racial and spiritual influences on working practices, beliefs and attitudes. This includes an appreciation of preferred modes of handling workplace tensions by way of conflict inducement or working towards consensus principles.

An overwhelming feature of 'acceptance' relates to a thorough appraisal of role limitations and boundaries, of what is impervious to change but may be manoeuvred around. Accurate assessments of situations enable practitioners to 'let go' of tensions and unproductive working practices, so that energy remains channelled towards constructive tasks.

Professional devices

First, acceptance in the professional arena involves a refusal to be ensnared by agency and societal expectations of social work infallibility in which errors of professional judgement are not permitted. Reflective practitioners recognise the limitations of current knowledge, analysing and employing available research findings to inform but not dictate their judgements (Taylor and White, 2001). This identification of uncertainty, with its lack of definitive solutions to unique situations, links closely with accountability; without this, professional autonomy is unachievable.

Second, an appreciation of uncertainty attunes reflective practitioners to their need for, and right to pursue, opportunities for continuing professional development. Despite low levels of available funding, attending conferences or debating issues with colleagues are vital developmental occasions. More accommodating workers sidestep training issues, thus avoiding the scrutiny of current practice often triggered through the acquisition of fresh knowledge. Third, most workers recognise their position within agency hierarchies. Accommodating practitioners bemoan their sense of powerlessness as 'cogs in the wheel', whereas reflective practitioners deploy their position to shape their professional boundaries, recognising achievable goals and how imaginative responses are possible within resource constraints. This stance opens up possibilities for users and carers, being the antithesis of paternalistic, controlling forms of intervention. They accept their organisational base, while confronting constructively the real nature of relationships between themselves, service users and colleagues. Acceptance of what is professionally 'doable' comes as a relief, generating creative energy for healthy survival in constraining and restrictive agencies.

Organisational devices

The themes identified through this analysis of personal and professional acceptance strategies reverberate through organisational life. Above all else, reflective practitioners learn to accept that hierarchical organisations are incapable of working constructively with emotions. Reflective action allows workers to maximise the benefits from personnel structures and rules surrounding employment protection, accepting agency provisions enabling them to look after themselves. Hence, reflective workers plan regular holidays and time off in lieu. In contrast, the harassed, accommodating worker does not create the necessary psychological space to unwind and relax. We would argue, therefore, that reflective processes push workers towards recognising the boundaries of their organisational manoeuvrability. Practitioners learn to accept agency policies, procedures and legislative context, over which they have limited impact, or to discern the influence of external, structural and political forces on their daily working practices.

How does this realisation operate? First, reflective practitioners reframe hierarchical decision making as being indicative of organisational complexity. Accommodating workers may grasp at the straw of conspiracy theory to explain decision-making processes, whereas reflection helps practitioners to untangle the threads of well intentioned but flawed ways of operating where the outcome may be the antithesis of sound organisational practice. Second, reflective practitioners accept the agency's tendency towards insularity and parochialism, where their own actions have little impact on the institutional image. Third, they learn to live within resource constraints, rather than bemoaning constantly how these restrictions limit their capacities to engage in creative practice. Finally, and most importantly, they accept the inherent contradictions within organisations, where, for instance, value statements are espoused about caring for and respecting individuals while staff care remains marginalised. Similarly, equal opportunities policies may be trumpeted while the organisation is riddled with inherent racism, sexism, heterosexism, ageism and discrimination against those with disabilities.

There is a common thread in this discussion of acceptance strategies, namely, social workers' ability to locate areas of policy and practice over which they have limited influence. This creates clear boundaries, within which practitioners can remain centred, letting go of unproductive activities, thoughts or emotions.

Conclusion

Practitioners constantly shift between patterns of accommodation and reflection-in-action in their daily working lives, as they juggle the different and competing value systems operating in agencies. This chapter has presented a framework for conceptualising practitioner behaviour emanating from the tension between social work ideals and practice realities. In so doing, we have shown how practitioners deploy a range of personal, professional and organisational devices to manage difficult, messy practice situations and organisational decision making. In Part 2, these dilemmas are explored in relation to specific practice contexts in order to illustrate more clearly how the devices can operate in practice. The unifying element in all of these chapters is the acknowledgement that skilled social work practice can make a difference in the various settings under discussion; however, unless social workers are able to manage the pressures that confront them within organisations they will be incapable of making that difference.

Part II

Part II

4

Social Work in the Voluntary Sector: Moving Forward While Holding On

Bill Badham and Tina Eadie

Introduction

> If anything is common to the (voluntary) sector it is a commitment to the preservation of diversity and above all to independence. And independence, if it means anything, must mean freedom to challenge the ideas and values, the policies and practices, and the activities and structures of other institutions in our society (Deakin, 1996a: p. 21).

The challenge facing the voluntary sector is to hold on to this independence while taking increasing responsibility for direct service provision, a space previously occupied by the statutory services. The government's commitment to this ever-increasing role of the voluntary sector in social care provision is set out in its Compact – an agreement drawn up with the voluntary sector in 1998, with separate documents for each of the countries in the United Kingdom (Stowe, 1998). Its guidelines define mutual expectations and good practice in areas such as contracts and funding. Further momentum was created after the government's July 2002 Comprehensive Spending Review. In September 2002, the Treasury unveiled its recommendations entitled 'The Role of the Voluntary and Community Sector in Service Delivery'. This three-year blueprint aims to enable the voluntary sector to play an increased role in public service delivery, pledging to fund properly the costs of providing services, encouraging more long-term contracts and promoting wider use of the sector's expertise.

Using a *macro* analysis, this chapter examines how the voluntary sector in the United Kingdom needs to move forward in taking account of the demands of contracts – which increasingly define the terms of reference of its activities. At the same time it argues that the sector must hold on to its campaigning function in pushing forward empowering services with, and on behalf of, disadvantaged and marginalised groups. Linked to this, the chapter investigates ways in which contractual relationships between the voluntary and statutory sectors affect radical and cutting-edge practice in relation both to campaigning and direct service provision roles. Drawing on the discussion in Chapter 3, the manoeuvrability of voluntary sector workers in the face of the increasingly heavy weight of contractual obligations to statutory partners is explored. A key tension highlighted for both practitioners and managers is the importance of working in ways which contribute towards alleviating structural inequalities – central to social work in the voluntary sector – while seeking to exploit the opportunities for developing a more secure funding base that are arising from the increased role of the sector in public service delivery.

The chapter begins by exploring briefly the concept of the voluntary sector and social welfare work within it. It focuses specifically on values underpinning practice at a *macro* level of analysis – those which support methods of working for social change. A model is introduced to examine the sector's shifting relationship with the state. In the light of this, the chapter concentrates on two specific ways of working which are central to effecting change at the *macro* level – campaigning and empowerment. Practice scenarios demonstrate workers' imaginative and creative approaches to the challenges presented by the current political and economic environment. Solution-focused practice as opposed to problem-based practice is highlighted and key values, knowledge, and skills underpinning *macro* level voluntary sector practice are drawn out.

The voluntary sector and social work

The roots of voluntary action in Britain can be traced back to the sixteenth century (Davis Smith, 1995: p. 9), encompassing the work of philanthropic organisations and individuals concerned with the relief of poverty and distress (see Owen, 1964) and the development of mutual aid, self-help and reform (see Beveridge, 1948). Kendall and

Knapp (1995: p. 66) note that observers and analysts of the voluntary sector often begin their accounts by remarking on its 'bewildering array of organisational forms, activities, motivations and ideologies'. Commentators find it easier to say what it is *not* – not for profit, not statutory – than what it *is* (Marshall, 1996: p. 46). Broadly, it includes trade unions, sports clubs, trade and professional associations, places of worship, universities and political parties (Perri 6 and Fieldgrass, 1992: p. 9). More narrowly defined it includes charities, and independent, not-for-profit and co-operative organisations. These range on a continuum from large complex bureaucracies whose internal hierarchies match those in the statutory sector to small, highly integrated organisations where policy making, management and practice might be undertaken by the same people, often unpaid. Functions include some or all of the following categories (Knight, 1993: p. 111):

- Service philanthropy – helping others in a less advantageous situation to oneself.
- Social solidarity – helping self and others in the same situation.
- Changing – altering the basis of society.
- Mobilising – rallying other people or resources to support a cause.
- Creating – bringing something new into play.
- Intermediary – co-ordinating or organising activities.

Our focus here is on organisations that address social need, specifically through 'changing', 'mobilising' and 'creating', and especially those at the cutting edge of promoting social justice. It is interesting that the current 'new' Labour government is acknowledging the distinctive value that these organisations bring, and promoting their crucial role in involving users in the design and delivery of services and acting as advocates to those most marginalised through poverty and social exclusion (Home Office, 2001: p. 3).

The voluntary sector has a long history of effecting change at the *macro* level. Examples from both the past and present include:

- The nineteenth-century pioneers of social action who saw themselves 'campaigning against evil' (Knight, 1993: p. 12).
- The nineteenth-century self-help movement (Knight, 1993; Davis Smith, 1995).
- Radical social work practice in the 1970s and the early 1980s embracing community work (Mayo, 1975, 1980), feminist

perspectives arising from the Women's Movement (Wilson, 1977; Barrett and McIntosh, 1982), anti-racism (Hall *et al.*, 1979; Sivanandan, 1982; Bryan *et al.*, 1985), and changing perceptions of sexuality (Hart, 1980) and disability (Oliver, 1983).
- Progress made in relation to Children's Rights in the 1990s (DoH, 1999a; Willow, 2001, 2002).

Value judgements about the nature of society underpin these examples. Values are moral principles or standards by which individuals and groups judge both themselves and others; therefore, social welfare practitioners must be clear about their own value base and its impact. This includes a recognition of potential conflicts, both within and between organisations (see Paton, 1996), and the ongoing tension in social work between focusing on individuals' welfare needs and tackling structural forces creating poverty and injustice (Jones, 1997). While people's motivation to voluntary action can range from sentiments of 'wanting to help others' to an all-embracing commitment to social justice, the value of much of the voluntary sector is its particular focus on tackling inequalities rather than blaming disadvantaged individuals and communities.

Holding similar values can act as 'the glue that binds the members of the organisation together' (Barnard and Walker, 1994: p. 58) and these will therefore influence the mission or purpose for which a group is established and to which their donors, volunteers and members subscribe. It is from this that voluntary organisations gain their legitimacy (Taylor and Langan, 1996: p. 28). Those working at the *macro/micro* interface as defined here will seek to address structural inequalities which disadvantage and exclude certain individuals and groups in society. These types of organisations could include a focus on:

- promotion of Black community development from a grassroots perspective;
- encouraging the development and management of good quality accommodation for people living with HIV or AIDS;
- establishing services for families of children with special needs because of developmental or learning difficulties, or a mental or physical disability;
- creating social activities to relieve isolation among lesbians, bisexuals and gay men;
- introducing formal structures to improve the economic, legal and social position of lone parent families.

Voluntary action has been influential in achieving social change and developing innovative services for marginalised groups in ways unmatched by the statutory sector. It has been argued (Jones, 1996) that mainstream social work has never succeeded in mounting a rigorous challenge to the legitimacy in which patterns of inequality and oppression systematically disadvantage specific groups of people. However, campaigns and pressure groups in the voluntary sector, particularly in the 1960s and the early 1970s, challenged the status quo and developed alternative structures outside of the existing system (Knight, 1993: pp. 23–4; Deakin, 1996b: p. 114). Much was achieved in the areas of, for example, family poverty, disability, homelessness, mental health, citizens' rights, community development and other local initiatives.

It would be wrong, however, to imply that the voluntary sector holds a monopoly on tackling structural inequalities. First, while the voluntary sector is generally regarded as a 'good thing' (Gann, 1996: p. 105) and 'value-led' (Hodgkin, 1993), research has found no shortage of values in other organisations (Taylor and Langan, 1996: p. 27). Second, voluntary organisations can also serve as 'mediators between the individual and the state, holding society together as well as lubricating it for social change' (Marshall, 1996: p. 45). Evers (1993) goes further and argues that the sector intercedes between three spheres in society – the state, the individual and the market. This role transcends differences in mission and function, giving individuals, groups and communities a vital role not only in social change, but also in society. Finally, if the voluntary sector ignores structural inequalities, then it can make them worse by pursuing its own self interest rather than tackling the underlying problems.

The voluntary sector, therefore, is diverse, dynamic, heterogeneous and covers a range of organisational structures from large national charities to small community groups. Social work within it reflects this, with social welfare services fulfilling a myriad of functions including mirroring those traditionally undertaken by the state, filling gaps in provision, identifying new needs and speaking out against social injustice. In this way, voluntary organisations have been well placed to experiment with innovative forms of provision, and to act as advisors or advocates for those seeking a particular service (see Deakin, 1996b: p. 114; Newman, 1998: p. 352). It is this relative autonomy and adaptability that has been threatened through an emphasis on contracts rather than more flexible grant arrangements. Although the Compact between the government and the voluntary sector

(Home Office, 1998a) validated organisations' rights to campaign against government policy without jeopardising their funding agreements, the extent to which this is achievable is still unclear. There is significant tension between government funding the sector by £4 billion a year to help the government achieve its objectives, and doing so in a manner which supports a key plank of its effective funding framework to 'respect the sector's independence' (Home Office, 2001). There remains concern about the extent to which the assumption of complementary interests between the government and the voluntary sector could negate some of the key roles and functions of the voluntary sector within society (Osborne and McLaughlin, 2002). The following section looks at the changing relationship between voluntary and statutory agencies in more detail.

Moving forward: the changing relationship between the voluntary and statutory sectors

The nature of the voluntary sector's relationship with the state changed dramatically during the 1990s, as outlined in Chapter 2. Statutory agencies took on specific roles of 'purchaser', 'regulator', 'competitor', 'collaborator', and 'commissioner' (Jones, 1996: p. 42). Voluntary and private sector organisations became providers of services previously the responsibility of the state. This mixed economy of care resulted in a major cultural shift (Means and Smith, 1998) for those involved and a blurring of responsibilities (Douglas and Philpot, 1998). As voluntary organisations, particularly those involved in the delivery of adult services, took on the role of 'alternative' rather than 'complementary' or 'supplementary' provider to the statutory sector, concerns were expressed about the impact on the nature of their activity (see, e.g., Lewis, 1993, 1996a; Deakin, 1996b). Although still heavily reliant on voluntary income – through individual and corporate giving – the contribution of central and local government grew (Hanvey and Philpot, 1996: p. 3). This was increasingly in the form of contracts bringing obligations and new responsibilities (see Lewis and Glennerster, 1996: pp. 105–12), rather than grants allowing greater discretion over spending.

The election of the 'new' Labour government in 1997 and the development of its 'Third Way' programme (Blair, 1998; Giddens, 1998) has resulted in a whole raft of initiatives (e.g., Quality Protects, New Deal for Communities, Education/Health Action Zones) relating to the Social Exclusion agenda. Rather than voluntary organisations and community groups bidding directly to local authorities for funding, they are increasingly making applications directly to central government *in partnership* with local authorities. Local Strategic Partnerships (LSPs) are seen as the overarching framework in the public, private, voluntary and community sectors. The emphasis is on resourcing communities to run their own projects through the funding of local small grant schemes. While it is hoped this will ensure that different initiatives and services support rather than contradict each other (Cabinet Office, 2001), there will be less opportunity for small voluntary organisations to set their own goals and objectives (Jordan with Jordan, 2000: p. 110).

There are also implications for social work; direct work with service users is increasingly being undertaken through a proliferation of new projects, units and schemes. Their overall aim is:

> . . . to get alongside service users, be available to them, work with them on their definitions of their current problems and give them lots of influence over processes of deciding on and progressing towards solutions (Jordan with Jordan, 2000: p. 130).

These initiatives are associated with social work in its broadest sense but are outside of formal social services structures. Furthermore employees are neither formally employed as social workers, nor see themselves as such (Jordan with Jordan, 2000; see also Garrett, 2002c).

One implication of these changed forms of funding is a shift in the nature and emphasis of voluntary sector activity. Most voluntary bodies would characterise themselves as 'multifunctional' (Kendall and Knapp, 1995: p. 67), and for our purposes here we have focused on two broad approaches – service provision and what Brenton (cited in Kendall and Knapp, 1995: p. 67) calls the 'pressure group function'. The former is 'a direct service to people, in kind or in the form of information, advice and support'. The latter includes direct action in the form of campaigning, lobbying and advocacy to achieve a desired change, including structural reform at the *macro* level. Many organisations combine both. As funding becomes increasingly tied to the provision of specific services, the allocation of resources to pressure group activities has declined (see Hanvey and Philpot, 1996: p. 5; Lewis and Glennerster, 1996: p. 111). Figure 4.1 illustrates this by means of a model in which the sphere of voluntary activity is shown as shifting from block 1 to block 2.

While acknowledging that private sector services have increased markedly over the past decade, this dimension will not be addressed

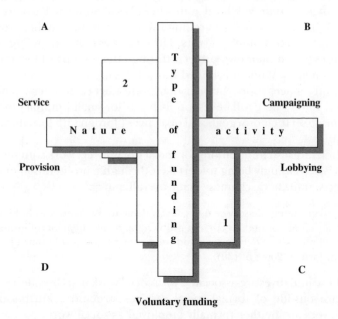

Figure 4.1 The interplay between voluntary sector funding and activity

here. For the purposes of the model, included in statutory income are forms of funding geared to achieving government determined goals, for example, the European Social Fund, the Single Regeneration Budget and the Children's Fund. Funding from Trusts is regarded as voluntary income, as is money from the Community Fund, while recognising that a significant element of the Community Fund is determined by government priorities.

The quadrants A, B, C, and D represent four broad positions in which voluntary organisations' work might be located:

A: Heavily reliant on statutory funding and providing a service in return.
B: Dependent on statutory funding for campaigning and lobbying activities.
C: Campaigns and lobbying resourced through voluntary funding.
D: Services provided through voluntary funding.

Voluntary sector activity takes place across all four quadrants. A service could be provided at full cost through a statutory contract to one group of service users (quadrant A), and at a nominal cost to another group, resourced through voluntary contributions and donations (quadrant D). The organisation might choose to use some of its donations to lobby for a change in legislation, or to campaign on behalf of specific service users (quadrant C). It might also, though less likely, be encouraged by its statutory partner to push for broader political changes in respect of its user group (quadrant B). Differing levels of activity in each quadrant are shown by blocks 1 and 2. Block 1 represents the locus of activity of an organisation which relies primarily on voluntary funding. It is in a position to choose how it manages its budget and the priorities placed on different aspects of the work. While it undertakes a range of activities, proportionately fewer are in the form of contracts with statutory agencies. Block 2 is more representative of an organisation which prioritises direct service provision by contract, including through local partnerships, placing its main locus of activity in quadrant A.

The 'mixed economy of welfare', referred to in Chapter 2, is not a new concept (Lewis, 1995; Douglas and Philpot, 1998; Johnson, 1999), but government enthusiasm for it in the 1980s and the 1990s led to a significant expansion in voluntary (and private) sector activity. There has been much concern about the potential loss of the multiple functions performed by the voluntary sector when basic welfare provision is prioritised by agencies seeking to secure contracts (Leat, 1993; Lewis and Glennerster, 1996). A concomitant reduction in emphasis on preventative work, campaigning and community development initiatives (Gutch *et al.*, 1990: p. 7) is demonstrated in the model by a shift from block 1 towards block 2. This rearrangement has implications for the voluntary sector's traditional role of pioneering new and innovative services not offered by the state but which, in time, statutory agencies might emulate (Hanvey and Philpot, 1996: p. 4). It brings into question whether groups would *be able to* continue campaigning against the state and lobbying for change if they are dependent upon it for its funding (Hanvey and Philpot, 1996: p. 5). A reduction in work being undertaken in quadrants B and C – where the strength of voluntary organisations in tackling social injustice at the *macro* level has customarily been found – presents a challenge to those determined to maintain this long-established tradition.

The move from Compulsory Competitive Tendering to Best Value, introduced by the Local Government Act 1999, established a new requirement for local authorities to carry out Best Value reviews of all their services, using the 'four Cs' – challenge, consult, compare and compete (Willow, 2002). This has brought both opportunities and threats. There are opportunities for greater accountability through the clarification of procedures, improvements in the quality of service and a developing sense of professionalism. Some organisations however, particularly smaller organisations, may feel threatened by tightly specified contracts which make demands they are unable to meet. Hedley (1995: p. 99) referred to research findings which reinforce the middle class nature of voluntary organisations. This highlights how working class and Black informal networks can often be ignored or bypassed by the 'organised' voluntary sector. The potential for these new arrangements to be experienced differentially might result in already marginalised groups being more vulnerable to the changes taking place.

Taking the example of Black voluntary groups, an important and growing part of the voluntary sector, it is difficult to establish whether these are facing the same or a greater threat to autonomy and resourcing. Research by Butt and Mirza (1997) showed that although the decline in local authority grant aid was less dramatic in Black organisations from 1995–96 to 1996–97, the overall impact was likely to be greater. This was due to higher dependence on local authorities as the main source of funding and a smaller average size of grant compared with white organisations. In inner city areas with a higher than average proportion of African-Caribbean, Asian and other minority ethnic groups, funding may be adequate, while other locations may be under-resourced, reflecting a recognition that funding might exhibit wider variation than for comparable white groups (Russell *et al.*, 1995: p. 28).

Yee and Mussenden (1998: p. 26) note that many Black groups fear they will 'turn into mini-Social Services Departments', losing their identities as community organisations. This reflects a stark choice of either switching to contract funding (represented in Figure 4.1 by the shift towards quadrant A) – risking uncertain consequences – or refusing to accept the new conditions (remaining predominantly in quadrants C or D) and chance endangering their whole future (Gutch *et al.*, 1990: p. 8). The overloading of the voluntary sector with statutory duties of local authorities puts in jeopardy their distinctive qualities, including an ability to innovate, challenge and pioneer new ways of improving services. The people who lose out will not be policy makers or politicians but service users, especially from disadvantaged groups.

An example of how this dilemma was resolved is the Social Care Provider Project (Yee and Mussenden, 1998), established in Wandsworth to meet Black elderly people's needs. The project helped to shape approaches to service delivery, rather than adopting them wholesale from the social services department – for example, through more joint working and sharing of skills between voluntary and statutory workers. This partnership approach offers voluntary organisations the opportunity to retain their independence while ensuring their users' needs are being met.

The threats and opportunities of shifting the locus of voluntary activity towards quadrant A is explored in relation to another marginalised group, gay and lesbian parents, in practice scenario 4.1.

PRACTICE SCENARIO 4.1

An emergency meeting has been called by a local voluntary organisation, *Children First*. Traditionally, the group has relied on voluntary funding to develop new services but this is becoming more difficult. A recently identified need has been for a lesbian, gay and bisexual support group. Following a wide-ranging debate, a decision was taken to approach the local authority for funding, even though this would be under contract to deliver specific services. Given its wider responsibilities to promote good parenting throughout the community, the local authority refused to dedicate this level of resourcing to a minority group. It has stated that it will reconsider the proposal if it is set out in more general terms. The motion proposed at the emergency meeting is as follows:

> 'We are not prepared to compromise further to secure funding for the identified support needs of lesbian, gay and bi-sexual parents in our community'.

Practice questions:
What opportunities and threats arise for service development at *Children First*:

- If they accept funding under contract to the local authority, marking a shift towards quadrant A of the model?
- If they refuse the money and retain their position within quadrant C and D?

Service provision is increasingly bound by funding imperatives and *Children First* has a difficult choice to make, with members needing to consider how to vote and why. Voting for the principled stance of the motion would maintain the activities of *Children First* in quadrant D in relation to resourcing the service for lesbian, gay and bisexual parents through its own funds. *Children First* might also decide to fund a campaign focusing on the particular needs of this marginalised group, an activity located in quadrant C. However, this position would risk financial vulnerability and being ignored by funders and policy makers. Securing statutory funding for a more general service would locate the activity in quadrant A, and, in the short term at least, ensure that an attempt would be made to include the needs of lesbian, gay and bisexual parents in the service provided. This would mark an overall shift in the locus of the organisation's activities from block 1 to block 2.

There are no easy solutions to this sort of dilemma. What is essential is that an open debate takes place in which members can reflect on the full implications of each option. Then, whatever the outcome of the vote, there will have been an opportunity to restate the values and overall mission of *Children First*, and to have considered these in the light of the current political and economic climate. Those voting against the motion in order to survive need to find ways of holding on to core values, knowledge and skills as practice shifts towards quadrant A. Bates and Pitkeathley (1996: p. 91) offer a salutary reminder that those working in the voluntary sector must beware of becoming too like the corporate sector – the skill is managing the balance between managerial and contractual imperatives and commitment to a cause and overall mission. How practitioners can retain cutting edge, radical practice and continue being a force for change while operating increasingly in quadrant A is illustrated in the following two sections.

Holding on: campaigning for change

Campaigning for change is where voluntary action in the United Kingdom began, with individuals committed to a cause turning a 'private trouble into a public issue to bring about changes in the law and in public opinion' (Bates and Pitkeathley, 1996: pp. 91–2). As such, it is central to the motivation of many in the sector and reflects key values underpinning voluntary action targeted at changing the status quo and challenging dominant norms of society. The campaign discussed in this section arose from workers suspecting an injustice and seeking ways of investigating it further. Their reflection-in-action, as discussed in Chapter 3, was demonstrated through their ability to look behind the facts being presented to them, to question certain information, to share hunches and ideas with colleagues and to lobby for action from their agency.

This example draws on the experience of a voluntary organisation whose mission includes campaigning for children's rights while also providing specialist child-centred services. Its justice orientation seeks to energise workers to reflect critically on their practice and that of others, noting inequalities and discrimination, and bringing these to the attention of managers. In the process, practitioners become a powerful force for change at the *macro* level. While the mediating role of the organisation is also important, the focus here is on the *macro/micro* interface, that is, how workers are able to contribute to this particular element of the mission. The issues raised are intended to be transferable and not specific to any one organisation.

The Children Act 1989, implemented in 1991, sets the scene for this practice scenario. The Act places a duty on all local authorities to introduce complaints procedures with a view to ensuring they are more accountable to 'looked after' children. These are aimed at enabling young people, their parents, carers or anyone with 'sufficient interest in the child's welfare' to make a complaint to the local authority about any aspect of the care received. On commencing a formal investigation, the complaints officer appoints both an investigating officer and an independent person who, as the name implies, is not a member of the social services department in which the complaint has originated and aims to provide an objective element. The two work alongside each other to ensure the complainant receives a fair investigation.

The Children's Resource Project, originally set up in 1992 with a consortium of 11 local authorities across Yorkshire and the North-East, is managed by The Children's Society. Committed to promoting justice for children and being a force for change, rather than becoming an extension of statutory provision by voluntary means, the Society aims to retain an overall funding ratio of 50/50 between voluntary income and all other external sources. It funds services for children, placed in quadrant D of Figure 4.1, from voluntary contributions, which also resource campaigning activities, located in quadrant C. The Children's Resource Project, however, is found in quadrant A of Figure 4.1 because the work is contracted by the

---

PRACTICE SCENARIO 4.2

Yasmin is a 13-year-old Muslim girl who has been in foster care for six months. She is concerned that her African-Caribbean foster parents have taken insufficient notice of her cultural needs in relation to religion, diet and dress. She was given information about the complaints procedure by her social worker but the explanation given had been brief and she remained unclear how to instigate the process. She tried to raise her concerns at her review but felt that no-one really understood how deeply she felt. Recently, she spoke to a different social worker who helped her make a complaint.

Practice questions:

- What action could be taken to explore workers' concerns that young people in foster care are even less well informed about the complaints procedure than those in residential care?
- What are the tensions arising from the fact that the Children's Resource Project is managed by a voluntary organisation but funded by the statutory agency against whom the complaint is being made?

---

11 authorities. Practice scenario 4.2 is used to demonstrate the potential for campaigning for change at a *macro/micro* level when the funding comes from statutory rather than voluntary sources.

In carrying out their task, and sharing their findings with each other, workers in The Children's Resource Project began to suspect that young people in residential care had more awareness of, and better access to, the local authority complaints procedure than those in foster care. (A major piece of research (Padbury and Frost, 2001) has in fact found that 55% of young people in foster care knew nothing about the complaints procedure.) An accommodating worker, as described in Chapter 3, risks missing the links between the young people being investigated. S/he would follow the procedure, not looking for the wider implications of issues being raised. The reflective practitioner, however, is interested more broadly in the young person's experience of the complaints procedure. In discussion with other workers, s/he develops a picture of complaints not being taken seriously, young people having a lack of knowledge about the procedure and what could be complained about, and insufficient attention being paid to generating satisfactory conclusions. Together, the workers question why this is happening and how it can be addressed. The workers pursue their concerns through managers, confident that what has been identified will be of wider interest within the organisation as it links to its values regarding justice for children.

Success in campaigning requires an ability to recognise and seize an opportunity to push forward a specific agenda, an issue about which there is growing concern but not yet a public outcry (Bates and Pitkeathley, 1996: p. 87). Project workers began to make connections, realising that the majority of complainants were from residential, not foster care settings, and were white, older and able-bodied. Procedurally, they noted unacceptable time delays – well beyond the 28 days allowed in the Children Act 1989. Responses to complaints by senior local authority officers were individualised, with little or no attempt at changing or even challenging the systems underpinning the issues raised. These concerns were discussed with line managers and taken up within the organisation as needing further investigation.

Arising from the reflective practice of the project staff, The Children's Society funded research focusing on five of the local authorities working with The Children's Resource Project over a five-month period in 1996–97. Data were collected about young people's perceptions and use of the complaints procedure, and their experience of making a formal complaint (Wallis and Frost, 1998: p. 12). The results showed that significantly more young people interviewed from residential care were aware of the procedure compared with those from foster care and no young person with a disability knew of its existence. Younger children appeared to be disadvantaged by the emphasis on formal, written information. In relation to timescales, only 18% of complaints made by young people were processed within 28 days, with over 50% of complaints taking more than 56 days. A series of recommendations were published with the report, including the introduction of a range of systems reflecting differences in age, ethnicity and ability (see Wallis and Frost, 1998: p. 68). The importance given to the results of the study are demonstrated in a letter by Paul Boateng, then Parliamentary Under Secretary of State, which states that the study '. . . indicates where changes are needed before we can be sure that looked after children are heard by those who care for them' (Wallis and Frost, 1998: p. vii).

As an example of reflection-in-action as depicted in Chapter 3, the project workers linked current instances of children looked after using the complaints procedure with their past experiences. Their intuition told them it was predominantly children in residential not foster care who came to their attention. The research project and the dissemination of its results not only raised issues about the operation of complaints systems but also identified wider implications for ensuring best practice in substitute care for children and young people. This moves the debate into the *macro* arena of equality of opportunity and children's rights to high-quality provision, protection and participation (Wallis and Frost, 1998: p. 73).

Nevertheless, how can workers manage the current tension between an organisation's right to speak out against certain aspects of statutory agencies' policy and its increasing reliance on them for funding? In our example of the research arising from The Children's Resource Project, a confrontational strategy could have alienated the 11 local authorities, preventing them from listening and being part of the change process. Their support for, and joint ownership of, the research might have been withdrawn, and with it their referrals of children and young people willing to be interviewed. Ultimately, The Children's Society could have lost the contract for the project. The scenario has shown that practitioners can act as change agents and promote their organisation's mission while working under contract to statutory agencies. What particular values, knowledge and skills relevant to campaigning for change can be drawn from the scenario and applied to other settings?

First, those involved need to be clear about the purpose of the campaign and its underpinning values. This requires energy and commitment to the promotion of the organisation's mission. The backing of those on whose behalf they are campaigning is needed, calling for an ability to take people along with them, to harness their support and enthuse them to the cause. Networking skills are involved – keeping in touch with sufficient numbers of individuals and groups to ensure that views are represented accurately (Bates and Pitkeathley, 1996: p. 83). Skills in verbal and written communication are essential, as is the ability to plan carefully, to organise time and personnel, and to negotiate access to people, information and resources. Research skills, as in the example, can also be utilised to achieve change.

Success is often measured by column inches (Bates and Pitkeathley, 1996: p. 86), therefore knowledge and skills are required in ensuring positive media coverage of the issue (Aldridge, 1994). It cannot be assumed that the local press will be sympathetic, nor that the national media will be interested. Getting to know local photographers is a start – they often gain access to the local press. Liaising with a particular reporter will establish rapport, helping to ensure that any article written gives an informed and accurate representation. Editors need to be identified and targeted, and the campaign explained with a clear and simple message. For overall success, an organisation must command the respect of its constituency *and* those it is trying to influence: 'Treading that tricky path between speaking with a confident voice and shouting so loudly that no one can or will listen to you is a skill which must be acquired' (Bates and Pitkeathley, 1996: p. 85). This is particularly important when a campaign arises from a project contracted by a statutory funder.

Workers in our example did not ignore the patterns of unequal access to the complaints procedure presented to them, neither did they just diagnose the problem; through campaigning activity within their organisation they became part of the solution. The organisation, while welcoming an income-generating project located in quadrant A of Figure 4.1, continued to seek ways of being a force for change. Locating itself primarily in quadrants C and D, The Children's Society was able to allocate resources to the research identified through its work with the statutory sector in quadrant A. In addition to demonstrating that voluntary organisations can continue to operate flexibly within a contracting climate, the research also gave children and young people looked after a voice. This is explored further in the following section focusing on service users' empowerment within the commissioning culture.

Holding on: empowerment in action

Like campaigning, empowerment is central to cutting-edge practice in the voluntary sector. This section explores the concept briefly and sets out a practice scenario which indicates some of the values, knowledge and skills required for empowering practice. It further demonstrates how principles of empowerment can operate within a voluntary sector project relying on a local authority contract for the majority of its funding. Reflecting on this at the *macro/micro* level, we argue that projects linked to broader social and political agendas, in this case the disability movement, are able to demand a high level of funding with fewer constraints than the nature of their activity might suggest. Regarded as a valuable and necessary service to vulnerable and marginalised people, they have more bargaining power – which workers should exploit.

Empowerment is a much-contested concept and, as Henderson and Pochin (2001: p. 76) suggest, is 'widely acclaimed but difficult to measure'. Maintaining our *macro/micro* focus, the definition employed here addresses power imbalances between individuals and groups in society and the means by which people become increasingly involved in issues affecting them directly:

> Empowerment . . . is a collective process on which the powerless embark as part of the struggle to resist the oppression of others, as part of their demands to be included, and/or to articulate their own views of the world (Oliver, 1996: p. 147).

While focusing on disability, this definition is applicable to other expressions of oppression including race (Solomon, 1976; Rooney, 1987; Ahmad, 1990), gender (Ernst and Goodison, 1981; Eichenbaum and Orbach, 1985), race and gender (hooks, 1982; Collins, 1991; Yuval-Davis, 1994), sexuality (Weeks, 1985; Corbett, 1994), poverty (Lister and Beresford, 1991), and children's rights (Willow, 2002). The value position underpinning the above definition reflects a belief that power can be 'given, granted or permitted', but is unlikely to be handed out to 'have-not' groups in society (Staples, 1990: p. 29). It must therefore be developed or taken by the powerless themselves (Hess in Staples, 1990: p. 29).

What is the role of practitioners if empowerment stresses the competence and rights of people to 'take charge of their own destinies'? (Staples, 1990: p. 31). In the classic text *Pedagogy of the Oppressed*, the Brazilian educator Paulo Freire (1972) made the important point that leaders must be careful not to dominate – either through greater knowledge or perceived understanding of their situation. This would be 'to deny true praxis to the people, deny them the right to say their own word and think their own thoughts' (1972: p. 97). Workers are responsible for co-ordination and, at times, direction but their opinions must not be imposed. Freire believed it to be essential that oppressed groups participate fully in any process of change, and that it is through increased awareness of their oppression that they acquire the ability to intervene and change the conditions in which they live (1972: pp. 80–1). Service users can be helped by workers to reflect critically, to make links, to take forward common issues, and to effect change, but they themselves must remain active participants in the creation and implementation of any policies, decisions, and processes affecting them (Staples, 1990: p. 31). Practice scenario 4.3 illustrates this.

PRACTICE SCENARIO 4.3: CENTRE ACTION

In 1989, a project worker was employed by MENCAP Homes Foundation to work with a group of adults with learning disabilities to clean up the derelict garden attached to one of its residential centres. Employing principles of empowerment, the worker used gardening as a means for the group to come together, rather than as an end in itself. Over time, the initial task was achieved and a garden maintenance service, Centre Action, was developed in the local community, being offered to those community members unable to do all gardening work themselves, and, through contracts, to local businesses. The majority of the group's funding is now obtained from the city council through a two year renewable contract.

Practice questions:

- What values, knowledge and skills of empowerment might the project worker have used?
- What are the potential problems arising from the funding arrangement and how might these be addressed?
- How might Centre Action be contributing to social justice and wider structural change?

Centre Action is an innovative project involving a group of people with learning disabilities facilitated by one paid worker. Run on principles of self-advocacy (see Brandon *et al.*, 1995), it is a radical alternative to a traditional day centre. Self-advocacy is about people speaking out and making themselves heard (with or without words), learning the skills needed to represent themselves and determining what happens in their lives. Reflecting this, Centre Action provides a unique opportunity for members to become actively involved in running their own gardening service. It is guided by values determining that work with people with learning disabilities should affirm their dignity and self-respect, enabling them to contribute to community life.

What knowledge and skills are required to realise these values in practice? The reflective worker will be knowledgeable about the different ways in which empowerment has been conceptualised, and the associated practice guidelines developed for its delivery (see, e.g., Solomon, 1976; Croft and Beresford, 1990; Beresford and Croft, 1993; Braye and Preston-Shoot, 1993; Ward and Mullender, 1991). These will not be accepted uncritically (see Fawcett and Featherstone, 1996: p. 54; Humphries, 1996b: p. 6; Page, 1992: p. 90) and the power imbalance inherent in the worker-service user relationship will be recognised. When faced with a dilemma, the reflective worker's skill is demonstrated by the ability to stand back, to facilitate the discovery of a resolution, one reinforcing the rights, requirements and responsibilities of the individuals involved. An accommodating worker, however, is likely to adopt a 'quick-fix, technical problem-solving approach' (Adams, 1996: p. 25).

In the context of Figure 4.1, Centre Action activity is located in block 2 as the majority of its funding is provided by the city council. However, the need to complete the city council's annual monitoring form presented a problem as its written style and use of jargon made it inaccessible to members. As a further example of 'reflection-in-action' (see Chapter 3), rather than simply filling in the form the project worker consulted with the group and acted on their collective decision that the form was a 'nonsense'. A city council officer was invited to visit the group and gain the necessary information through the means agreed by its members – a presentation achieved through pictures, video and their own words. The officer agreed to adapt the method of determining and reviewing Centre Action's contract by making regular visits. Bureaucratic, unintelligible and imposed systems of accountability were therefore replaced by dialogue, dignity and increased mutual understanding.

Everyone at Centre Action might dislike the language of contracts, the 'jumping through hoops', but they have demonstrated their ability to engage with the contract culture while maintaining their integrity. The worker's skills were crucial in this process. By holding on to her core belief in the group's capacity to empower itself, not dominating but enabling group members to create and give their presentation, the worker ensured they were in control, not her. While having some concerns about whether the group would give a comprehensive account of their activities, the stance taken affirmed her belief in Centre Action as a means for individuals to explore their strengths, to gain status and develop a positive view of themselves through their own accomplishments. Members have stated that the group is where they can make self discoveries, 'be who we are', rather than moulded by society's definitions. Describing her role as being 'a supportive person standing back', the worker said: 'You listen, you watch everything and you assume nothing'.

By involving everyone in the process, from the actual physical work to administering the office-based scheme as a business, individuals at

Centre Action experience increased confidence and skills, leading to greater independence. The solution-focused as opposed to problem-based approach reflects key aspects of empowering practice interacting at the *macro/micro* interface. Specifically:

- People have rights, including rights to be heard and to control their own lives (Human Rights Act 1998; Disability Discrimination Act 1995).
- Practice can effectively be built on the knowledge that people acting collectively can be powerful (Mullender and Ward, 1991, p. 31).

One expression of this collective power is the 'Equal People Statement' developed by Centre Action members which reads:

> We work together and respect each other for who we are. We have decided that putting people down because of their race, colour, or religion is wrong. Putting people down because they are women who are lesbian or men who are gay is wrong. Putting people down because they have a disability or find anything hard to do is wrong. We do not want this to happen here. We do not like the feeling of being put down, it makes us angry and unhappy. We try not to do it to anyone else.

What the project officer saw reflected the group's collective power. If workers play into the system by completing inappropriate forms and going to the city council as 'professional to professional', the oppression of specific groups of people will be perpetuated. In contrast, empowerment is a way of life, a way of acting, a way of being. All practitioners have values, knowledge and skills but central to the process is the skill of knowing when to make them known and when it is more appropriate to wait and allow others to work through a process of developing their own.

When large numbers of groups and organisations are promoting the same cause in their own way and often in isolation from each other, they can become a new social movement (Davis in Oliver, 1996: p. 149), impacting on public attitudes and national policy. Centre Action, as part of the wider disability movement, has contributed to placing on the political agenda their right to be heard and taken seriously, to participate and to have access to decision-making processes.

Conclusion

There is a risk that contracting for services absorbs the vibrancy, creativity and independence of voluntary action; that the voluntary sector sells out to the state, loses its way and becomes no more than a cheap alternative to public services, held to ransom by local and national government reluctant to let go of the purse strings (Whelan, 1996). This chapter has sought to demonstrate that, despite the emphasis on best value, efficiency and effectiveness, workers in voluntary sector social welfare agencies continue to work in innovative and creative ways. The values, knowledge and skills they use to challenge statutory norms and accepted practices achieve changes that have the potential to impact positively on those with whom they work at individual, group, institutional and structural levels.

The sector's current interdependence with the state is not new, but is taking a different form. The voluntary sector can be compared to a chameleon changing its colour to suit the particular backdrop of the times. As discussed, this offers both opportunities and threats. While for some, particularly larger organisations, there will be advantages such as further expansion and a reliable source of income, there is also the risk of losing sight of their original mission, their independence and incentive to campaign. While the voluntary sector needs to demonstrate flexibility to rise to the new challenges, success in the new culture should not be at the expense of diversity and independence, challenging existing approaches and drawing new issues into the public arena.

The chapter has shown that voluntary sector social welfare agencies can rise to the challenge, to demonstrate that voluntary action is not static but is able to pioneer change (Knight, 1993). They can hold on to their roots as promoters of social justice, while adapting and moving forward within new parameters set by the government in its Compact with the sector. Groups are showing that it is possible and essential to embrace what is most dear to them – promoting the needs of marginalised groups, influencing public opinion, campaigning for policy change, ensuring empowering practice, and encouraging active citizenship.

It has been stated that independent voluntary organisations are 'the backbone of a civil society and a vital indicator of democratic health' (Joseph Rowntree Foundation, 1996: p. 1). This chapter has shown that practitioners who retain their values, maintaining the organisation's mission while working to new priorities and within new constraints, will achieve a more skilled, reflective and empowering level of practice and present a model to other sectors of how to provide effective services *and* effect change at the *macro* level.

5

Community Connections and Creative Mental Health Practice

Peter Bates and Sandra Butler

Community recovery begins when the community and its leaders understand both the effects of mental illness and the societal impact of not delivering effective, efficient services. Recovery begins in earnest when the community and its leaders find ways to harness the potential contribution of service users in every aspect of community life (Silvestri and Jue, 2002: p. 32).

Introduction

There is a history of distrust between the people who use and those who provide mental health services. Despite this, user consultation and empowerment have become critical themes in mental health, generating efforts to produce user-centred services, generally concentrating upon either training the users to help reform existing services or creating new organisations unpolluted by traditional values, policies and practices. There are alternatives to these options, such as training the traditional power holders to let go, creating new patterns of decision making, or re-interpreting the notion of empowerment so that it relates to independent living rather than service design and delivery. It is this last strand that we pursue here by examining the development of community inclusion as a viable option for service planners in constructing alternatives to heavily congregated mental health services. The chapter uses the pioneering work of the Community Connections Project, Nottingham, as a practice scenario at various points in the chapter to illustrate many of the themes for discussion. Because of this, the various practice scenarios in this chapter are different from those found elsewhere in the book; as they refer to the establishment of a specific project they do not contain separate practice questions, but refer to the various issues confronted when establishing the project. It should also be noted that while this scenario outlines the development of a particular service (a *mezzo* response), it was established because of the effects of the *macro* level on people experiencing mental health difficulties. However, there are other responses that individual practitioners could make to these circumstances: the approach outlined does not represent the only possible 'solution'.

PRACTICE SCENARIO 5.1: INTRODUCING THE COMMUNITY CONNECTIONS PROJECT

In 1993, the first author became increasingly aware of the failure of traditional psychiatric day services to tackle community inclusion. Day centres could be empowering and participative but they failed to build a bridge into ordinary relationships with citizens outside of the mental health system. At that time the local further education college wanted to provide opportunities to people with mental health difficulties and appointed an education counsellor for a six-month trial period. Linking with one day centre, she gradually developed suitable pathways into college for numerous people, many of whom participated as individual students in mainstream classes. The vision grew to identify similar links into sports activities, cultural pursuits, and so on, with the model of Community Connections evolving incrementally (Bates, 1996). By 1998, the project had its own office base, was appointing its first full time team leader, building collaborative arrangements with learning disability services and had worked with over 300 service users and 50 community organisations. This work has since then been ongoing.

Utilising a *macro/micro* analysis, this chapter identifies the key theoretical strands that are woven into community connections work. Having outlined a values and policy framework for community inclusion of mental health service users, we present a model of community participation alongside practice issues and dilemmas emanating from the role of Community Bridge Builder. The arguments explored reveal how innovative practice is achievable within the confines of traditional psychiatric systems. They also illustrate that creative work in the field of mental health can stem directly from *macro* concerns about the place of people with mental health difficulties in society.

Consequences of using mental health services

As mental health reforms have progressed it has become obvious that breaking down institutionalisation involves more than just demolishing bricks and mortar. Service users have been excluded from increasingly complex, multiracial and multicultural societal contexts. As a result, they commonly experience a number of factors that constrict their social roles and sense of identity. Within the psychiatric system, the damaging effects of a strong patient identity and an unequal power relationship with staff compounds the problem. The focus on care facilities and care planning which prioritises survival needs and symptom management often avoids any recognition of users' strengths or their contribution to family and community life. Few expect or support users to take on positive roles in the community. In addition, the mystique surrounding mental illness, the community safety shroud-waving of the media, the mantra of confidentiality and the blaming of families all reinforce the illusion that professionals – and no one else – must deal with every problem encountered by service users.

Day services have been particularly slow to develop options that address equal opportunities and users' social exclusion. Their aim has been skill development, behavioural management and change of service users in a depoliticised arena where few centres have created multiracial and woman centred environments. In response to this, African-Caribbean and Asian communities have developed their own autonomous, physically distinctive organisations as expressions of their aspirations, expectations and self-definition of their own experiences, while striving to fulfil the duties and responsibilities of their communities. Indeed, Black users have repeatedly asked for Black centres in user surveys (McGovern and Hemmings, 1994; Radia, 1996), as this provides an opportunity for mutuality and sharing (Sassoon and Lindow, 1995).

While it is necessary to ensure that existing day services provide both Black and women only spaces and times, the establishment of a more community-based, individualised approach for everyone is long overdue. Irrespective of the quality of provision, long-term mental health problems and institutionalisation are associated with a range of features that affect social contact. These include:

- self care, as neglected personal hygiene can offend others (Bates and Pidgeon, 1990);
- home management, as hospitality is a valued feature of friendship;
- unemployment;
- poverty;
- restricted use of educational and leisure facilities.

Relationships may well be characterised by dependency, damaged during acute episodes of disturbance, inhibited by low self-confidence and experienced as stressful. Institutional care is likely to offer a restricted set of models of appropriate behaviour (Goffman, 1961), severe role constriction (Estroff, 1989) and shrunken social circles (Brugha, 1991). Taylor and Huxley (1984: p. 28) observed that the social networks of users with schizophrenia are small, especially in relation to non-kin members. Network members are also poorly connected, having asymmetric relationships where others, rather than the service user, largely direct the relationship. Indeed, the picture is so depressingly uniform that Wilcox and Bellamy (1987) have asserted that people with severe disabilities will experience few relationships, these will most probably be of an impersonal and temporary nature, and that those contacts will be restricted to other users, providers or kin.

The circles network diagram (Figure 5.1) may be used to illustrate the social situation for many long-term service users. Family members may occupy the circle of intimacy while the circle of exchange is populated by staff who are paid to be there, but it is entirely possible that the circles of friendship and participation will be unoccupied. How would we feel and act if these circles were empty in our lives? Some people who have traditionally been blamed for their awkward behaviour might achieve an improved quality of life if their networks included people in every circle. The overriding evidence suggests that people with support needs lead isolated lives and formal services do little to ameliorate the problem.

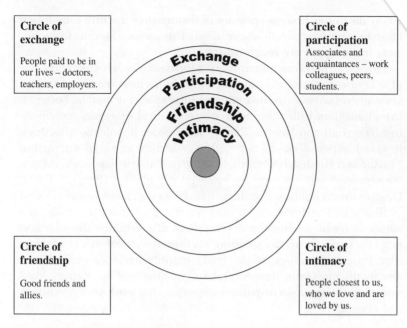

Circle of exchange

People paid to be in our lives – doctors, teachers, employers.

Circle of participation

Associates and acquaintances – work colleagues, peers, students.

Circle of friendship

Good friends and allies.

Circle of intimacy

People closest to us, who we love and are loved by us.

Exchange
Participation
Friendship
Intimacy

Figure 5.1 The circles network diagram

Impact of social contact

Sociologists have attributed a range of problems to isolation, segregation and alienation – for example, House *et al.* (1988) concluded that socially isolated people were twice as likely to die at a given age compared with those who enjoyed strong social ties. The MIND inquiry (Dunn, 1999) provides substantial evidence from service users to show the impact of discrimination and exclusion (see also Sayce, 2000). Psychiatric literature acknowledges the complex relationship between social inclusion and mental distress. Poverty and disadvantage deny people opportunities to develop and sustain community participation (Holloway, 1988), while relationships with family members, neighbours, work or leisure associates can provide a monitoring function, alerting the helping agencies when required. Isolated persons are without the benefit of this monitoring function and therefore problems remain undetected until they become critical (Hughes and Gove, 1981), while people with few social networks are at more risk of abuse. Psychiatric crises can precipitate withdrawal by others, and the social drift hypothesis (Hollingshead and Redlich,

1958) illustrates how, as episodes of disturbance fracture established lifestyle patterns, people move down the socioeconomic scale and away from supportive relationships.

However, this is not an entirely uniform picture. Hughes and Gove (1981) also note that relationships with household members are not always conducive to positive mental health, and it may be better to live alone than with those who are too critical or emotionally over-involved (Leff and Vaughn, 1985). Some older people associate high levels of personal satisfaction with a reduction of social interaction (Taylor and Huxley, 1984) and, in some psychiatric diagnoses, relapse is correlated with an increase in social stimulation (Brugha, 1991). Despite these cautions, Brugha generally sees social isolation as a sign of illness and inclusion as an intervention goal, since it usually con-stitutes a buffer against the development of psychiatric disorder and is a crucial factor in determining successful survival in the commu-nity. Indeed, Burchard *et al.* (1991) identify having a social life as among the most critical aspects relating to quality of life. Being locked out of community participation, therefore, has profound psycholog-ical effects.

The policy context

There has been a substantial shift in both social policy in general and mental health policy in particular since the early 1990s when the Nottingham Community Connections project begun. The 'new' Labour government adopted European ideas about social exclusion from 1997 (Pierson, 2002), establishing the Social Exclusion Unit within the Cabinet Office. Social exclusion was defined as follows:

> . . . a shorthand label for what can happen when individuals or areas suffer from a combination of linked problems such as unemployment, poor skills, low incomes, poor housing, high crime environment, bad health and family breakdown (Social Exclusion Unit, 1999).

This definition concentrates attention upon material deprivation rather than social isolation and upon specific neighbourhoods rather than 'communities of experience' such as mental health service users. However, the Social Exclusion Unit has had such a pervasive effect that almost all UK social institutions now proclaim that it is 'combat-ing social exclusion'. The European Union has continued to apply leverage and the Nice Summit in December 2000 required Member States to develop National Action Plans for tackling social exclusion.

While social inclusion is about opportunities, the Disability Discrimination Act 1995 and the Human Rights Act 2000 have combined to safeguard some civil rights of mental health service users.

In mental health policy, a number of high profile tragedies led to the introduction of the Care Programme Approach, which required statutory agencies to devise comprehensive and co-ordinated care plans for people with severe mental illness. Subsequently the National Service Framework for mental health insisted that the plans for people on the 'enhanced' Care Programme Approach should include action for employment, education, training or other occupation (DoH, 1999b). Opportunities for employment have been given additional attention by the NHS (DoH, 2000c), and by social services authorities through the 'Welfare to Work for Disabled People' plans (SSI, 2001).

The National Service Framework for mental health includes seven standards, of which standard 1 relates to mental health promotion, requiring social services authorities and the health service to promote the mental health of local communities – including tackling discrimination and exclusion. Mental health professionals are clearly being required to develop a new range of skills. In addition, the NHS Plan (DoH, 2000b) substantially increased the number of Assertive Outreach Teams to work with people who are perceived as hard to engage with services. The work of these inter-agency teams has been increasingly linked with psychosocial approaches and informed by perspectives from the recovery movement (Deegan, 1996), again strengthening the level of interest in social inclusion. These developments in the mental health world are scrutinised by a number of quality assurance mechanisms such as Best Value that require evidence of achievement. This in turn demands a rigorous analysis of what is meant by inclusion.

Community participation

If we accept the imperative to reduce mental health users' involuntary social isolation, what does it mean to participate in community life? Policies based upon the assumption that informal supports will spontaneously emerge are overambitious (Wenger, 1993), so a sophisticated vision of community must be established which embraces a range of interlocking features. Such a model may emerge from the evolving work on social capital (Putnam, 2000), although much more work is needed to move this analysis forward from passively observing the features of community life to demonstrating how particular groups can strengthen their position.

For some service users, their primary identity is with the locality in which they live, while others will identify with a community of interest. A much more limited definition of community inclusion is offered by Norris (1984), who, addressing the needs of people discharged from secure hospitals, considers 'community tenure' as merely avoiding recall to hospital, and by Reiter and Levi (1980), for whom 'community integration' means no more than attendance at a work training scheme. By contrast, Perske (1988) writes of the lives of disabled people 'interweaving emotionally with the lives of others in the neighbourhood'. The underlying difference between these narrow and wide definitions is whether the focus is upon service utilisation or upon citizenship. Four theoretical streams have added to the complexity of our understanding about the meaning of community participation for mental health users, namely, normalisation, the five accomplishments, friendship and inclusive community.

Normalisation

For normalisation theorists, inclusion in society is promoted as a means of achieving valued lifestyles for people who are traditionally devalued. Nirje (cited in Ramon, 1991: p. 6) perceived normalisation as making available to the devalued person patterns and conditions of 'ordinary life' closely resembling the norms of mainstream society, including privacy and access to social, emotional and sexual relationships with others. Indeed, Wolfensberger (1980) rejects any kind of congregated service and asserts that the only helpful programmes are those based on positive one-to-one relationships between ordinary unpaid citizens and those with disabilities. Thus, Wolfensberger would close all specialist residential and day care facilities and retrain the staff to deliver a service in non-specialist community facilities.

Critics of normalisation reply that congregated services have the potential to offer a safe place for participants to acknowledge their disability, talk through the emotional and practical consequences of the loss of their 'healthy selves', face stigma, swap coping strategies, set realistic goals and redefine their experience as a political rather than merely a personal struggle (Hendrix, 1981; Chappell, 1992; Szivos, 1992). According to Chappell (1992), normalisation theorists depreciate relationships between devalued people. More critically, normalisation is accused of encouraging people to deny their experience and conform to dominant cultural values, ignoring in the process the diverse lifestyles of a multiracial and multicultural society. Brown and Smith (1992b) assert that its emphasis on conformity undermines any recognition of women's oppression – women's self-validation should be the goal, rather than encouraging accommodation to the culturally valued norms that contained them in the first place. Given the structural dynamics outlined in Chapter 1, although normalisation or 'social role valorisation' (Wolfensberger, 1983) has been influential in disability services since the 1980s, its failure to address the effects of oppression seriously limits its potency.

The five accomplishments

In attempting to operationalise Wolfensberger's approach, O'Brien (1987) focused on five accomplishments that have an important influence upon quality of life and community membership. These are community presence, choice and autonomy, competence, respect, and community participation. Community presence means that people with disabilities use the same geographical space as everyone else, by living in ordinary streets, using local shops, public transport and so on, while community participation requires people with disabilities to engage in valued roles and relationships in those communities. In this analysis, while community care has achieved community presence it has done nothing for community participation, and little to understand and respect users' hopes and desires.

Friendship

Friendships occur when there is an exchange of practical help, shared company or intimacy (Richardson and Ritchie, 1989). While occasionally developing when people meet in formal relationships (co-worker, relative, carer, student, neighbour, flatmate), these roles are insufficient to ensure that friendship actually occurs. The building blocks of valued interpersonal relationships include: choosing and having the opportunity to meet, sharing in common experiences and activities, continuity, reciprocity, the skills to build and maintain the contact, and a belief that each has something to offer. It is perhaps the element of choice that marks friendship out as distinctive from more formal roles, enabling aspects of each other's identity to be revealed.

It is possible to imagine a mental health service that is designed to promote friendship between people experiencing mental distress and other citizens. However, there are a number of important themes that intersect with this issue, including:

- The dominant values and inequalities in society that shape our understanding of the nature of friendship.
- People with mental health problems are negotiating friendships from a position of marginalisation and perhaps multiple oppression (Traustadottir *et al.*, 1994).
- A preoccupation with risk and community safety has made other citizens fearful of forming friendships with people known to the mental health service.

Inclusive community

The literature on inclusion is fragmented, being full of nuances and conflicts of understanding; contributors do not speak with a single voice. However, in the past twenty years a group of 'inclusive community' writers have emerged with a common view on disability issues (Beeman *et al.*, 1989; Carling, 1995). Despite this, the application of inclusion concepts and practices to the British mental health sector has been weak for five key reasons.

- There is limited transfer of learning between service sectors.
- Mental health services have been slower to develop normalisation and advocacy than the learning disabilities field.
- Historically, inclusion in mental health has had no national champion, as is the case with learning disabilities' National Development Team (Wertheimer, 1992; Simons, 1997).
- Working with people with enduring mental health difficulties to build community participation is a long-term task and is low priority given the 'tyranny of the immediate'.
- Given high levels of institutionalisation, users have often not seen the possibilities of community inclusion, and, within the context of hostile communities users have been concerned about finding safe, non-stigmatising settings.

So what is unique about the inclusion movement and why can it generate creative mental health practice? First, it is profoundly – perhaps naively – hopeful and celebratory. While the proponents of inclusion are keenly aware of stigma and rejection, they tend to focus most of their efforts on people who will welcome others, and hope that good news will spread by example. They do not castigate people for behaving inappropriately towards those with disabilities, or view this as wilful oppression. Instead, they assume people are well motivated and offer training to enhance the community's capacity to welcome disabled people. In addition, the strengths model (Rapp and Wintersteen, 1989) assists human service staff to shift from a problem focus to a concentration on the assets, capacities and positive achievements of both users and the community.

Second, person-centred planning approaches focus on the individual's dream of an improved quality of life and then work backwards ('What do I want? How do I achieve this? What support will I need?'). This contrasts with the traditional approach of human service professionals who assess the present and then plan each step forwards ('What is available now?'). Participants in the inclusion movement are united by a shared dream of a future where there is a place for everyone (Bates, 2002).

Third, it does not distinguish between people labelled disabled or non-disabled. Instead, everyone is using their skills to work for a more inclusive world, where interdependency is valued and social exclusion is outlawed. Fourth, inclusion is about friendship and validation by others, with an attendant emphasis on the centrality of relationships. The best inclusion projects (O'Brien and O'Brien, 1992) seem to be those where ordinary citizens value the person with a disability for themselves and are not particularly motivated by altruism. Finally, inclusion is a right, not a privilege. Inclusion enthusiasts argue that since society has been learning about social exclusion for two hundred years it will be a protracted process to end fragmentation, let go of disabling practices, and learn how to support people effectively (Asante, 1997).

Inclusive writers believe that there are potential roles and relationships in the community for people with disabilities and these can be located and unlocked by emphasising our common bond of humanity and interdependence (Mount *et al.*, 1988; Beeman *et al.*, 1989; Ludlum, 1993). In the person-centred plan (Mount and Zwemik, 1989) self-determination and relationships are prioritised with the objective of changing the environment and attitudes as a way of integrating users. Focused effort on the part of workers is directed towards increasing opportunities and choices for service users, rather than prescribing a certain kind of lifestyle or degree of social inclusion.

Community inclusion is attractive for its optimism about the capacity of ordinary citizens and those with disabilities to build mutual, valuing relationships with each other. This vision has fuelled efforts to provide opportunities for disabled people to integrate into activities such as further education, employment and recreational pursuits, and has affirmed the sociological hypothesis that, for many users, social isolation and role constriction is a consequence of the service rather than the person. These four theoretical strands – normalisation, the five accomplishments, friendship and inclusion – are not clear and distinctive in their identity or their effect upon community care services, but each has strengthened the case for tackling the deficit in community connections experienced by people with disabilities. While each stream is subject to criticism the overall argument for developing such opportunities remains strong, and the poverty of contact which is a feature of the lives of people with enduring mental health difficulties demands careful but determined action.

The four dimensions of community participation

We have demonstrated how community connections work is visionary and idealistic and this confronts social work with considerable dilemmas in bridging the gap between these ideals and practice realities. For mental health users in receipt of community care services, Figure 5.2 presents a framework of four elements to be used in assessing different kinds of contact with the community. These are not mutually

GOING OUT – leaving the residential or day care building for any reason	COMMUNITY AMENITIES – places to shop, eat, drink, walk, look
GOAL/RATIONALE – To enlarge experiences, develop interests, gain respite from other household members, acquire topics for conversation, add to collection of 'safe places'.	GOAL/RATIONALE – To develop independence in activities of daily living, to reduce use of specialist services, to develop existing acquaintances into friendships.
INTEGRATED PURSUITS – joining a group of citizens without apparent disabilities to work, learn or enjoy leisure time	SOCIAL NETWORKS – relatives, friends, neighbours, colleagues who care
GOAL/RATIONALE – To socialise into valued roles, to make acquaintances who have common interests, to pursue skills and interests with those people over a period of time, to develop an active life and support network apart from formal welfare services.	GOAL/RATIONALE – For companionship, practical help and emotional support, to buffer against stress and illness, to connect with a growing network of contacts.

Figure 5.2 The four elements of community participation

exclusive, and a single activity may well include two or three elements, but it is helpful to think about them separately.

Going out

Research in this area has generally been applied to residential situations. For example, Firth and Short (1987) found that the number of outings and their duration increased by over 50% after people had moved from hospital to a community hostel. Adding a layer of complexity to this kind of study involves listing and perhaps categorising the destinations of the outings (Lowe and de Paiva, 1991). However, such a list tells us little about the *meaning* of those excursions to the person concerned. Outings of almost any kind can be enriching, enlarge the repertoire of topics for conversation, and stimulate interests. Organised visits, repeatedly using the same destination, can establish a sense of familiarity with the aim of adding these venues to an individual's personal map. Staff or other allies can often help in this field by assisting with the arrangements, providing transport, or serving as an escort.

Community amenities

Some people highly value the contact they have with shopkeepers, hairdressers and others who staff community amenities. Saxby *et al.* (1986) examined the way in which people with learning difficulties used shops and cafes and they offer the notion of 'substantive participation' to describe actively engaging in appropriate behaviour in a particular setting. This would distinguish, for example, passively accompanying someone who was shopping, from an occasion where the disabled person was pushing the trolley, selecting items, offering money to the cashier and packing bags. A distinctive factor in these environments is the nature of contact with others. Although interaction with non-disabled people does take place, it tends to be instrumental, brief and impersonal. However, people who already know each other might use these community amenities together to develop their friendship; acquaintances may go for a drink, walk in the park or spend an afternoon shopping.

Integrated pursuits

While the use of community amenities is characterised by brief contact with other citizens, this element is concerned with longer-term membership of social groups. The pursuit might be remunerative employment, further education or a recreational activity and may provide a social role that is highly valued in the community. Those attending have some sense of group identity and are bound together by a common interest or activity, rather than a medical diagnosis. The role of a carer or ally may range from companionship to making introductions or repairing an activity when it appears to be in danger of breaking down. Both Evans *et al.* (1992) and Schalock and Lilley (1986) note that disabled people sometimes achieve geographical integration by attending the same group as other citizens, but fail to integrate socially. It is therefore easier to create the illusion of inclusion than the reality.

Social networks

Willmott (1986) analysed the frequency of contacts with relatives, neighbours and friends among the general population. He found that men had more contact with others than women; that African-Caribbean and Asian elders had less than average contact with neighbours; and that young people had more contact with friends than older people. However, support is a combination of both *quantity* and *quality* of contact. Tolsdorf (1976) examined the social networks of psychiatric in-patients and found that their relationships were less intimate than a comparison group. Furthermore, they were less likely to draw on network resources due to anxieties about the ignorance or insensitivity of network members. Silberfeld (1978) found that his group of psychiatric patients were in touch with as many relatives as the control group, but met them less frequently and spent less time at each encounter.

In contrast to these findings, Nelson *et al.* (1992) examined the networks of several people who were receiving psychotropic medication and found considerable evidence of reciprocity in relationships. Transactions between patients were characterised by a higher level of emotional support than relationships with relatives or professionals. Relationships with kin, neighbours and associates confer a sense of identity, value and role. Allies can use a wide range of strategies to support people who wish to expand branches of their social network, increase the degree of intimacy or replace negative exchanges with more positive ones. Community inclusion cannot mandate or legislate for intimacy (Asante, 1997), but it can create the preconditions from which friendships can emerge.

Adopting an inclusive approach is a valid approach in an age of shrinking welfare expenditure, as it transfers some of the professional support to unpaid informal systems, with a concomitant need for professional humility. Community care practices often see professional

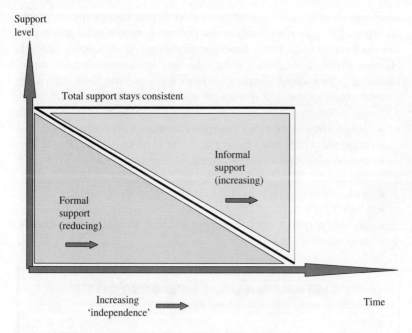

Figure 5.3 The balance between formal and informal support

support as diminishing over time, akin to the lower triangle in Figure 5.3. If, however, the person's need for a fixed amount of total support is recognised, illustrated by the whole rectangle, then the shift over time is to see the professional contribution gradually replaced by informal supports – self help skills, relatives, friends, work colleagues and others.

However, Community Connections does not involve abdication by the state of its support role. Rather, it involves innovative services in forging new types of relationships between providers and users, to which we shall now turn.

Person-centred or service-centred design?

Service-centred systems need to be replaced with person-centred approaches. The 'person-centred' approach means supporting a specific person, along with members of their informal network and other agencies, to live the life they want. Flexible service responses mean being available when, where and how it makes sense for the user. This challenges workers, who must be skilled at providing support across an array of different environments. Few workers can offer a comprehensive map of community-based possibilities to their clients. Indeed, Horton (1996) recognises the challenges in designing and implementing personalised support services for a racially and ethnically diverse group of users. She expects competent staff to:

- utilise anti-oppressive strategies that start with the person;
- understand lifestyle choices and factors affecting quality of life;
- provide access to communication, including use of preferred language;
- seek out key people in the informal support network;
- challenge systems that inhibit innovative service practices;
- be held accountable for user satisfaction and outcomes relating to community inclusion.

PRACTICE SCENARIO 5.2: DECIDING ON THE BASIC APPROACH

In deciding the appropriate direction for the Community Connections project, there needed to be a core agreement concerning the foundations on which it was based. The key aspects of this were defined as follows:

- A commitment to social inclusion and person-centred approaches.
- Avoidance of responsibility for buildings or for providing support to regular groups as this would divert effort away from inclusion work.
- A life domains approach in which workers were recruited to specialise in a nominated layer of community life.

In urban areas with reasonably good transport systems, it is possible to slice the community by topic, such as employment, education, volunteering, arts, faith and cultural communities, sport and exercise, and local neighbourhoods. For instance, one worker can become knowledgeable about employment and build relationships with the chamber of commerce, the Jobcentre and so on, while another worker can investigate cultural opportunities. These life domains provide a focus for worker and user alike, enabling marketing to be targeted, referrals to be made, and achievements to be recognised. As projects progress, the life domains can be split and re-combined as new staff arrive and others leave. Community Connections work can be co-ordinated across a range of mental health settings using dedicated staff time, where a percentage of the working week is allocated to life domain activities. Such a strategy demystifies this approach, reduces the risk that it will be dismissed as idealistic and unachievable, and prevents this developmental work being squeezed out by short-term activities (a risk implicit in the changes and pressures on social workers which were identified in Chapter 2). A team approach is needed to ensure that learning gained in one life domain is shared with staff and users engaged in other domains.

Community Connections interventions are akin to community development work in the voluntary sector, as outlined in Chapter 4. Indeed, the voluntary sector is well placed to contribute imaginatively to the totality of users' life domains because small-scale community projects often have a better sense of locality than the monolithic psychiatric system. Inclusive values and devolution of power to service providers and users are in harmony with social work values, although many experienced practitioners may need to re-learn underused skills.

PRACTICE SCENARIO 5.3: STAGES OF DEVELOPMENT

The Community Connections Project involved three stages of development:

- In Phase 1, faced with a unique practice situation, ideas developed out of reflection, conceptualisation and active experimentation. The project rested on the energy and enthusiasm of a small number of key people acting as instigators, with supplementary help arising out of goodwill gestures by others. This was a loose network with a limited capacity to resolve conflict, agree on a common direction or guarantee quality. Marketing of the project was intense in order to secure support and resources.
- The pioneering work in this phase provided the launchpad for phase 2 when staff were employed to work within the project. Individuals were selected, trained and then managed in order to build a team that delivered high quality work to service users.
- At this point project staff could look toward phase 3, when the roles will be well established, support networks in place, and community bridge builders employed by host organisations in each life domain as part of their access and equal opportunities support.

In order to maintain community links and ensure that staff are accountable for their work a transparent structure needs to be set in place. Reflective practice necessitates more democratic forms of organisation where users have a direct input in policy formation, the mechanisms for consultation and participation are clear (Shaw, 1997), and users have maximum ability to define issues and identify appropriate action (Brandon, 1991; Braye, 2000). This entire process is characteristic of professional reflexivity (Taylor and White, 2000), a highly developed capacity to reflect on the implementation of change and adapt the processes accordingly.

In view of the pioneering nature of this work, there are few eclectic projects across the UK. Some comparatively restricted projects work:

- in a particular life domain (e.g., offering cultural opportunities to mental health users in museums and art galleries – see Dodd and Sandell, 2001);
- with a specific user group, such as people with learning disabilities only (McIntosh and Whittaker, 1999);
- with a particular strategy for inclusion, such as jobcoaching (Rusch and Hughes, 1989) or 'circles of friends' (Bates, 2000).

The limited range of opportunities is exemplified by available volunteering projects. A few volunteer bureaux offer specific support to people with mental health difficulties, and many of those are dependent on short life funding. The majority view marginalised groups as potential recipients of voluntary effort, rather than as possible sources of volunteers, with communities and users being mutually enriched by the experience (Bates, 2001).

The fragmented pattern of project development points to the multiple dilemmas involved when steering a course through the unsettled waters of short life funding and organisational politics. Nevertheless, enacting inclusion principles in diverse and flexible ways symbolises the creativity involved, further illustrated by the 'bridge builder's' practice skills and qualities.

Role of the bridge builder

The worker for each life domain adopts a role as a bridge builder (Mount *et al.*, 1988) and may be employed by agencies other than health and social services. Her/his job involves exploring the particular life domain, locating allies, developing a strategy and offering pathways into that area of community life to users. Bridge builders work as both 'travel agents' and 'travel companions' (Deitchman, 1980). Travel agents know what is available in the community, provide comprehensive information about opportunities and occasionally create new locations, while travel companions accompany the person into community settings. For socially excluded people who have engaged in demeaning or self-destructive behaviour, supporting the placement will include assisting users to learn appropriate behaviour in organisations where they will not be judged as morally inferior if they make a mistake (Davey, 1998).

Agencies have to learn new things too. One study of supported employment found that the traditional inequalities were being played out in the new 'inclusive' locations of ordinary jobs in ordinary workplaces. Women, who were placed in traditional sectors of food and clerical services, typically worked less hours and at a lower hourly rate of pay than men and had less positive relationships with their co-workers than male supported colleagues (Olson *et al.*, 2000).

Travel agents and travel companions need to vary their strategies for individuals across life domains. For instance, the negotiating skills required in the education life domain, where the bridge builder may be working with large further education colleges, will be vastly different to those needed in small community groups in the local neighbourhood. Therefore, it becomes essential to catalogue available strategies, identifying the skills that maximise their success as well as the hazards to be avoided. For example, one user joined a local residents' association with a worker who believed that his role was to provide intensive support at the beginning and then taper away, leaving the user attending the group independently. Unfortunately, this was not explained clearly enough to the user at the outset, and, in his eyes, the worker modelled poor commitment to the group. As a result, the worker's withdrawal from the group was shortly followed by the user's. This demonstrates how crucial it is for bridge builders to meet periodically in order to report progress, gather stories, swap strategies and celebrate success so that they develop competence and confidence. Through teamwork, a reflexive approach becomes interwoven in the project's evaluation.

A short repertoire of inclusion strategies and skills

Bridge builders in the Community Connections Project clarified their thinking, located allies who had developed specific placements in each location, learnt the language of the placement setting, and acquired a sense of being connected to a wider inclusion movement. As a result they developed a repertoire of inclusion strategies and skills, as follows:

Accommodation:	Changing the physical or social environment to make it more accessible.
Befriending:	Bring together a service user and a citizen from outside of the care system who are both interested in becoming friends.
Circle of friends:	Enlist a group of friends, relatives and colleagues to work with the focus person in defining and achieving his or her ambitions.
Curriculum differentiation:	Broaden the range of opportunities within a particular community setting so that the person can succeed when her/his ability fluctuates.
Deliberately integrated group:	A group that is developed with the aim of providing a forum where people from services and the community can meet as equals.
Enclave:	A group of service users who stay together but use an ordinary setting and remain socially segregated.
Escort:	Accompany the service user on the journey to the activity.
Expanding community capacity:	Inclusion training and support for host organisations will resolve anxieties and help them to welcome people with support needs
Interpretation:	Present the service user to others as interesting and capable.
Just visiting:	Going to the target location beforehand in order to become familiar with the journey, the place and the people.
Know the community:	Gathering information about community activities and networks.
Look-alike escort:	A citizen who accompanies the service user into a community setting where they are perceived as two friends, rather than an incongruous couple.

Natural supports:	People already in the host setting can be the best supporters.
Progression routes:	The way in which activity at one level of community integration can be planned to lead into the next level.
Registering together:	An ally signs up to the community activity alongside the service user.
Systematic instruction:	A coach accompanies the service user into the placement setting, analyses the tasks to be undertaken and steadily trains the person to carry out more and more of them until the user is free standing and independent (Gold, 1976).
Welcoming host:	An ally already in the host setting who will look out for the service user and introduce her/him to others.

McKnight, in O'Brien and O'Brien (1996), lists several paradoxes for community bridge builders, including being professional and using sophisticated skills while promoting a view that ordinary citizens can make an invaluable contribution; and working oneself out of a job. Because the role of bridge builder requires grappling with the dynamics of oppression and discrimination (highlighted in Chapter 1) and the internalisation of stigmatised identity, the effective practitioner must be capable in these areas. For example, in wrestling with the challenge of tackling racism and sexism, competent bridge builders will create pathways into Black or women-only settings.

The focus on community connections challenges bridge builders to rethink the notion of professional distance as they face issues that engage the heart as well as the head. They must also build access to faith communities and demonstrate respect for users' spirituality, which requires:

- The capacity to listen to the service user's history and current faith experience;
- Willingness to explore the universality of spiritual questions;
- Sensitivity to the range of meanings ascribed to psychiatric diagnosis and recovery by various faith systems;

- Knowledge of the most effective ways of harnessing goodwill within each faith community.
  (Mental Health Foundation, 2000)

The bridge builder therefore has a complex and difficult set of tasks. Indeed, as is also implicit within the work settings outlined in chapters 7 and 9 in this volume, there is no guarantee that social work training would be seen as a requirement for this role. However, there are numerous reasons for this task being best undertaken by social workers as service providers, or as co-ordinators of community connections projects.

- There is a need for a high level of sensitivity to anti-oppressive practice and empowerment values in community connections work. Social work is the only training amongst the caring professions that focuses on this topic (CCETSW, 1995).
- The knowledge base draws heavily on community development theories, requiring a thorough assimilation of community resources, and having an overview of users' structural and societal contexts, alongside co-ordination and negotiation skills. These areas are traditionally the province of social work, placing them in a strong position to respond to social exclusion (Washington and Paylor, 1998).
- Mental health social workers use systemic thinking to assess users' quality of life and undertake risk analyses. Smith (1993) reports a difference between social workers and health professionals in their approach to risk taking, with Ryan (1996) observing that risk is often viewed negatively by health practitioners. In addition, they bear formal responsibility for their judgement in matters concerning the safety of both the individual and the community, especially in work related to the Mental Health Act 1983, to a greater extent than any other discipline except psychiatry. This combination provides a secure foundation for the innovative work of building inclusive communities.

However, the field is open to pioneers from any discipline who have vision, courage and perseverance. Evidence from early British experiments shows that most work is being developed by people whose common bond is that they share ideals, optimism and determination, rather than a particular academic or employment background. However, we would argue that the skills of a social worker are particularly appropriate for a bridge builder.

PRACTICE SCENARIO 5.4: MEASURABLE COMPETENCES FOR A COMMUNITY BRIDGE BUILDER

Whatever the professional background of a bridge builder, it is vital that s/he possesses a range of knowledge, skills and values. These can be are expressed as measurable competences, as follows:

- Work flexible hours to enable support to be offered when needed.
- Demonstrate an understanding of the range of mental health problems and their effects.
- Promote service user's freedom of choice, independence and community inclusion.
- Build partnerships with other agencies to identify and develop opportunities for service users.
- Offer mental health awareness training to potential hosts.
- Maintain good knowledge of community opportunities.
- Share learning with others involved in community connections work.
- Sensitively use all appropriate strategies to support community inclusion.
- Monitor service user satisfaction and amend support packages as required.

Ethical dilemmas in community connections work

Given the contested nature of this form of intervention, the life domains perspective helps to escape the trap of perceiving locality as the only valid concept of community. It also takes us straight to the heart of three key hazards: inclusion as assimilation, as subjugation, and as containment.

First, inclusion does not mean assimilation. In the 1990s, efforts were made to include multiculturism in disability services (Baxter *et al.*, 1990; O'Connor, 1992, 1993; Traustadottir *et al.*, 1994) after recognising that community integration had been implemented using an assimilationist framework (Racino, 1994). When arranging a community opportunity with a user the goal is more than assimilation. At one level, the service user may need to learn appropriate behaviour in order to 'fit' into the placement. In order to meet this target, s/he may be tempted to deny her/his experiences of mental distress in order to 'pass' as non-disabled, or to see themselves as a lone champion for the rights of service users and so feel permanently exhibited. The insidious and damaging effects of an assimilationist approach are readily apparent. The host environment therefore needs to change to become enriched by the addition of new experiences and inter-pretations brought by users, with a view to embracing and actively fos-tering diversity and celebrating difference.

Second, inclusion is not subjugation. There is an implicit belief that inclusive projects will be intuitively responsive to minority ethnic groups and women, but qualities of friendliness and welcome are not enough to overcome structural inequalities and social injustice. What do community bridge builders do when offered a placement which positions the user in a powerless role, but reflects where other dis-abled people, women, or Black people are likely to be found? The Community Connections Project could become so focused upon achieving placements for users as volunteers that only traditional placements for women are forthcoming, for example. By adopting the macro perspective outlined in Chapter 1, oppression in all its forms can be recognised and challenged.

New forms of decision making need to be harnessed so that users are not excluded from positions of influence in the organisations they join. This relates to users learning the skills to participate in com-munities, service providers changing the decision-making machinery and service managers widening the decision-making arena. One of these mechanisms is groupwork (Butler and Wintram, 1991), which has been vital for Black men and women's consciousness-raising and politicisation. Bridge builders therefore need to offer support to everyone and particularly women and Black people real choices based on positive action principles. Otherwise, service delivery will be hallmarked by the same patterns of paternalism inherent in con-gregated services, which will then be translated in an unreconstructed fashion into the community.

Third, inclusion is not containment. It offers a range of new roles and relationships for service users that transcend the traditional and controlling patient or client status. Users are perceived as citizens first, people who bring the richness of their human experience to the wider community. Professional norms have to be reworked as users begin to make real friendships with neighbours, fall in love at work, or argue with the manager of the local community centre. All of these events create a dilemma for the traditional concept of user/professional relationships, which therefore have to be renegotiated.

PRACTICE SCENARIO 5.5: SUCCESS FACTORS IN NEGOTIATING FOR CONFIDENTIALITY

In what ways, for instance, does the practice of confidentiality need to be redefined within an inclusion project? A user may simultaneously link with bridge builders operating in the education and volunteering Life Domains, employed by the college and local volunteer bureau respectively. What communication and information sharing should take place between the two bridge builders? Does the psychiatrist communicate with either of them? What does the education bridge builder say to the college tutor? In negotiating for confidentiality (Soler *et al.*, 1993), the following guidelines need to be debated:

- Explicit negotiation with the user to agree the boundaries and content of disclosure.
- Discussion of the user's support needs with the host agency prior to arranging a particular placement, to discover how the placement setting treats issues of confidentiality and disclosure, and to explain the project's perspective.
- A focus on practical behaviours rather than medical diagnoses.
- A detailed and time-limited written agreement authorising the mechanisms of disclosure, signed by the user.
- Ongoing support for the placement host and service users.

In any inclusion project, the dilemmas surrounding confidentiality are clarified incrementally as workers and users confront particular practice scenarios. Reflection-in-action recognises that maximum experiential learning is generated through facing up to the mistakes, the unique practice situations which challenge traditional organisational responses.

Conclusion

In this chapter, we have demonstrated the deleterious effects of exclusion on people's mental health and made a case for designing services that offer users the opportunity of social inclusion. Having constructed the arguments for the participation of mental health service users in community life and activities, we have recognised the barriers that confront users and service providers alike in attempting to include users in community-based pursuits and social networks. By presenting a model of community participation, we have sought to capture the dilemmas and nuances of the inclusion movement, with a view to articulating how reflexive processes can be utilised to create an innovative, creative mental health project. Community inclusion work draws on idealistic dreams and values, and translates these into the small, incremental steps of practice realities, transforming users', workers' and community placements' lives in the process.

The context has dramatically changed over the decade since this project was pioneered. While the government is contemplating more restrictive legislation to replace the 1983 Mental Health Act and additional beds are being set up in secure units, there is a simultaneous drive to promote inclusion. The Social Exclusion Unit is working on a major project to identify and harness the efforts of all government departments to combat the exclusion of people with mental health problems. Within mental health, the lack of formalised duties in respect of day care is allowing funds to be diverted into alternative services that are deemed to be essential, and, at the same time, there is widespread interest in the community connections approach. There is a clear tension within government policy; as the choices become starker, the consequences of these decisions for service users become more explicit.

Acknowledgements

We are grateful to Jane Danforth, Volunteer Co-ordinator, Nottingham Community Connections Project, and Kathryn James, Development Officer for Learning and Health at NIACE, for sharing with us their insights, reflections, hopes and fears about their Life Domains work.

6

Exploitation, Protection and Empowerment of People with Learning Disabilities

Pam Cooke and Rachael Ellis

Introduction

This chapter connects the *macro* and *micro* levels of analysis, focusing specifically on issues related to adults with learning disability – their abuse and exploitation, protection and empowerment. The *macro* examines how society treats learning disabled people, while the *micro* is concerned with individuals' feelings about their abuse and place in the community and the consequent implications for social work practice. First, the chapter will explore the meaning of, and society's contribution to, exploitation; how this impacts on learning disabled people in their homes and in public places. Second, it considers the balance between protection and the rights of users to take risks. Finally, it concentrates on empowerment, with particular reference to the role of self-advocacy. Throughout, we will address how social work practice can contribute to a new relationship based on opening up choices to disabled people while ensuring their safety. Social work agencies walk a tightrope between the provision of protective strategies and the type of services contributing to the prevention of abuse, while enabling vulnerable adults to make their own informed decisions wherever possible.

For illustrative purposes, the chapter includes insights gleaned from consultations with five self-advocacy groups concerning their perceptions of service delivery alongside safety and protection issues. Having practised self-assertiveness and self-protection exercises, the groups generously offered examples of their work, including newsletters, leaflets and drawings about their activities. We have also drawn on the Ann Craft Trust's training and consultancy experiences with social workers and other professionals concerning adult protection. Due to our greater familiarity with the legal and policy content of England and Wales, this chapter is most directly applicable to social work in these two countries. However, we believe that the general issue of the exploitation of people with learning disabilities is transferable to other countries and cultures, as are the core themes with which social workers are engaged through the practice scenarios – protection, advocacy and empowerment.

Exploitation

In the current climate, people with learning disabilities are frequently ignored, socially excluded and rendered powerless. Such undervaluing leads to exploitation. Our discussions with self-advocacy groups revealed that exploitation in its broadest sense was the 'norm' in their everyday lives; often seen as easy targets in the community, namecalling and theft of small amounts of money or possessions were commonplace. Invariably, exploitation is used as a diluted word for physical, sexual and financial abuse, while the term 'abuse' itself is often a 'soft' description for crimes of assault, indecent assault, rape and theft. In order for social workers to appreciate the pernicious nature of structural inequalities (outlined in Chapter 1), we will examine four key manifestations of exploitation in the lives of those with learning disabilities and their effects on contemporary practice:

- The resonance of historical legacies concerning disability in current exploitative behaviour.
- How the disabled population is affected by sexism and racism.
- The occurrence of exploitation in public places.
- The roles of institutionalisation and normalisation in perpetuating exploitation.

In relation to the historical manifestation of exploitation, many cultures have seen disability as punishment either of the person, parents or society, creating an atmosphere of condemnation or disgust, and a desire to keep the contamination of disability away from the rest of the population (Reiser, 1995). Violence masquerading as medical treatment can be seen in the history of eugenics, a powerful reminder of the inhumanity directed against those least able to defend themselves (Shakespeare, 1998) resulting in isolation, segregated space (Kitchin, 1998) and involuntary sterilisation (Park and Radford, 1998). With claims of biological inferiority, such attitudes have legitimised discrimination for centuries, and at their worst, gained expression through the Third Reich's label of 'unworthy beings' with experimentation, euthanasia and the death camps (Sherman Heyl, 1998). Nor is our own recent history free of controversy regarding the involuntary sterilisation of women (Carson, 1992; Lyon, 1994). Similarly, current debates on genetic screening raise many ethical dilemmas, such as the suggestion of choice for parents in aborting damaged foetuses, challenging the right to existence for individuals with disabilities (Shakespeare, 1998).

Whichever historical epoch is scrutinised, disability-related exploitation and violence (Waxman, 1991) stems from a combination of *fear* and *hatred* among the majority population. Fear originates from the association between disability and loss of control, humanity and social relations, characterised by Hahn (1988) as 'existential anxiety'. Together with 'aesthetic anxiety', or the fear of others whose visible traits are perceived as disturbing or unpleasant, it is the source of hatred towards people with learning disabilities. Consequently, by focusing on the traits ascribed to disabled victims of exploitation, society blames the targets of violence, abuse and institutional practices, rendering them responsible for their own suffering (Ryan, 1971).

Anti-disability fear and hatred also permeate the second factor of exploitation, namely the differential effects of racism and sexism on people with learning disabilities. Such additional jeopardy may exacerbate individuals' sense of low self-esteem while increasing their *vulnerability* as targets of abuse. By defining people as 'other', their 'difference' is accentuated, 'division' is established, while their potential contribution to 'diversity' is underplayed (see Chapter 1). Acceptance of disabled people, for instance, may be no better in Black than in white communities (Begum *et al.*, 1994). At the same time, the specific needs of Black learning disabled users do not receive the same amount of attention as the needs of people from the white community (Lewis, 1996b). The multilayered interplay of such disadvantage may, therefore, be difficult to untangle. For example, research demonstrates how women with learning disabilities are more likely to feel powerless and at risk in the community than men (Hendey and Pascall, 1998). Yet, men with learning disabilities also suffer from sexual abuse and they are just as vulnerable in decision making about whether or with whom they have sex, especially in situations where they lack status and power (Cambridge *et al.*, 1993; Brown *et al.*, 1995). Given the heterogeneity of the learning disabled population, adult protection services need to be reviewed to ensure that they meet the requirements of a diverse group (Walker, 1998).

Societal denial of the scale of violence against disabled people (Waxman, 1991) is illustrated by our third concern relating to the exploitation of men and women in public places (Flynn, 1989; Williams, C., 1995). This was a significant factor in the self-advocacy group members' lives, where women especially – and some men – feared going out alone during the evening due to their perceived lack of safety. Group members had experienced verbal abuse, harassment and theft on the streets and in public buildings. Research (Wilson and Brewer, 1992) has demonstrated how disabled people are twice as likely to be victims of crime against the person, while C. Williams (1993, 1995) has confirmed that threatening, abusive and insulting behaviour in public places are the most frequent forms of victimisation experienced by people with learning disabilities. While such incidents are not usually pursued through criminal or civil actions, and are therefore rendered invisible, this exploitation constructs a *culture of vulnerability* among people with learning disabilities. Being socialised into compliance and self doubt, an under-reporting of crime due to threats from their attackers, and the stigma of victimisation (Waxman, 1991) are all contributory factors (Wilson *et al.*, 1996). However, the contention that vulnerability is the primary explanation for disability-related violence is too superficial and ignores the socio-political context shaping people's lives. Waxman (1991) asserts that powerlessness only yields opportunities for perpetrators to express their hatred, but opportunism is legitimised by wider structural forces and institutional behaviour.

What, then, has been the impact of these *macro* dynamics on our fourth area, professional behaviour and institutional practices? These historical trends, coupled with their ideological and theoretical underpinnings, were officially sanctioned in past legislation, in the establishment of asylums, segregated institutions and special hospital care. These were largely medical solutions to human conditions, enabling society to keep 'mentally handicapped' (*sic.*) people out of sight for life, to avoid the general public's embarrassment and distress. This 'care' ensured that society's failure to adapt to the needs of this section of the population was ignored (Shearer, 1980). The subsequent move away from the old asylums and institutions has been characterised by paternalist attitudes; "*We* know and will provide what is best for *them*". Such historically grounded ideas and feelings contribute to the discounting of individuals with disabilities, thereby feeding into exploitative behaviour and institutional actions.

A critical appraisal of the influential principle of 'normalisation' (Wolfensberger, 1972; O'Brien, 1981) also reveals a tendency to reinforce exploitation. The critique has been thoroughly rehearsed in recent literature (Brown and Smith, 1992c; Chappell, 1992c; Brown and Walmsley, 1997) and can be identified as follows:

- Services based on normalisation principles assume that to be acceptable, the 'abnormal' (disabled) group must be rendered 'normal'. Moreover, this concept discounts those who wish to carve out a different lifestyle acknowledging and valuing their disabled identity (Ellis, 1990); ignoring this is yet another form of exploitation (Bano *et al.*, 1993).
- More specifically, it implicitly identifies the preferred ideological and service model as that of the dominant white population. Therefore, it does not fully recognise and support the concepts of diversity and difference central to this book. Those who do not conform by virtue of 'race' and ethnicity, sexuality, culture or class are less likely to be catered for.
- It is dominated by professional vested interests and authority over the lives of people with learning disabilities (Chappell, 1992).
- It is a *laissez-faire* model, denying support to people even where this is indicated (Brown and Walmsley, 1997).
- Most critically, it has failed to acknowledge the impact of socio-economic factors – outlined in Chapter 1 – on people's lives. Chappell (1992) observes that unless structural factors are addressed, the potential gains from normalisation are limited.

In rising to the challenges of the contemporary disability movement (Campbell and Oliver, 1996) and the critique of normalisation, there is increasing recognition of individuals' rights to make their own informed decisions; this marks a positive shift in social work policy and practice. Practice scenario 6.1 highlights these dynamics of oppression requiring considerable social work skills and knowledge

PRACTICE SCENARIO 6.1

Anita (white, aged 28) has mild to moderate learning disabilities and has lived most of her life in a small, private residential establishment, returning home to her family at weekends. A care assistant has become increasingly concerned about conversations occurring after Anita returns from weekend visits. Anita has indicated that she has accompanied her sisters on their Saturday nights out to meet some men. She says she now has boyfriends, and one man in particular is important to her. She is not distressed by this new experience; indeed, she is pleased to be considered 'grown up'. However, she discloses that her sisters are including her in their prostitution. Anita seems unaware about the real nature of the Saturday 'dates' and of any dangers in this behaviour. She wants to continue going home at weekends, particularly to see her special boyfriend, although she has admitted she does not always wish to do what he says. Her family may not protect her; the residential home perceive their behaviour to be central to the problem. The decision to place Anita in residential care originally related to difficulties in family relationships. There have been a number of 'fathers' with a lack of boundaries between adults and children. Although she now an adult, staff are concerned about Anita's safety and have contacted the local social services field team.

Practice questions:

- What attitudes and values about learning disability, sexual rights and prostitution would affect a social worker's understanding and responses to this scenario?
- What knowledge and skills are needed to formulate a risk assessment?

to move beyond normalisation principles in determining if, how and in what ways Anita can be protected from sexual exploitation.

A reflective practitioner will have to disentangle a number of conceptual strands here. First, the social worker will recognise that women with learning disabilities are over-represented as victims of sexual assault (Sobsey and Varnhagen, 1989), framing information gathering within feminist knowledge and research concerning the politics of sexual violence (Rhodes and McNeill, 1985; Kelly, 1988).

Second, the practitioner must work with the tension between the right of women with learning disabilities to have sexual relationships and the *culture of vulnerability*, heightening as it does their risk of being sexually assaulted with a concomitant concern for their protection. Therefore, the worker's reflexive awareness is crucial in recognising how s/he has been influenced by conflicting heterosexist/sexist stereotypes and false assumptions. On the one hand, these are rooted in the fear of women with learning disabilities' uncontrolled sexuality and uninhibited behaviour (Carmody, 1991). On the other hand, perceptions of their asexuality abound, with considerable curiosity as to why they are targeted for sexual violence anyway (Waxman, 1991).

Third, in formulating a risk assessment, the social worker must deduce the extent to which Anita understands her actions alongside the potential consequences. Does she have the capacity to consent to sexual acts (Churchill *et al.*, 1996) and to distinguish between different forms of sexual activity? Can she comprehend the notion of selling sex? Brown and Turk (1992) have stressed that a woman cannot give meaningful consent if she is unable to understand the various elements that constitute sexual behaviour. If Anita is unaware of her own sexual feelings and her human rights in relation to choice of sexual partners, the risk of sexual exploitation is considerably increased. She may not recognise her status as a potential or actual victim of crime or her entitlement to police assistance. If she *has* withheld her consent to sexual activity then, theoretically at least, she is protected by rape and sexual assault laws, although securing a conviction in such cases is difficult (Green, 2001). At least in partial recognition of these problems the government is reviewing the issue of the legal response to sexual offences, with the aim of placing a new sexual offence bill before parliament.

Even if Anita has made a judgement about her involvement in prostitution, the power imbalance between herself, her 'boyfriend' and the sisters will affect her capacity to give meaningful consent. The social worker and police must assess whether force has been used, with any injuries sustained. Anita's powerlessness is underpinned by the likelihood that her past experiences have proffered minimal opportunities for constructive friendships, a phenomenon also discussed in Chapter 5 in relation to people with mental health problems. A longing for intimacy may reinforce her naivety about the good intentions of others, with a desire to please permeating her gratitude for any sexual attention (Carmody, 1991).

An abusive situation which may not constitute a breach of the law creates difficulties for practitioners. Under the Street Offences Act 1959, while soliciting is illegal in the United Kingdom, prostitution is not. Anita may claim this is her life choice and resist any attempts to persuade her away from prostitution. As she is over 16 years of age, she is beyond the protection of the Children Act 1989, used occasionally with young people drawn into prostitution (Gregory *et al.*, 1998). Additionally, the legal powers protecting adults from abuse are largely fragmented and framed so as to exclude the majority of learning disabled people. A guardianship order under the Mental Health Act 1983, for instance, is probably not applicable because Anita is not 'mentally impaired' under the terms of the Act (Vernon, 1993). Similarly, the Sexual Offences Act 1956, sections 7 and 43(1), provides powers in relation to sexual intercourse with a 'defective' (*sic.*), usually defined as a woman with severe learning disabilities (Churchill *et al.*, 1997), which is irrelevant to Anita. (However, as noted above, the law on sexual offences is under review.)

Of more use might be section 3 of the Act, where it is an offence to 'procure' a woman for immoral purposes by false pretences or false representation. In these situations, it must be proved, with corroborative evidence, that the alleged acts occurred but not that the victim withheld her consent (Churchill *et al.*, 1997). For criminal law, there must be a complainant, with the police being prepared to take the matter further (Gunn, 1996). In any case, the police will need to investigate whether Anita has been involved in a commercial transaction and whether any individuals have been living off her immoral earnings; this emphasises the importance of the police in securing justice for people with learning disabilities (CPS/ACPO 2000; Sharp, 2001). Consideration of these pieces of legislation, combined with the general need to support vulnerable people in such circumstances (Home Office, 1998b), must be balanced against the removal of Anita's civil liberties; in such circumstances an understanding of the Human Rights Act 1998 is essential (Lilley *et al.*, 2001).

The practitioner, therefore, can explore with Anita and her family the implications of her actions, with the aim of facilitating her understanding and developing strategies to reduce risk (Wilcox, 1994). Skills in accurate communication become essential alongside the sensitive handling of sexual information and avoidance of imposing judgemental attitudes (Craft, 1987). S/he can actively use materials from the field of personal and sexual relationships (Craft and Hitching, 1989; Craft, 1991), adapting these for Anita's purposes.

McCarthy (1993) and McCarthy and Thompson (1992, 1994, 1996) also present strategies to reduce risk including programmes of sex education and suggestions for staff responses. For instance, Anita can be offered assertiveness exercises with regard to safer sex and personal safety. As she increases her awareness of the nature of the Saturday 'dates' she may ask for support in extricating herself from this activity while retaining contact with her family on her terms. In using advocacy and negotiating skills, the social worker should always be prepared for the possibility that Anita, when weighing up the situation, regards the retention of her 'boyfriend' and the expectations of her family above any discomfort about prostitution.

There is considerable risk of sexual exploitation for young women with learning disabilities. Therefore, effective assessments of situations involving substantial power imbalances require diligent handling and a range of protective strategies, to be explored in the next section.

Protection

The role of societal protection is ambiguous; why, for example, has child protection been afforded such high priority, with a national network of sophisticated policies and procedures, in comparison with adult protection, with its relatively low status and underdeveloped social policy responses? There remains little awareness of the needs of vulnerable adults experiencing violence and abuse. While some of this ignorance can be attributed to a failure to recognise the pervasiveness of abuse (Carmody, 1991), it still constitutes a denial of human rights. Indeed, the underlying rationale for adult protection services is that society owes a duty of care to those less able to keep themselves safe. Abuse in this context involves a whole range of damaging experiences, which could be avoided, resulting from the actions or omissions of others. These range from criminal acts at one extreme to poor practice involving a failure to provide, or prevent others from providing, proper care (UKCC, 1996: pp. 10–12).

Nevertheless, perceptions of abuse have a subjective dimension that is context and culturally specific. For example, the pervading culture in an institution may result in abusive practices becoming an unquestioned norm (Morton, 1998). In these circumstances, 'protection' acquires a wider meaning, involving the establishment of co-ordinated, multi-agency systems with a shared philosophy, strategy and procedures directed at identifying and intervening effectively when abuse has occurred. As society allows itself to 'think the unthinkable' (Brown and Craft, 1989) so individuals may feel empowered to report abuse perpetrated within institutions. Resultant enquiries, for example, the Independent Longcare Inquiry (Burgner *et al.*, 1998), have become catalysts for practitioners and services, placing greater emphasis on the need for protection at both individual and organisational levels. Of even greater importance is the fact that guidance on the development and implementation of multi-agency policies and procedures (DoH, 2000d) now emphasises the role that local authority social services departments should play in co-ordinating policies to protect vulnerable adults from abuse and identifies their responsibility to investigate and take action when a vulnerable adults is believed to be suffering abuse. The guidance also offers a structure and content for the development of local inter-agency policies, procedures and joint protocols that will draw on good practice locally and nationally.

In practice scenario 6.2, we emphasise how practitioners may tolerate or fail to recognise abuse concerning an adult with learning disability; the resultant 'accommodation' (see Chapter 3) means that protection issues may be ignored until crisis point. Reflective practice, however, involves the practitioner acknowledging and questioning what is happening at an earlier stage.

There is a temptation here to focus on Dionne's 'challenging' behaviour, enacting a medicalised response in keeping with the fourth manifestation of exploitation mentioned earlier. Her mother's request for the doctor's assistance, the subsequent hospital admission and medication, the potential for exclusion from college, are indicative of the pathologising tendencies of organisational practices. Moreover, the college's failure to report these incidents to the lead agency for adult protection, thereby colluding with the perpetrators' actions, is symptomatic of general dissatisfaction among users and carers with how allegations are handled. 'Accommodating' practice easily slips into lack of institutional safeguards and denial of human rights. If, however, a social model is adopted – and it is important to note that learning disability is often neglected within the social model of disability (Chappell *et al.*, 2001) – then the focus moves from Dionne being perceived as the 'problem' to the college's response to the group of men perpetrating the harassment and alleged sexual abuse. In so doing, Dionne's behaviour may now be seen as a form of communication (Lovett, 1996). She, in effect, has 'turned up the volume' in an effort to be heard, with her behaviour becoming a 'reasonable'

PRACTICE SCENARIO 6.2

Dionne, aged 19 and of dual heritage (African-Caribbean father and white mother), has moderate learning disabilities and some autistic features. She lives with her mother who is separated from her father, with whom there is little contact. She attends a college for young people with learning disabilities. Over the past year, she has complained to her mother of bullying by young men at the college. They have been verbally abusive, with this escalating into some physical violence. Her mother reported this to the college on each occasion but felt no action had been taken and the incidents continued. Dionne's behaviour then changed abruptly from being anxious into complete withdrawal, a refusal to speak, and periods of anger towards her mother, occasionally including physical violence. Her mother asked her GP for assistance in approaching social services in relation to the abuse at the college. After an investigation in which Dionne did not disclose any further information, the college agreed to review its policy on bullying and abuse. No further action was taken in respect of offering Dionne or her family support. However, Dionne has now refused to return to college and is not eating. Her aggressive outbursts have increased, and she has been admitted to a learning disability psychiatric ward in the local hospital for observation and to give her mother some respite. Three days after admission, Dionne tells a nurse that some men at college had trapped her in the toilets and touched her 'boobs' and 'Mary', which had been very sore.

Practice questions:

- Which factors should be taken into account in making an assessment of seriousness?
- What supports will Dionne need to ensure her protection and emotional wellbeing during the investigative process?

---

response to an unreasonable environment where she feels threatened and unprotected by both the college and her mother.

An assessment of seriousness is the adult protection equivalent to 'significant harm' in the child protection arena (Brown *et al.*, 1998: p. 36) and should include an evaluation of:

- The individual and her/his vulnerability.
- The nature of the abuse and its impact on the individual.
- The context, including historical information, which may indicate a pattern of abuse.
- The power dynamics in the abuser/victim relationship, including possible coercion or risk resulting from an investigation.
- The nature and motivation of the alleged abuser(s) (if known).
- The actual or likely risk to other people.

Operating within adult protection policy, the practitioner, in collaboration with the police, can use the above framework to assess whether Dionne has been the subject of abuse, with the young men's actions amounting to criminal offence(s). The practitioner can operate within a four stage procedural model (Churchill *et al.*, 1996) – alerting, reporting, investigating and monitoring – to acquire a comprehensive picture of the situation and its chronology. This will involve multi-agency working, gaining the best from other professionals and agencies through joint value checks and teasing out disablist assumptions permeating the four manifestations of exploitation, mentioned above. If the college is the primary source of Dionne's difficulties, then the social worker needs to establish how far it has followed its own policies on bullying and abuse. Given the family's alienation and distress, an important objective will be to involve Dionne and her mother throughout, providing them with clear explanations about what is happening while reassuring them of the appropriateness of their disclosures.

In responding to Dionne's allegation to the nurse, an investigation into possible sexual abuse should be jointly planned with the police from an early stage, as in child protection practice (Home Office, 2000). The investigative team should appreciate that information gathering is distinct from, and a preliminary to, assessment and planning and should meet both police and social services' objectives (Home Office and DoH, 1992; Brown *et al.*, 1996; Home Office, 1998b), including:

- To find out what, if anything, has happened to Dionne.
- To protect her from further harm.
- To acquire any associated and corroborative evidence available.
- To interview and obtain statements from anyone able to assist the investigation.

- To assess whether Dionne, as the victim, will be a competent key witness in court and be able to withstand cross-examination.
- To assess the abilities and culpability of the suspects who also have learning disabilities.
- To consider the formulation of an aftercare and therapeutic plan for Dionne.

The social worker, in assessing the possible implications of Dionne's ethnic origin, will need to investigate whether the abuse and harassment are imbued with racism. The Stephen Lawrence Inquiry recommends that a racist incident should be defined as one which is perceived as such by the victim or others (MacPherson, 1999). Dionne may be experiencing stigmatisation through racism, sexism and disablism, all contributing to a distorted perception, by her college and others, of her 'challenging' behaviour (Baxter *et al.*, 1990). Her distress and disturbance through victimisation will need to be considered in relation to her sense of ethnic identity and self-worth, and her ability to learn coping skills in a racist environment (Ince, 1998).

Creative use of investigative interviewing techniques is therefore vital in minimising Dionne's stress, vulnerability and confusion as the police and social work enquiries evolve (Cooke and Davies, 2001). Additionally, accuracy of her memory, alongside her potential acquiescence may be queried when assessing her capacity to give evidence as a witness (Clifford, 1997). It is often presumed that people with learning disabilities have unsophisticated memory retrieval strategies relating to context and cue (Fisher and Geiselman, 1992; Milne *et al.*, 1997). Nonetheless, research (Clare and Gudjonsson, 1993) indicates that many witnesses with learning disabilities, when appropriately interviewed using cognitive techniques, are able to remember core events (although, in some cases not the chronology or sequence), and are resistant to suggestibility when recounting traumatic episodes. Recall of detail is more problematic and pressure for such information may result in confabulation (Tully and Fritzon, 1996).

Interviewers, then, need to enhance their communication with, and facilitation of, Dionne as a potential witness through their *own* behaviour, rather than presuming the limits of her capability or reliability. The following model identifies two areas, environment and supports, where the team can play a pivotal role in enabling Dionne to tell her story (Seiter, 1992).

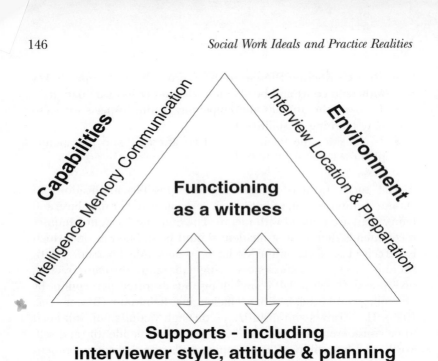

Figure 6.1 Model of joint investigative interviewing (adapted from the American Association of Mental Retardation) (*sic.*) (Seiter, 1992)

This model provides conceptual guidance to the investigative team by emphasising Dionne's abilities alongside her deficits, thereby avoiding labelling her solely as someone with communication difficulties. The focus shifts to the interviewers' joint responsibility in being sensitive to and appropriately skilled in appraising her needs. In assessing whether a victim/witness is 'capable' of being interviewed (the triangle's left-hand side), the following minimum criteria are suggested (Brown *et al.*, 1996). Does Dionne:

- Have a reliable, intentional and intelligible method of communicating?
- Signal 'Yes' or 'No' in a recognisable way?
- Communicate specific information purposefully?
- Remember recent and more long-term events?
- Understand the concept of telling the truth?

It will also be necessary to consider whether the application of the 'special measures', as defined in the 'Youth Justice and Criminal

Evidence Act' (HM Government, 1999) and explained in 'Achieving Best Evidence in Criminal Proceedings' (Home Office, 2000), will enable Dionne to give her 'best evidence'. The Court makes this decision and again expert assessment will be required at an early stage in the investigation.

Information gathering must be influenced by the triangle's right-hand side, environmental features. The organisation of the interview, whether non-verbal prompts and aids need to be available, who should be present and how they should be prepared, must all be decided (Home Office and DoH, 1992; Morris, 1998c). The base of the triangle considers the interview itself, in terms of adapting standard interviewing skills and techniques (Tully and Cahill, 1984; Bull and Cullen, 1992) to meet the requirements of people with learning disabilities (Fisher and Geiselman, 1992; Milne and Bull, 1999). Particular care will need to be exercised in questioning styles, as Dionne will have difficulty in communicating her experiences clearly, especially when under stress (Carmody, 1991). Perpetrators' threats against the victim will also hinder disclosure of details. Nonetheless, everything possible should be done to enable expression (Marchant and Page, 1993; Burke *et al.*, 1998) by approaching Dionne with an open attitude (Jackson and Jackson, 1998). Indeed, layers of injustice will accrue if the investigation compounds Dionne's experiences of exploitation.

By the end of the investigation, in making professional judgements within a legal framework, the worker should demonstrate that her/his conclusions are well founded and reasonable through:

- An ability to recognise relevant and exclude irrelevant information.
- Recognising when desirable information is missing and making adjustments accordingly.
- Utilisation of contemporary research, taking account of important cases, reports, Home Office (1998b) guidance and the Independent Longcare Inquiry (Burgner *et al.*, 1998).
- Knowledge of the criminal law and the rules of evidence, referred to above, in conjunction with appropriate detailed information from the police.

Dionne's needs will have confronted the practitioner with a unique situation, deeply affected by entrenched and accommodating professional behaviour. Through the process of reflection and inquiry, s/he should be open to acknowledging any deficiency in her/his knowledge base, acquiring advice and information accordingly (DoH/SSI, 1991a; Spicer, 1995). Without the accomplishment of reflective practice, it will be difficult for the practitioner to enable users facing exploitation to embrace empowerment and self-advocacy.

Empowerment and self-advocacy

A key problem in social work with people with learning disabilities is the balance between users' empowerment and the responsibility of ensuring that users have as safe an environment as possible. This is made more complex by the fact that 'empowerment' is in danger of becoming a debased term because of its definitional imprecision. For example, there is a world of difference between the consumerist vision expressed in the practitioners' guide to assessment and care management (DoH/SSI, 1991b: p. 9), and the radical perspectives propounded by the disability movement (Henderson and Pochin, 2001). Practice scenario 4.3 in Chapter 4, for instance, demonstrates a more consciously 'political' approach to empowerment of people with learning disabilities, drawing on the work of Freire (1972). However, various writers have helpfully drawn attention to how these different interpretations can coexist (see, e.g., Taylor *et al.*, 1992; Means *et al.*, 1994; Means and Smith, 1998; Henderson and Pochin, 2001).

Means *et al.* (1994) have defined three distinctive strategies for empowerment through 'exit', 'voice' and 'rights'. The first implies a market orientation; the user is enabled to exercise choice between alternative service providers, and switch from one to another if dissatisfied with the service received. This is an explicitly consumerist model and is close to the Conservative government's intentions in developing community care. The core weakness of this conception is that the assumption of free choice is nonsensical when applied to people with learning disabilities, since it assumes a level of power that has been systematically stripped from them. This clearly demonstrates the central fallacy underpinning market theories in social care (Lymbery, 2000).

Empowerment through 'voice' is defined by Means *et al.* (1994) as a democratic approach, where users are given an opportunity to transform their services by speaking out about them. As Means and Smith (1998) indicate, this can take place at individual and collective levels;

indeed, the consultation requirement in the production of community care plans is an example of 'voice' empowerment in action. The core limitation of this approach is that it leaves the power relationship between service users and professionals *in situ*; the mere fact of being offered an opportunity to express an opinion on services does not equate to having the power to effect change.

The third approach, empowerment through 'rights', is the disability movement's preferred strategy (Means *et al.*, 1994). Since it is based on the adoption of universal rights for all it has been strengthened by the passage of the Human Rights Act 1998. However, under existing community care legislation, people with learning disabilities have relatively few rights, with local authorities retaining considerable discretionary powers (Mandelstam, 1999); this situation is unlikely to be amended because of its financial consequences (Means and Smith, 1998). Despite this, a rights-based approach is essential for the empowerment of users and carers, particularly in terms of guaranteeing a reasonable income and in protecting the individual against abuse and exploitation (Means and Smith, 1998: p. 100).

In the light of the conceptual and practical limitations of the different versions of empowerment, Means and Smith (1998) suggest that for many people empowerment can only be achieved through a process of 'struggle' in challenging the realities of power relations (see Chapter 1). Social workers have a crucial role in this, as they occupy a position of power that can be deployed either to assist or obstruct this struggle. Taylor *et al.* (1992) have usefully defined empowerment on a continuum or 'ladder' which outlines the degree of power given to or taken by users.

HIGH   Users have the authority to take decisions

        Users have the authority to take some decisions

        Users have an opportunity to influence decisions

        User views are sought before making decisions

        Decisions are publicised and explained before implementation

LOW   Information is given about decisions made

Figure 6.2 Ladder of empowerment (Taylor *et al.*, 1992: p. 3)

People are empowered in different degrees when they have access to information, control over money and resources, alongside the power and authority to use these in achieving their purposes (Wilcox, 1994). While all these represent rungs on the 'ladder', the social worker needs to ensure that each user is as near the top as possible. An important prerequisite for empowerment is the ability to identify and state what you want, or complain about injustice. This is not always easy for people with learning disabilities, many of whom have been systematically denied the chance to advocate on their own behalf, and who may also have communication difficulties to overcome. The development of advocacy (Brandon *et al.*, 1995; Sim and Mackay, 1997; Henderson and Pochin, 2001) and self-advocacy (Aspis, 1997) has been part of a process aiming to help people access supports, articulate their needs, receive the services they require, and secure their rights. The Ann Craft Trust's experiences, and our meetings with the self-advocacy groups, have demonstrated that levels of empowerment are directly related to each individual's comprehension and conceptual abilities, alongside their social aptitude. Without knowing a great deal about the individual, it is difficult for the social worker to be sure whether a person is making an informed choice. If her/his capacities are restricted, the need for an independent advocate to represent the interests of the vulnerable individual is paramount (Sim and Mackay, 1997: p. 5). Self-advocacy is linked, through self-determination, to empowerment, both individually and collectively: 'It's helped me to stand up for me rights . . . it's helped me to be more confident . . . I'm not frightened of confrontation now' (Atkinson and Williams, 1990: pp. 166, 192). However, self-advocacy may appear more powerful than it really is; Aspis (1997) alerts us to its potential use as a tool for ensuring that people with learning disabilities accept 'a bad deal' rather than offering them an opportunity to challenge the society which still labels and stigmatises them. In such circumstances it does not necessarily move people several rungs up the 'ladder' since existing power relations are left intact.

Given these tensions, how can empowering social work practice with people with learning disabilities be identified? The starting point is a willingness and confidence to use precisely the same skills, knowledge and experience utilised with any other community member. The Ann Craft Trust, in facilitating training courses for qualified social workers and other professionals, has discovered that many practitioners feel unable or unwilling to do this. In the minutiae of the social work relationship, empowering practice lies in a good understanding of the importance of pace, a willingness to alter practice in response to feedback and reflection and in an acknowledgement of the unique identity of each individual, including their abilities and disabilities. It involves sensitivity, sharing and relinquishing control according to individual needs and wishes, relationship and trust building, developing two way communication and perceiving each experience and interaction, however trivial, as an opportunity for personal/political development. Herein lies the dilemma for social workers operating in a service ethos of brief interventions and time limited care plans which, as described in Chapter 3, impinge negatively on reflective practitioners (see also Chapter 7). Nevertheless, empowerment is crucially dependent on recognising power inequalities and a commitment to combating them.

An example of the dilemmas involved in empowering practice can be seen in practice scenario 6.3, involving a couple's desire for independence in the community. Here, the social worker can offer information, enhancing the couple's coping abilities and decision-making skills, while respecting their privacy and right to refuse help.

It can be difficult for practitioners to allow people to take charge of their lives and the services they need, which professionals have traditionally determined and controlled. Practitioners, in operating a 'professional gift model' (Duffy, 1996), assume complete responsibility for assessing user needs. This model threatened Brenda's autonomy by presuming the right to make decisions on her behalf, thereby undermining her ability to make choices for herself.

The first social worker was working within an overall plan to develop Brenda's capacity for independent living, seeing the services offered as necessary for her skill enhancement and future life. An additional subtext may well have been distrust of Richard, concerns about the power dynamics between them and unwillingness to accept their relationship. The first social worker accepted neither the right of the couple to marry nor the reality of their married existence. She missed the opportunity to make an assessment of Brenda's changed circumstances in a way that respected her rights and choices, acting in a manner perceived by them to be intrusive, disrespectful and threatening. A rigid adherence to the previously agreed care plan blocked her ability to communicate effectively with Brenda, with the management of risk assuming paramount importance. The practitioner was therefore unprepared to take a flexible approach to Brenda's burgeoning relationship with Richard – something that should have been cause for celebration.

PRACTICE SCENARIO 6.3

Brenda, a younger white woman with moderate learning disabilities, who lived in residential care, met Richard, a white man in middle age with mild learning disabilities. They wanted to get married, with Brenda moving into Richard's flat. Brenda's social worker, from a community resource team, expressed doubts about these plans, being concerned about her ability to assess her own wants in the face of Richard's capabilities. The practitioner was working with Brenda to prepare her for living independently in supported accommodation, as part of an agreed care plan. The couple did marry, and the social worker continued to visit Brenda; however, the couple felt she was still organising Brenda's life, without reference to them. Richard was also angry that the social worker came into his flat without invitation and looked through his bills. He wanted to look after both himself and Brenda without interference. The couple spoke to their self-advocacy group who helped them to write a letter to the social worker asking her to withdraw from Brenda's life. The practitioner met with the couple to try to resolve the situation, but both parties found this a frustrating experience. Soon thereafter, the social worker left and the case was held temporarily by the team manager. A further meeting occurred between the couple and social services, with subsequent negotiations about the possible termination of services becoming protracted. In the meantime, Brenda continued attending the day centre arranged by the first social worker, where she took part in a programme specifically designed to help her with independent living skills – cooking, budgeting, shopping, and so on. However, her attendance at the day centre was poor. After a gap of three months, a new social worker was allocated to Brenda.

Practice questions:

- What are Brenda's needs and rights, and how can these best be supported?
- How can the second practitioner offer Brenda a service that will empower her to achieve independence?
- What is the best way of involving Richard in the process?
- What knowledge, values and skills does the social worker need to apply?

The second social worker will face difficulties inherent in a situation where trust has been lost, but by adopting an empowering social model of intervention, s/he can acknowledge Brenda's status as an adult and act to facilitate her consideration of important issues. In order to accomplish this, the practitioner must recognise existing dimensions of power, particularly in respect of sexism. Possession of a learning disability will have led to a negation of Brenda's right to make decisions, compounded by overprotectiveness – exemplified by the first social worker – derived from her gendered socialisation. While accepting the risks in developing a sexual relationship, the social worker should not be deterred from working sensitively with both Brenda and Richard in the areas of sexuality and intimacy. This means acknowledging that their needs may conflict; for example, Richard may be replicating Brenda's oppression by 'taking over' – this is implied in his comment that he wants to 'look after' her, and manage all finances. The social worker will also need to interrogate the extent to which Richard has assumed a patriarchal role in relation to Brenda, highlighting the obvious – if little expressed – fact that members of oppressed groups can also act in oppressive ways as individuals.

Consequently, the social worker's practice must be governed by principles of user involvement and rights, ensuring that Brenda is the focus for assessment and planning. S/he must enable Brenda to give 'voice' to her needs, actively seeking the services of an independent advocate to fulfil that role (Cambridge, 1999). Richard should also be encouraged to contribute through recognition of his relationship with her. In this respect, his learning disability is less important than his status as marital partner, and he has the right to be as fully involved as any other person occupying a similar relationship. However, the social worker must be wary of two parallel possibilities. While it should not be assumed that Richard necessarily has the right to speak for Brenda in all matters, neither should the social worker ignore the possibility that what Richard is saying might accurately represent her wishes. Stanley (1999) has noted that users with the ability to express their needs strongly are most able to exercise choice, but users' voices can be lost when dominated by more eloquent carers. However, disregarding the voice of the carer in such a situation has the potential to be profoundly unhelpful and patronising.

Given that a key goal of social work intervention is to enable Brenda's ascent up the 'ladder of empowerment', it is vital that issues of autonomy, protection and empowerment are kept in balance

(Stevenson and Parsloe, 1993; Braye and Preston-Shoot, 1995). The practitioner's role is to assist Brenda in making decisions that not only respect her right to autonomy but also keep her safe. However, simply giving her a 'voice' in decision making is a partial view of empowerment, as already indicated. Social work practice must also enable Brenda to exercise her choice to 'exit' from the service if she does not want it. The social worker should explain fully the purpose of the independent living programme, and the potential benefits to Brenda – and Richard – if she continues to attend, ensuring that her 'rights' are secured.

It will take considerable delicacy to renegotiate the social work relationship with them in order to encourage Brenda's assertiveness. Moving further from the professional gift model is likely to be a learning experience and a cause of anxiety for all parties. The practitioner may be able to help Brenda to move higher on the 'ladder' of empowerment by supporting her in taking control of her care services through direct payments, although its application for people with learning disabilities is relatively underdeveloped (Cambridge, 1999). Part of the social work task is to inform her about, and assist her in considering, her options, for example, using service brokerage or a trust fund.

In terms of skills, good communication is the key to empowering social work practice, as illustrated in our discussions with the self-advocacy groups. People unanimously talked about the importance of having someone who listened to them; they strongly disliked the worker, from whichever service, who only spoke to their families or carers. The most valued professionals were perceived to be those who maintained contact. This is not surprising when many people with learning disabilities are acknowledged as having problems in communication, language and in forming and sustaining relationships. Therefore, skills in developing relationships with individuals who may not be immediately forthcoming or open to reciprocation are vital. If the first rungs on the ladder of empowerment are based on receiving and understanding information, then a key social work task must be to offer information in a manner that people with learning disabilities can actively use.

In order to practice reflectively in this scenario, the social worker requires considerable knowledge about the impact of structural oppression on the lives of people with learning disabilities and the legal basis for action (discussed earlier in relation to practice scenario 6.1). Her/his value base will reflect a capacity to understand the complex layers of empowerment and the difficulties of balancing autonomy with protection. Additionally, the practitioner must deploy the full panoply of social work skills – assessment, communication, relationship-building, liaison, negotiation and the identification, management and resolution of conflict (see Coulshed and Orme, 1998). Finally, s/he will need to identify the political dimensions of the empowerment process, more fully addressed in practice scenario 4.3. In this situation, the potential for collective action deriving from Brenda's involvement in self-advocacy needs to be explored through discussions about the group's role in facilitating the raising of Brenda's consciousness and skill development in challenging social injustice. The group could offer a vital forum to examine the nature of power relationships, assisting her in the process of negotiating for – or 'exiting from' – services.

Conclusion

In this chapter we have examined how social attitudes towards learning disability and structural forces, the *macro*, condition users' experiences of exploitation, protection and empowerment as well as direct social work practice, the *micro*. On a historical basis it is clear that the circumstances of people with learning disabilities have improved. Indeed, the White Paper *Valuing People* (DoH, 2001a) reflects this, but it is clear that its rhetoric needs to be matched by action (Gates, 2001). Negative views of learning disability still interact with models of normalisation and professional control to promote often untested assumptions about incapacity and incompetence, undermining their rights to have appropriate supports and still be able to make decisions about their lives (Leicester and Cooke, 2002).

Inevitably, social workers' interventions are constrained by the structures, resources, policies and procedures of their employing agency. While operating within these systems, our stance throughout this chapter has been to affirm how effective social work practice involves deploying models of intervention which challenge existing assumptions and test boundaries. The investigative interviewing model is one such example, encouraging practitioners to take a more positive and flexible approach to users' abilities and to accept personal responsibility for enabling communication. In contemplating the model of empowerment outlined above, social workers will be drawn to the practice dilemma of balancing a moral and legal duty of care, the ability of an individual to make any particular decision, and their personal autonomy and right to take risks. These complex issues also lie at the heart of adult protection work. For the self-advocacy groups, satisfaction with professional intervention involved being listened to carefully. Such workers afforded them respect and the confidence to ask for what they wanted, building foundations for empowering and protective social work practice.

7

Managerialism and Care Management Practice with Older People

Mark Lymbery

Introduction

The purpose of this chapter is to analyse the impact of community care policy on social work practice with older people. Given the different legal systems that support community care, the arguments in this chapter are directly applicable to England, Wales and Scotland. However, the more general theoretical background of managerialism is accepted as a more international phenomenon (Pollitt, 1993), and the chapter's themes will therefore have resonance beyond national boundaries. It will focus on the introduction of care management, and the extent to which the practice of the new care managers has become dominated by organisational priorities, to the overall detriment of service quality. In the overall schema of the book, the chapter focuses primarily on linking the *mezzo* and *micro* levels of analysis of Chapters 2 and 3. However, it is prefaced by a brief discussion of the *macro* context of community care policy, and therefore draws to some extent on the analysis developed in Chapter 1. It argues that creative social work should be a central component of care management with older people, and that routinised responses to need are inadequate when confronted by complex sets of human circumstances. Indeed, as Johnson (2002) argues, the state of care management for older people is simply incompatible with notions of social justice.

The chapter starts by analysing the extent to which the implementation of community care represents the primacy of budgetary and resource considerations over the principles that secured widespread political and professional support following the publication of the White Paper *Caring for People* (DoH, 1989). The systems of care management that have been established, based on government guidance (DoH/SSI, 1991b, 1991c), attempt to apply universally what has only been tested for fragments of the population (Huxley, 1993). The practice that has developed contains strong elements of what Sturges (1996) has defined as an administrative model (see Chapter 2), creating many dilemmas for the care manager who wishes to practise reflectively.

The chapter concludes by identifying, through the use of practice scenarios, individualised responses to need where care managers recognise the unique nature of each person's circumstances, while conforming to their employers' requirements. It is suggested that creative care management can help to ensure that the 'realities' of the organisational context do not necessarily stifle good practice. The existence of stringent bureaucratic and procedural requirements is acknowledged, but the chapter proposes that these need not dictate the content and style of practice. Care managers' ability to develop imaginative ways of working is critical, as high quality practice creates the best defence against managerialism.

Community care policy in context

This section sets out to clarify how community care policy has affected the development of care management, rather than to provide a detailed analysis of its history and background (for such an analysis, see Means and Smith, 1998). The idea of 'community care' was a core aspiration of welfare policy from the late 1950s, but lacked a national policy to enable its systematic development. Two themes underpinned the debate in the 1980s. First, there was concern about the welfare of people cared for in large institutions. Second, there was anxiety about the high cost of institutional care, which led to a search for less expensive solutions. The alteration in social security regulations in 1980 provided the final impetus for change. The modifications enabled people in receipt of state benefits to claim the full-board and lodging charge and freely enter residential or nursing homes with state support. This precipitated a rapid increase in expenditure on institutional care from the social security budget from £10 million in 1979 to an estimated £2,480 million by April 1993 (Wistow *et al.*, 1994).

Economic imperatives therefore stimulated much concern about community care policy. Several reports were particularly influential in its development (see Wistow *et al.*, 1994). The most significant is the Griffiths Report, the primary task of which was to review 'the way public funds are used to support community care policy' (Griffiths, 1988: p. iii, para. 1). Griffiths warned that the proper implementation of community care would not be a cheap option, and that 'ambitious policies' should not be embarked upon without 'appropriate funds' (Griffiths, 1988: p. ix, para. 38). The community care White Paper (DoH, 1989) accepted the bulk of the report's recommendations, with one or two exceptions. It aimed to ensure the general principle of 'promoting choice and independence', and contained six key objectives which combined care principles with political and organisational priorities (DoH, 1989: p. 5, para. 1.11). *Caring for People* differed significantly from the Griffiths Report in its failure to accept the recommendation for comprehensive ring fencing of the financial resources for community care (Wistow *et al.*, 1994), which has had a major bearing on the adequacy of funding since.

The White Paper was translated into legislative form in 1990. There was a general political and professional welcome for its objectives, and for most of what the government sought to introduce. The academic community was markedly more sceptical, with several writers criticising the predominantly financial motives which underpinned the policy (Means and Smith, 1998). The main concern was that since the 'deep normative core' (Lewis and Glennerster, 1996: p. 195) of community care was the need to control the increase in expenditure on social care, the entire policy was unlikely to be properly funded. Therefore, 'if the Treasury managed to give local authorities anything less than £625 million a year in the early years of the scheme, it would be saving money on what it would have had to pay under the old arrangements' (Lewis and Glennerster, 1996: p. 29). In addition, concern was voiced regarding the extent to which the passage of the reforms would serve to perpetuate the 'hidden policy conflict' (Lewis, 2001) between health and social care. The additional money to implement community care was transferred to local authorities through a Special Transitional Grant (STG) in 1993–94 and the subsequent two years. The cumulative total for the first three years was £1,568 million, substantially less than what would otherwise have been spent from the social security budget. This simple calculation does not represent

the full extent of the financial problem for social services departments (SSDs), being complicated by a number of other factors. The
first of these is in the way in which the STG was distributed. The settlement in 1993–94 was only ring fenced for that particular year; for
subsequent years it transferred into the local authority's base budget,
with no requirement that it be spent on community care services. The
same was true for the settlements of the two following years. This presented a particular problem for local authorities confronting major
resource problems.

Community care policy, therefore, stemmed from primarily economic considerations. As Lewis and Glennerster (1996) conclude, the
policy has been successful in this respect, with no public outcry concerning the adequacy of its funding. This achievement has not been
straightforward for SSDs. Several of them have experienced problems
in balancing their community care budget, resulting in the public's
increased expectations and demands not being met (Hadley and
Clough, 1996). In addition, there have been clear cost transfers from
health to social care as health authorities substantially reduced their
provision of long-term care (Lewis, 2001). All of this is particularly
significant in relation to the growing levels of poverty and inequality
that characterise British society, as identified in Chapter 1. State-
funded community care services are of most benefit to those people
who have limited economic and political power, or who have experienced various forms of societal oppression. The mechanism of care
management was established to help balance the tension between
needs and resources; the following section reviews how this aspect of
policy has developed.

The development of care management

Care management was the creation of the new community care policy,
and it is important briefly to consider its antecedents. There has long
been a terminological confusion between care management, referred
to in the Griffiths Report (1988), and case management, the desig-
nation applied to both American and British pilot projects, and subsequently used in the White Paper (DoH, 1989). From 1991, and the
publication of government guidance on community care (DoH/SSI,
1991b, 1991c), the preferred term has been 'care management'. This
is technically accurate; as Griffiths suggests, the 'care manager' will
'oversee the assessment and re-assessment function and manage the
resulting action' (Griffiths, 1988: p. 14, para. 6.6). However, when

'case management' was used in the White Paper, this was more in tune with the definitions inspiring its development. Huxley (1993) is suspicious of this shift, believing that 'care management' has no agreed definition and can therefore be twisted to suit several perspectives – particularly the managerialist priorities that have come to dominate community care (identified in the following section: see also Chapter 2).

Analysing care management from a social work perspective helps to illuminate this debate. In America, the social work role in case management was equivocal. For example, Moxley's (1989: p. 11) definition of case management practice as a 'client-level strategy for promoting the co-ordination of human services, opportunities, or benefits' does not lead to the conclusion that social work skills are necessarily central to this process. However, Moxley's interpretation focuses on the primacy of meeting client need, not the efficient administration of scarce resources predominant in community care (Payne, 1995). A similar point was evident in influential British case management pilot projects (Challis and Davies, 1986; Knapp *et al.*, 1992; Challis *et al.*, 1995). These were tightly controlled and organised, with clearly defined research objectives; the role of skilled social workers as case managers was critical, as the counselling, therapeutic and interpersonal aspects of the role were considered to be vital (Payne, 1995; Sheppard, 1995a). Indeed, Challis *et al.* (1995) note that care management requires skills in excess of those which would normally be used by a social worker.

Some of the problems that have beset care management for older people in practice derive from the model that has been adopted. Payne (2000b) notes that different approaches have been deployed for various client groups. For example, a multiprofessional model distinguishes high risk mental health services and a model of service brokerage has been developed to meet the needs of adults with disabilities. A defined professional role is implied in each (Payne, 2000b). By contrast, the model that has come to dominate work with older people is that of social care entrepreneurship, where the availability of services is tightly constrained by costs. This has brought about a great increase in the level of bureaucratisation of care management for older people (Sturges, 1996; Lymbery, 1998a; Postle, 1999, 2002; Payne, 2000b). Indeed, some practitioners have expressed the view that the introduction of care management heralded the demise of social work with older people (Postle, 2001).

Therefore, although the benefits of the pilot projects were well documented, they have not necessarily proved capable of emulation when applied more widely, particularly in administratively driven models of practice. The published guidance (DoH/SSI, 1991b, 1991c) defines care management as a seven stage process; there is nothing in this which is unfamiliar to social workers, as it describes standard social work activity (Payne, 2000b). However, the cycle can be interpreted mechanistically, ignoring the necessary interactions between different stages. Equally, overemphasis on assessment to the exclusion of other elements of care management – particularly monitoring and review – can serve to fragment the process. Sturges (1996) argues that fragmentation is a worrying feature of British care management, increasing its administrative nature as characterised by the following features:

- Routinised working – swift assessment, unimaginative planning and cursory review.
- Large caseloads, with the emphasis on processing a high volume of work rather than client outcomes.
- Proliferation of forms for various aspects of practice.
- Tasks are split, and provided by different workers, leading to a general deskilling of the workforce.
- Emphasis on formal services rather than the linking of formal and informal services.
- Discouragement of the counselling and interpersonal aspects of social work.

(Sturges, 1996: p. 49)

Research on care management emphasises the disparity that exists between local authorities (Challis *et al.*, 2001). For example, in their research within five SSDs, Lewis *et al.* (1997) note that 'overly mechanistic' forms of care management were not widely evident, and that social work values underpinned its development to some degree. However, they also identify some issues that illustrate Sturges' concerns, including the increase in bureaucratisation, routinisation and proceduralisation (see Chapter 2). On a more general level, they also highlight disturbing issues of low morale and cynicism among care managers; this reflects similar findings in other research (Pahl, 1994; May and Buck, 2000), and contrasts markedly with the relatively high morale of those managers who set community care policy. Postle (2002) argues that while the work required of care managers is increasingly complex the processes that they have to follow are reductionist, leading to assorted problems in practice. McGrath *et al.* (1996) identify lack of resources as the critical problem for care managers; Ramcharan *et al.* (1999) confirm this finding, adding that assessment tasks appear to be consuming even more care management time, to the detriment of care planning and direct work with service users. Baldwin (1996) concludes that while many practitioners have been resistant to the managerialist approach accompanying the introduction of care management, they also cling to forms of practice that have not responded to the challenges of community care and are therefore in need of improvement.

This brief summary is inconclusive; while it appears that care management has a more administratively driven orientation, social work skills still influence its practice. However, the following section will argue that there has been a shift in the way care management is controlled with an increase in the power of managers relative to social workers.

The impact of managerialism

This section will identify those aspects of policy that have increased managerial power, and hence have decreased care managers' autonomy. Key arguments were introduced in general terms in Chapter 2; here, they are applied to the specific circumstances of community care. Particular attention will be given to increased managerial dominance over practice, as evidenced by financial controls, fragmentation of the social work process and proceduralisation. This is framed within an analysis of managerialism, largely derived from the work of Clarke and colleagues (Langan and Clarke, 1994; Newman and Clarke, 1994; Clarke and Newman, 1997; Clarke, 1998; Langan, 2000). The financial imperatives of community care have created an organisational climate where budgetary management takes highest priority. This preoccupation stems from the impossibility of what SSDs have to do – that is, to reconcile the inadequacy of resources with apparently infinite demand. This has created fertile ground for managerialism, as managers have set the agenda for the way in which SSDs engage with the requirements of policy (Langan and Clarke, 1994). It is important to recognise the twin elements of managerialism (Clarke, 1998; see also Chapter 2), and apply these specifically to community care.

First, managers have brought about a fundamental transformation of welfare organisations in order to carry out government policy requirements. For community care, this has had several consequences.

New forms of budgetary management have been introduced, including quotas for admissions to residential and nursing home care. To administer this system, many SSDs have created panels to authorise placements and (indirectly) to monitor care managers' work. Similar thinking has led to cash limits for care packages to maintain service users in their own homes. This is particularly significant in that the lack of community-based alternatives ensures high levels of admission into institutional care (Netten *et al.*, 2001).

Second, managers have directly increased their own power in relation to front-line social workers, whose capacity for the exercise of professional discretion has been limited (Lymbery, 1998a). Fragmentation of the work process is a good example of this. Many SSDs have created separate jobs to monitor and review care packages, usually occupied by unqualified staff, and hence (implicitly, at least) not regarded as needing the same level of skill. Conversely, in authorities where care managers retain responsibility for monitoring or review, this is likely to be as part of a high caseload – which, as Challis (1994) observes, will reduce the effectiveness of work performance. In the former case, the lack of continuity is in opposition to the essential principles of care management. In the latter, workload pressures make it difficult for care managers to deliver effective practice. As Postle (2002) has discovered, many practitioners are dissatisfied with the compromises that are routinely forced upon them as a result of this pressure.

Community care has also heralded more detailed and potentially prescriptive procedures, symbolised by copious assessment documentation. As seen in Chapter 3, if these are used in an accommodated fashion, a form can dictate the content and style of assessment rather than fulfil its primary purpose as a means by which relevant information can be gathered, combined and subsequently analysed. The resultant 'checklist' practice is driven by SSDs' priorities, not by service users' needs. While the establishment of the single assessment process for older people ought to ensure that there is a genuinely person-centred approach (DoH, 2002a, 2002b), there is an apparent danger that this process will simply replicate many of the existing problems and concerns. The proliferation of assessment documentation is not the sole manifestation of proceduralisation. Many workers new to care management are astonished by the weight of paperwork, where forms are required for every aspect of service provision, as well as for monitoring and review purposes. This further reduces the time available for face to face work, still the core social work task.

Generally, as with assessment, administrative tasks have the effect of dominating – rather than serving – the professional dimensions of practice. This problem is compounded by the fact that social work with older people is less professionally developed than other areas (Lymbery, 1998a; Thompson and Thompson, 2001), thus making it even more difficult to resist managerialist processes.

However, simply accepting managerialist supremacy does not represent an adequate response; as was pointed out in Chapter 3, there are long-term consequences for an individual who is forced to conform to practice dissonant with her/his values. Care managers need to be able to work imaginatively within organisational constraints, and urgently require guidance as to how such inventive work can be achieved and sustained.

Care management practice

Through the medium of selected practice scenarios, this section will identify facets of creative practice. The framework used will be the seven stages of care management (DoH/SSI, 1991b, 1991c), with particular emphasis on the elements of assessment, planning, implementation and evaluation. As Taylor and Devine (1994) point out, this model represents the 'basic helping cycle' that is used throughout social work (see also Payne, 2000b). The scenarios illustrate the range of need with which care managers are confronted and the challenging nature of practice. However, in all cases it would be possible to reduce the level of complexity to a simple service-driven, accommodated response, as defined in Chapter 3, thereby denying the individuality and depth of the problems presented. Excellent practice is based on an acknowledgement of the singular nature of each set of circumstances, with a response based around the uniqueness of need.

PRACTICE SCENARIO 7.1: ASSESSMENT

Mr Pat Clifton is a 75-year-old, widowed Black man. Born in Jamaica, he came to work in Nottingham in the 1950s, accompanied by his wife, who died nine months ago, following which he moved to live with his son and daughter-in-law and their two teenage children. He occupies a separate part of their house, extended and converted to provide him with his own space.

Continued

His daughter-in-law, Gloria, has referred him to the social services office; as the main carer, she has requested three weeks' respite care for Pat in an older people's home while the family goes on holiday. Gloria has also taken responsibility for managing Pat's finances. In the referral papers, Pat is described as 'depressed' and 'socially isolated'. Reference to case files indicates that Pat currently receives the support of a home care assistant for one hour each morning to help him get out of bed, washed and dressed and once a week, to help him have a bath. Pat's main physical problems are associated with arthritis in his knees and hips, which severely restrict his mobility and give him constant pain.

Practice questions:

- What information will help you to assess Pat's needs successfully, as well as those of Gloria as the main carer?
- How will you seek this information?
- What theoretical perspectives can be utilised in this situation?
- In particular, what is the potential impact of Pat's past life history on his present circumstances?

The initial referral information will generate hypotheses concerning the nature of the situation – the apparent problems and strengths available within the family to deal with it. There should be sufficient detail for a skilled worker to identify key topics on which to focus. The process of developing hypotheses and identifying core issues to pursue is not neutral (Munro, 1998b); it is informed by the values and theoretical orientation of the social worker concerned. In the light of this, a care manager must be careful not to develop closed perspectives, which s/he is incapable of revising in the light of experience.

Several possibilities are evident here. It is important to be clear about the ways in which the process of ageing can be understood (Thompson, 1995: pp. 23–42), and to consider how different theoretical insights may help to inform Pat's situation. In essence, this means reflecting on the range of factors which have impacted upon Pat, creating his current experience of old age. His 'race' and country of origin are key issues; the specific experiences of African-Caribbean people must be fully explored. As Blakemore and Boneham (1994) suggest, the fact that Pat is a member of a 'migrant generation' is likely to be important to him, with many of his memories rooted in Jamaica. They suggest that it is vital to understand the specific experience of each individual, what Thompson (1998) terms the 'ontology of ageing'. In this respect, it is important to explore his multiple experiences of loss (Marris, 1986; Worden, 1991), which include continuing grief for his wife, compounded by the recognition that he will never again go 'home', as well as a lack of cultural understanding of how he may feel and express his bereavement (see Field *et al.*, 1997; Hockey *et al.*, 2001). This may help to explain his reported depression; as Parkes (1986) has shown, there is a clear link between bereavement and both mental and physical illness, with multiple losses also exacerbating the effects of the grieving process (Sidell, 1993; Dickenson *et al.*, 2000).

The care manager should ensure that the assessment process involves Gloria as well as Pat, while guarding against assuming that their needs and wishes are compatible. Wistow and Barnes (1993) argue that professional responses should extend service users' control over their lives, and choice regarding the use of services. This implies maintaining a vision of the overarching aims that are being sought while engaging in specific activities contributing to those goals. A number of skills are required to undertake this effectively. As with all social work, the act of assessment is critical. Smale *et al.* (1993) have suggested that there are three general assessment models, as follows:

- *Questioning model* – where the care manager seeks to elicit information from the service user, and employs professional expertise to interpret it.
- *Procedural model* – where the assessment is primarily governed by the agency function, so that the care manager gathers information to judge the service user's eligibility for services.
- *Exchange model* – where the service user is perceived as having expert knowledge about her/his own circumstances. The pattern of assessment is of an exchange of information where worker and user jointly identify the internal and external resources to be brought to bear on a problem, and develop a plan which drawing upon those resources towards an end identified by the user.

While Smale *et al.* (1993) clearly consider the exchange model to be preferable, they acknowledge that other models may have legitimate uses. Care managers should not allow their practice to become dominated by the procedural model, which reflects the managerialist devices discussed earlier. This model is unresponsive to service users, offers limited scope for the exercise of professional judgement, and represents the antithesis of reflection-in-action (Schön, 1991; see also Chapter 3).

A reflective care manager must ensure that the assessment goal is to produce an action plan reflecting the needs and wishes of users and carers, and with which they feel satisfied. In this scenario, the exchange model is clearly to be preferred. It is for Pat to define his physical and psychological problems, especially since the care manager is unlikely to share his racial or cultural background. Only Pat has the capacity to identify the extent to which the hypotheses about loss (identified earlier) are applicable to him, or articulate the impact of arthritis on his daily life. The practitioner must acknowledge the inherent problems that older people have in understanding the assessment process where their lives are already in crisis (Richards, 2000). Similarly, the care manager needs to have a broad understanding of cultural traditions that affect both the giving and receipt of care services (Alibhai-Brown, 1998). Finally, the practitioner must be clear about the limitations of her/his professional knowledge. The establishment of the single assessment process for older people (DoH, 2002b) is intended to ensure that a more explicitly multidisciplinary approach is taken, with the contributions of other professionals – doctors, community nurses, therapists, etc. – being central to it. Social workers, who are likely to lead the assessment in many of the more complex cases (DoH, 2002c), must recognise where needs indicate that the involvement of other professionals would enhance the assessment outcome. In addition, they need to recognise the specific contribution that other professionals could make to the assessment process (Worth, 2001). In this case, for example, it will be vital to establish clearly what Pat's medical and nursing needs might be. Despite its inherent difficulties (Hudson, 2002), effective inter-professional work is a prerequisite for good quality assessments in cases such as this.

In order to achieve all this, a practitioner must allocate sufficient time to accomplish the work satisfactorily, paying appropriate attention to Pat's emotional as well as physical needs. For example, it is important to work with bereavement at a pace that is sensitive to the individual (Lloyd, 1997), accepting the complexity of Pat's feelings. In doing this, the care manager will need to present a convincing argument as to why the assessment cannot be simply concluded in a matter of days. The basis of this lies in acknowledging the emotional impact of the assessment process on Pat (Middleton, 1997; Richards, 2000). Similarly, the care manager must demonstrate analytical skills whereby Pat and Gloria's needs can be identified and then held in balance.

This is clearly a complex set of circumstances, which should be reflected in the depth of the assessment and subsequent care plan. The managerialist pressure will be to complete the assessment quickly, in line with the high turnover of work that is often required. To combat this, the care manager must present a reasoned and well argued assessment and care plan, as this is more likely to be approved. Three particular factors can assist the creative practitioner:

- Although the loyalties of first-line managers are divided between service users and organisational priorities, many of them have a commitment to the importance of meeting user need and will respond positively to a well-constructed plan.
- Therefore, it is essential that the quality of the care manager's work be of the highest order, as this represents the best defence against managerialist intrusion.
- The core argument is that investment of time in the relatively early stages of a problem may help to improve the situation such that future financial expenditure can be minimised.

In this way, social work values – the centrality of service user need, the importance of good assessment, and the benefits of preventative work – are invoked to support the case for the detailed care plan.

PRACTICE SCENARIO 7.2: PLANNING AND IMPLEMENTATION

Mrs Winnie Holmes, an 86-year-old white woman, has been referred to the care management team by a local community hospital. She has recently experienced a series of falls and has had numerous infections; these have affected her ability to care for herself, placing stress on her informal carers. Winnie currently lives alone, but receives considerable support from Albert, who is 78-years-old, with whom she has had a seven-year relationship, and Albert's daughter, Connie. Albert is himself quite frail, having restricted

Continued

vision and hearing capacity. From the assessment, it is clear that while Winnie would like to continue to live at home, her fluctuating health means this may not be possible; Albert and Connie are unable, realistically, to continue to provide adequate support.

Practice questions:

- To what extent could Winnie benefit from a programme of rehabilitation?
- How will you plan the decision about where Winnie is to live?
- Who will be involved in this decision?
- Once the decision has been made, what are the key elements to consider in enabling all parties to get to grips with Winnie's changed arrangements?
- How will you secure the resources to meet Winnie's needs? What theoretical perspectives will inform your thinking?

As far as planning is concerned, the unifying principle must be to ensure that Winnie remains the central focus, being not just the subject of the plan but also instrumental in its development. Additionally, the process must actively involve both Albert and Connie, who have been providing considerable unpaid care. Theoretically, the care manager could be helped by systemic approaches (Evans and Kearney, 1996; Bilson and Ross, 1999) identifying the key elements of Winnie's life, while assisting all parties to explore the practical and emotional impact of her changed circumstances. Systemic approaches recognise that people exist within complex social worlds, and should help the care manager to understand the perspectives of different parties and secure an agreed course of action. Meeting(s) with all parties would provide an opportunity to explore the various possibilities, so they are aware of the range of available options, and their merits and demerits. Evans and Kearney (1996) lay particular stress on the importance of 'convening' in helping to reach agreements.

In all social work, an essential prerequisite for good planning is the accumulation of high quality information from the assessment process (Milner and O'Byrne, 1998). In this case, it is important first to determine whether or not Winnie has the capacity to benefit from rehabilitation; most SSDs have now instigated various forms of rehabilitation, taking advantage of the injection of cash into intermediate care (DoH, 2000b). It is possible that Winnie could regain many of the skills of daily living that she has lost, for example; as noted in the previous section, the need to involve other professionals in the assessment – in particular, occupational therapists – is paramount. If rehabilitation and continued independent living is not an option, the next area for consideration is Winnie's future housing. The care manager needs to consider the available alternatives, ensuring that Winnie is fully engaged in the process with a view to reflect her wishes and securing her ongoing commitment to the plan. If Winnie cannot remain in her own home the next possibility is to check out the feasibility of Winnie moving in with Albert. This is complicated by two key issues – does either party want to consider this, and is it practicable given Albert's own health and care needs? The next option is to consider a move into some form of supported housing; the attractiveness of this would depend on Winnie's wishes and an accurate assessment of her capabilities. It should not be a straightforward choice between remaining at home and entering residential care, particularly if there are intermediate care (Audit Commission, 2000) and supported housing options available (Means and Smith, 1996). Although the potential impact of budgetary restraints on Winnie's preference must be acknowledged, a care manager should not restrict the range of options at this stage, since the priority is first to ascertain what Winnie wishes to do.

Social work skills are a key aspect of the planning process (Hughes, 1995; Payne, 1995). Communication skills are vital, both in the practical sense of being able to convey complex information but also more generally in building and developing a profitable working relationship (Lishman, 1994). The care manager must be prepared to balance any conflicts that may arise and be skilled in managing the tension between the wishes of Winnie, Connie and Albert. Negotiating skills are core for social work with older people (Hughes, 1995) and are fully evident in this scenario. Equally, as Orme and Glastonbury (1993) recognise, the construction of a care package involves the exercise of liaison skills. In addition, it requires a creative engagement with the circumstances with which the care manager is confronted, in order to avoid the trap of offering a 'set menu' of services (Hughes, 1995). The more effective the process of planning, the more likely it is that the strategy will prove to be sustainable.

The creative care manager needs to be alert to the contributions of other professional disciplines in accumulating data to inform assessment and planning (Evers *et al.*, 1994; Wilson and Dockrell, 1995; Payne, 2000a; Lymbery, 2003b). As Øvretveit (1993) has observed, effective practice requires the active co-ordination of different occupational groups (see also DoH, 2002c). In this case, a care plan must take account of information about Winnie's health – her medical prognosis and the pattern of nursing care indicated by her health needs. This material should be interpreted in the light of the extensive literature on carers and caring (Finch, 1990; Twigg and Atkin, 1994) which raises numerous key points:

- The provision of informal care for older people is usually undertaken within the context of a continuing relationship.
- No societal norm underpins informal care; while a sense of family obligation is commonly felt, this should not be treated as unproblematic.
- Much informal care is provided by women, with men tending only to be active as carers within the context of 'spousal' relationships.

In this case, caring responsibilities are not derived from a straightforward sense of family obligation; the relationship between Winnie and Albert is of relatively recent origin, while Connie is the direct kin of Albert, not Winnie. It is vital to enable them to indicate whether they can continue to provide the level of informal care that Winnie needs, and to build a realistic plan about their continuing contributions.

Therefore, the practical expression of empowerment is both through the achievement of an outcome with which all parties are satisfied and in the means by which that outcome is attained. Attention must therefore be given to the process of the work as well as to the final goal (Stevenson and Parsloe, 1993). Good practice must recognise the emotional intensity that is inherent in this situation, and allow scope for its expression (see Chapter 3). For example, if the agreed plan involves Winnie moving house, the care manager needs to allow space for this major life transition to be explored, and its implications fully discussed. Winnie is likely to find this possibility distressing, even though she may acknowledge its inevitability. It is important that she is able to view this in a positive light; as a major life event, its impact should not be minimised (Marshall and Dixon, 1996).

The framework of good practice outlined above will inevitably take time to implement. This may be in direct conflict with the organisational priority for work to be completed speedily, noted earlier. In particular, there is a potential conflict between the needs identified and the budgetary resources available to meet those needs. The strongest arguments to combat a managerialist approach can be summarised as follows:

- The assertion, with accompanying data, of the reasons why the process should be constructed so as to give Winnie, Connie and Albert proper time to explore their responses to the changing circumstances which are confronting them. This rests on a clearly articulated plan, where the different stages, and the actions required at these points, are well integrated into the whole.

- Clear evidence that the plan outlined is the most effective way of meeting assessed need. It is essential that this includes the interpersonal support that has traditionally characterised social work, without which the care package will not function effectively (Payne, 1995).

- The care manager needs to mount an argument to justify the commitment of resources, recognising that financial considerations cannot be ignored. This involves accepting that it is necessary to present good quality evidence as justification for proposed expenditure.

PRACTICE SCENARIO 7.3: MONITORING, REVIEW AND REASSESSMENT

You are a care manager located within a local health centre, attached to a GP practice, working with Mrs Ada Perkins, a 77-year-old white woman. She lives with her husband, Walter, in a ground floor council flat. The couple have been married for 54 years. You were first involved with Ada two years ago, where the introduction of home care support enabled Walter to continue his caring role in managing his wife's physical needs and undertaking housework. However, Ada has been increasingly forgetful in recent months, having been diagnosed with Alzheimer's disease. She is also physically frail. In addition, Ada has had long-standing mental health problems, requiring periodic hospitalisation. These started before her marriage, and Walter had been unaware of them at the time. There has been a history of domestic violence, with them both describing 'flaming rows' during which Walter has

Continued

hit Ada; this violence has recently recurred. Walter also has health problems, having been diagnosed with angina eight years ago, and having a weak
back that is exacerbated by the amount of lifting and movement that he
has to do. Walter does not believe that Ada can still remain at home,
whereas she is insistent she can. The GP feels that referral to hospital for
a full assessment of her physical/mental condition is indicated; Ada regards
that prospect with horror.

Practice questions:

- What are the main sources of information on Ada's ability to manage
  at home?
- How will you engage with Ada to discuss this, given her increasing
  levels of dementia?
- What inter-professional and multidisciplinary factors should be taken
  into account?
- What theoretical models underpin the review process and will
  inform subsequent action?

This scenario is incapable of being understood unless the care
manager considers the impact of past life experiences on Ada and
Walter, and moves beyond the 'surface' of the presenting problems
to the 'depth' which places these problems in context (Howe, 1996a).
For example, the violence within the relationship originates earlier
in the marriage, and should not be mistakenly viewed as 'elder
abuse' (Kingston and Penhale, 1995), but rather as domestic
violence. It is predominantly men who perpetrate abuse on women
(Mullender, 1996) as an expression of patriarchial power inequalities
(Morley, 1993; Mullender, 1996). Therefore, the violence is clearly
Walter's responsibility – he has chosen to be abusive towards Ada, she
has not invited it. However, as Frude (1994) indicates, the social
worker must also reflect on aspects of the relationship that may aggra-
vate Walter's violence. Two factors should be considered. First, Ada's
mental health problems were concealed from Walter before their
marriage. Second, Ada's dementia could have contributed both to
the resurgence in violence and to Walter's failing health. The stresses
on carers of people with dementia are well recognised (Goldsmith,
1996), and these are complicated by the nature and quality of the
past relationship (Marshall, 1990).

Similarly, Ada's resistance to the idea of entering hospital may be linked to her prior experiences of medical treatment. Therefore, she may associate hospitals with extreme unpleasantness, especially given the fact that her increasing dementia will fracture her reasoning processes (Marshall, 1990). No practical tasks can be completed successfully unless these significant contextual issues are first addressed. A full reassessment of Ada's circumstances is indicated, thereby moving into a fresh part of the care management cycle. The situation has changed since the initial referral, with the decline in Ada's mental capabilities coinciding with a decrease in Walter's ability to provide care and support. Similarly, the recurrent violence from Walter to Ada has created another pressing problem.

While Ada and Walter will have to be assisted in coming to a decision is acceptable to them both, the care manager's primary responsibility is to secure Ada's welfare. The first priority is to address the domestic violence, to which she is highly vulnerable due to her age and health: 'older women have the same right to leave or to stay, to have action taken against their partners or not, as other women' (Mullender, 1996: p. 132). The care manager must explore a range of options with Ada, including working with Walter to reduce his violence. This cannot be rushed, due to the intense emotions likely to be generated through the process, plus the complicating fact of Ada's dementia.

Communication skills are significant when working with people with dementia (Goldsmith, 1996). There are two key elements for a care manager to consider. First, s/he must judge the effects of the dementia, and adjust her/his means of communication accordingly. Second, s/he must recognise the importance of non-verbal communication, as people with dementia can quickly sense when they are genuinely valued (Marshall, 1990). Assessment skills are clearly required, as is the ability to deploy skills of resource management to identify and secure appropriate services.

Perhaps the most difficult requirement for a care manager is maintaining the ability to work with both Ada and Walter to resolve this situation, despite their conflicting needs. A reflective practitioner will explore the dynamics of the relationship, developing the ability to use growing knowledge about this in the ensuring practice (Taylor, 1996). Professional actions will not be programmed, but will be a creative response to circumstances. Practice based on technical rationality (Schön, 1991; Adams, 1996) would search for the 'correct' solution to Ada and Walter's dilemma; practice grounded in reflection-in-action will seek an outcome deriving from the uniqueness of their experiences.

In identifying and managing conflict the care manager must make it clear to Walter that his violence is unacceptable, while respecting his right to be involved in decision making about their future. It is important to avoid the trap of being overprotective or paternalistic (Bennett *et al.*, 1997); while her/his primary role is to ensure Ada's protection, s/he must also recognise her right to self-determination. As with much social work, maintaining this balance between autonomy and protection – made more complex by Ada's dementia – involves a question of judgement that cannot be managerially pre-scribed. The care manager's co-ordinating responsibilities will be useful in helping to combat abuse and violence (Biggs *et al.*, 1995) in that s/he retains an oversight of the situation drawing on the multi-ple perspectives of care providers.

In conferring with a variety of sources to supplement existing knowledge, detailed information about the likely progress of Ada's dementia, and how this will affect the couple, must be acquired. The care manager must also understand Ada's past history of mental health difficulties, and requires knowledge about Walter's health. The physical location of the care manager within primary health care may yield considerable benefits. Ready access to information from the GP and community nurses is imperative, and there is evidence that this is eased by a care manager's direct proximity to such professionals (Hudson *et al.*, 1997; Lymbery, 1998b; Lymbery and Millward, 2000). More specifically, such arrangements have been found to create a more holistic assessment and speed up the response time (Hardy *et al.*, 1996; Lymbery and Millward, 2000). In addition, the process of monitoring and review of care packages is also enhanced (Hardy *et al.*, 1996). Therefore, effective co-operation should lead to a more planned and coherent service outcome (Wilson and Dockrell, 1995), while being entirely in line with the collaborative principles outlined in the NHS Plan (DoH, 2000b).

There are numerous ways in which this scenario presents a chal-lenge to managerialist dominance in social work. Once again, prac-tice must not be rushed to fit time management priorities. Continuity is essential; this is not a feature of much care management (Sturges, 1996). The processes of review and re-assessment require interper-sonal skills of the highest order and should not be dominated by pro-cedural requirements. Finally, although resource management is an important factor to be addressed – particularly if admission to

residential care or an extensive package of home care is to be considered – it should not be the worker's central preoccupation. The
following factors may serve to justify the professional dimensions of
practice that have been outlined:

- The care manager must be explicit about the potential consequences of hurried and hence inadequate decisions. For
  example, a possible outcome could be to increase the home
  care package. However, if Walter is not fully engaged in this
  decision, it is unlikely he would be committed to it, with a
  greater likelihood of its failure, thereby leading to increased
  financial costs to the SSD. A successful outcome is based on the
  intensive support offered by the care manager to Ada and
  Walter, clarity about the home care package and the establishment of a level of trust in, and respect for, the care manager.
  Therefore, time spent in securing an effective re-assessment of
  need can in fact be justified on financial grounds.
- The care manager's location within the health centre has two
  potential benefits. The first has already been noted: it should
  facilitate effective inter-professional work. The second is equally
  significant, however. Experience suggests that care managers
  within primary health care settings can help to ensure constancy
  of support since all cases are the responsibility of a named individual (Lymbery and Millward, 2000). This is a shift from the
  bureaucratised models of allocation existing in many SSDs,
  which serve to fracture that sense of continuity.
- The appropriate location of social workers is part of a debate
  about the ways in which SSDs' organisation can facilitate rather
  than stifle creative practice. In this example, it is likely that
  changing needs would be brought to the attention of the care
  manager at a relatively early stage, when there is still some
  flexibility to accommodate and resolve the changes.

Conclusion

This chapter has sought to delineate the parameters of good care management practice with older people. The development of managerialism within SSDs has created a climate often experienced as both
hostile and controlling by practitioners (Jones, 2001). As Postle (1999)
observes, this does not help those workers to develop high quality
services for older people. However, since social work knowledge,

skills and values are vital in ensuring that service users have the best opportunities to maximise their independence and control over their destinies, it is important that practitioners are enabled to feel positive about their work and its potential. Given the tension that exists between managerialism and practice, care managers must develop strategies for articulating the importance of their work, and of justifying their actions within managerialist frames of reference.

The main ways of accomplishing this refer back to traditional professional skills. As indicated in Chapter 3, social workers operate within the 'swampy lowlands' (Schön, 1991: p. 42) of practice, where they respond to unique circumstances in ways that cannot be prescribed. They must retain the capacity to respond flexibly to these situations. For example, in constructing a care package, a social worker needs to accept that it must be presented in ways that maximise its prospects of being approved. Poor practice will increase the chance of resources not being made available, thereby penalising the service user concerned. Similarly, in assessing need, implementing and monitoring a care plan, a practitioner must be concerned with the whole person in their social world, ensuring an appropriate response to the user, his/her assessed needs and available resources. In this way, there is a genuine opportunity to create an empowering form of practice with older people (Thompson and Thompson, 2001). It is the argument of this chapter that such practice remains possible within care management with older people, that it is positively in the best interests of service users and that it can help to ensure that their fundamental rights and needs are protected (Johnson, 2002).

8

Creativity and Constraint in Child Welfare

Marian Charles with Jane Wilton

Introduction

In recent years child welfare services have been dominated by child protection with a consequent deterioration in the understanding and execution of social work responsibilities for 'looked after' children. This is due in part to the growing gulf between case management and therapeutic work, but also relates to the perceived downgrading of the status of work with children 'looked after' compared to the specialisms of child protection and substitute home finding (Utting, 1997). Social workers have become ill equipped for direct work with children and unable to communicate with those with special needs (SSI, 1997). Such a decline is hardly surprising in a climate where the emotional elements of social work practice are devalued or denied in environments dominated by managerialism and bureaucracy (as outlined in Chapter 3).

By exploring the interplay between the *mezzo* and *micro* levels, this chapter focuses on how child welfare practitioners manage to bridge the gap between the organisational realities of proceduralisation and standardisation and the practice ideals of working creatively with children and young people. Concentrating on statutory fieldwork, the chapter considers the accusation that local authority social workers 'just fill in the forms'. The Assessment and Action Records from the *Looking After Children: Good Parenting, Good Outcomes* materials (DoH, 1995a) are used to demonstrate how an essentially bureaucratic

179

device (widely deployed across the United Kingdom) can act as a vehicle for reflective practice.

The chapter first reviews the current tensions facing child care workers, identifying four major themes. Then, acknowledging the disadvantages faced by children and young people 'looked after' and how these are compounded by their experiences of public care, it considers the development and use of the action and assessment records. These provide a basis for scrutinising practice, examining how imaginative work with children, drawing on social work values, skills and knowledge, is still possible. However, practitioners must recognise and deal with the emotional aspects of engaging with children and refuse to allow simplistic completion of the documentation to dominate the interventive agenda.

Current tensions facing child care social workers

Four themes currently dominate the experiences of statutory child care social workers:

- The conflicting needs of organisations and families;
- Resource constraints;
- The marginalisation of relationship skills;
- Lack of attention accorded to the 'how' of social work practice.

First, there is the tension rooted in the conflicting needs of the organisation and those of the child and his/her family. In his review of local authority services, Utting (1997) concluded that work with children in care is directed more towards organisational goals than to those relating to the child. Children's needs can only be addressed through child-centred practice in which their welfare is given paramountcy in decision making and resource allocation processes, where their individual requirements and differences are valued, and where their disadvantage and powerlessness are countered and their rights promoted. Child-centred practice (Hohmann and Weikart, 1995; Bray, 1997) means working at the child's pace, irrespective of organisational timescales, listening carefully and actively to the individual child or young person, and valuing his/her views and opinions. Organisational agendas with demands for paperwork completion, speedy throughput of work, conformity and adherence to systems and reduced costs are in direct opposition to such practice. The social worker is in the middle of this 'tug-of-war', wrenched in one direction by professional knowledge, skills and values relating to the interpersonal, therapeutic and nurturing aspects of practice and hauled in the other by the economic, regulatory demands and bureaucratic controls of the organisation. Freedom of manoeuvre is limited by these managerialist forces as the 'surrounding belt of restriction' (Bamford, 1989: p. 137) is ever tightened by fresh procedures and additional departmental guidance.

Second, resource constraints, alongside increasing expectations on social services departments, have created a mismatch between the volume of work and resources necessary to deliver effective services. This inevitably has knock-on effects on practice, especially when the emotional and practical demands make social work with children 'looked after' particularly challenging. This is evident in agencies with high staff turnover and shortages, huge caseloads, significant numbers of children in care without allocated social workers and a lack of residential and fostering resources (Laming, 1998), resulting in a work culture characterised by a sense of hopelessness (SSI, 1998). Workers in these settings struggle to find time, the physical and emotional energy to work directly with children, especially when hours are absorbed in efforts to shore up collapsing foster placements, conduct child protection enquiries, or cover the duties of absent colleagues.

Third, the emphasis on efficiency, economy and effectiveness combined with notions of measurable outcomes has led to the marginalisation of relationship skills. Research studies have consistently demonstrated that service users both want and value the relationships forged with practitioners (Rees and Wallace, 1982; Thoburn *et al.*, 1995). The tug-of-war continues for the social worker. On the one side, there is relationship building, based on establishing trust, with recipients of child welfare services who want to be involved in decision making processes and cared about as individuals (DHSS, 1985; DoH, 1991b, 1995b). For children 'looked after', with their likely distrust of adults and problems stemming from abuse, separation and rejection, connections with practitioners, evolved through joint activities and spending time together, are fundamental to their well being. On the other side, there is the organisational bureaucracy that accords little value or allocated hours to the key task of developing positive interactions with children. The difficulties in gaining children's trust when they picture their social workers as unavailable, always 'on the run', turning up to see them unexpectedly, yet not when arranged (Butler and Charles, 1996), and wanting to talk about their adult, bureaucratic preoccupations, are given scant recognition. Hence, the process of devoting time 'which will yield most benefit to children' (Ryan and Walker, 1993: p. 5), rather than finished products like completed documentation, remains largely hidden.

Lastly, there is the relegation to the edge of the organisational playing field of the 'how' aspect of practice, to the extent that social work is in danger of becoming a 'lost art' (Platt, 1998). As Davies (1994: p. 155) argues: 'What makes something social work is not *what* is done but *how* it is done'. Procedures and bureaucratic processes cannot achieve good practice on their own (Gibbons, 1997); attention has to be directed to communication patterns, family dynamics and feelings. In an environment where systems are accorded maximum importance and crisis driven practice is the norm, little prominence is attached to the detail and skills of practice. This experience is mirrored for frontline practitioners in formal supervision sessions, where bureaucratic *mezzo* priorities can too often dominate the supervision agenda. Supervisors concentrate on the managerial functions, checking out that tasks have been completed and procedures followed, leaving little or no time to address the restorative and formative needs (Hawkins and Shohet, 2000) for reflection and emotional expression evidenced at the *micro* practice level. In this way, a further contribution is made to the culture of emotional 'dumbing down' created by individual and organisational defences to demands from politicians, users and others (Davies, 1998). Yet all workers, whether newly qualified or more experienced, need support to practise and develop skills in direct work with children (Marsh and Triseliotis, 1996). Without this, practitioners are left with an ever increasing lack of confidence in their skills, knowledge and self-efficacy, pushing them into avoiding communication and engagement with children. Ironically, completion of administrative tasks, initially seen as bureaucratic burdens, creates an illusion to the worker, his/her manager and the organisation of social work well done, of partnership and agreement, and of risks assessed and managed, yet their fulfilment may have nothing to do with the real needs of service users.

Despite the difficulties inherent in maintaining a consistent child focus in the face of the tensions outlined above, our intention is to demonstrate the scope for creative practice and management of these difficulties and dilemmas between the *mezzo* and the *micro* in the application of the assessment and action records. Designed 'to measure children's progress, to assess the standard of care which they are receiving and to plan improvements' (DoH, 1991b: p. 3), these lie at the heart of the *Looking After Children: Good Parenting, Good Outcomes* materials (DoH, 1995a). Since the end of 1998, these are reportedly being used by more than 90% of English authorities and the majority of those in Wales, Scotland and Northern Ireland (Colton *et al.*, 2001).

The Assessment and Action Records

The impetus behind the development of the Assessment and Action Records stems from the 1980s, when a growing body of research highlighted the weaknesses in the services provided by local authorities. Studies illustrated that the difficulties facing children 'looked after', an already disadvantaged group, are compounded by their experiences of public care. They became isolated from their families due to neglect of the maintenance of significant links and contacts (Rowe and Lambert, 1973; Millham *et al.*, 1986), leaving parents feeling devalued and helpless (Packman *et al.*, 1986; Fisher *et al.*, 1986); their health and education needs received little priority (Knapp *et al.*, 1985; Jackson, 1987; Simms, 1988); evidence of active social work planning for children once in public care was rarely demonstrated (Vernon and Fruin, 1986); and those leaving the care system were poorly prepared and ill equipped for independent living (Stein and Carey, 1986; Bonnerjea, 1990; Garnett, 1992).

Increasing concern for the position of children in the care system raised questions about the standard, quality and costs of public care. An independent working party, established by the Department of Health, considered earlier research illustrating the defects of state care. The resultant publication (Parker *et al.*, 1991) highlighted seven major developmental dimensions crucial for positive outcomes for children and young people:

- health;
- education;
- identity;
- family and social relationships;
- social presentation;
- emotional and behavioural development;
- self-care skills.

In addition, schedules of questions, based on the best available research evidence about parental behaviour (e.g., see Herbert, 1989;

Burghes, 1994; Pugh *et al.*, 1994), were devised as a means of assessing whether appropriate action has been taken to ensure the likelihood of good outcomes for specific age groups of children 'looked after', thus improving their chances of reaching their potential and achieving an acceptable quality of adult life. The schedules were subsequently tested (Ward, 1995) to determine the validity of the dimensions identified, with 'ordinary' parents (Jackson, 1998: p. 49) being asked which developmental aspects were important to them and how good outcomes were promoted for their own children. Despite some variation in emphasis, results were said to indicate few ethnic or social class differences concerning parents' beliefs about significant factors in healthy development (Ward, 1995). Parents were generally in agreement with the goals specified in the Assessment and Action Records. Thus, the foundations were laid for the current documents, stressing these critical developmental aspects for 'looked after' children and providing key foci for assessing the level of 'good parenting' within social work practice (see Appendix 1). Furthermore, the same seven developmental dimensions now form the components of the child's developmental needs domain in the *Framework for the Assessment of Children in Need and their Families* (DoH *et al.*, 2000).

To date, the Assessment and Action Records have not been subjected to extensive scrutiny on either a theoretical or operational level, although they have been open to a number of criticisms (for a more detailed discussion, see Knight and Caveney, 1998; Garrett, 1999b, 2002e):

(1) They hold a 'normative view of parenting and family life' (Knight and Caveney, 1998: p. 29) with the imposition of white middle class assumptions which ignore the context within which individual development takes place.

(2) This 'normative' view is presented as an apparently 'objective' outcome. Garrett (2002e) has labelled this as an 'objectivist illusion', pointing out the tendency to treat alternative perspectives and approaches as ideologically driven.

(3) The basis for the construction of notions of 'good parental care' can be criticised. 'In some of the more deprived (*sic.*) districts, substantially few families were willing to participate' (Ward, 1995: p. 25). This raises questions over their validity in terms of a class and/or 'race' bias (Garrett, 1999b).

(4) The overly directive checklist approach is unlikely to be child friendly and lends itself to pure data collection and 'process-

ing' of children. This is seen as increasing the bureaucratic character of being in public care and thus eroding the principle of partnership embodied in the Children Act 1989 (Knight and Caveney, 1998), and marginalising 'children's subjective experiences and right to identify relevant issues for themselves' (Garrett, 1999b: p. 36).

(5) Further to this, Garrett (2002e) has suggested that there was inadequate involvement of key stakeholders – including children, families and social workers – in the development of the documentation, leading to what he terms its 'arid' approach.

(6) The documents fail to define what is meant by terms such as 'reasonable' or 'adequate', or to consider the context in which these terms are applied.

Using the Records in practice

It should be noted that the original intention behind the development of the Assessment and Action Records was not that of a bureaucratic form filling exercise, despite the criticisms noted above. Indeed, it was recognised that the Records would be of little value if so employed, although the danger of ticking boxes rather than using the Records as a framework for good practice was acknowledged (Ward, 1995). The Records are intended to be essentially practice tools, designed to elicit discussion and exploration of the action required to achieve positive outcomes for children. As such, they are only as good as the skills and knowledge with which they are exercised. However, their application depends upon the degree to which individual child care practitioners have accommodated to organisational requirements and have been able to develop reflective skills (see Chapter 3), as the balance achieved between these two influences the worker's scope for manoeuvrability and creativity in practice.

Form filling is part of organisational life. Reflective practitioners accept this facet of their daily existence, appreciating the benefits of consistency and standard setting inherent in a well completed document. In addition, they identify the positive aspects of the Assessment and Action Records, acknowledging the opportunity to ground their professional judgements in study findings, understanding their research based nature. They welcome the chance to subject these to critical scrutiny rather than accepting them as 'self evident truths' (Trinder, 1996: p. 238) impacting little on practice. Spotting opportunities to connect the 'what' with the 'how' of social work, reflective practitioners regard the completion of the forms as a flexible means of purposeful questioning and exploration of aspects of children's lives: a task engaging children, their parents, carers and significant others in stimulating discussion and debate. Such discourse leads to joint decisions about what action needs to be implemented, and by whom, to improve an individual's life chances. They are also aware of the potential authority of well documented, detailed, accurate records, demonstrating the complexity of children's lives, to influence the allocation of resources, the formation of agency policies and modes of service delivery. Above all, reflective workers pinpoint the professional control and autonomy they possess over the process, the manner and methods by which the forms are completed.

Reflective practitioners recognise the Assessment and Action Records as potential child-focused tools readily applicable to unique practice situations. They use them as such, seizing the chance to spend more time with children. They build on their experience of completing the materials as they go along, using the reactions of children and others to the issues under discussion to reframe questions or try fresh approaches to the exploration of sensitive subjects. The Records become a means of combating the scant periods formally devoted to relationship building at the *mezzo* level. They evolve into a communication tool, validating time spent with children even if there is no immediate or visible outcome, and giving increased opportunities to involve children in planning and making decisions (Thomas and O'Kane, 1998). Concern for both outcomes *and* processes ensures that the physical completion of the forms does not dominate the work with the child. Alert to the dangers of the task becoming mechanistic, reflective practitioners use the Records as a means of gathering qualitative rather than quantitative data. The wishes of a child or young person not to discuss or to have his/her views formally recorded about specific aspects of his/her life are respected, with the practitioner adapting the materials to address items s/he identifies as important. Over time, reflective practitioners amass the necessary details at the individual's pace, setting the information within the cultural and structural context in which s/he lives and identifying resource inequalities. Rather than the completed documentation being the sole purpose of the exercise, the outcome of the interactions is of equal importance.

In contrast, accommodating workers, falling prey to our fourth tension and discarding the 'how' of social work practice, concentrate on meeting agency requirements. We have been dismayed by stories of social workers visiting children with the announcement that: 'We must fill in your LAC forms today'. It seems clear that for these workers, the form filling has become an end in itself, 'the source of action' (Knight and Caveney, 1998: p. 39). Completion of the Records, an agency requirement and used by management as a measure of competence, may hold a certain appeal for stressed, under confident workers, who are then able to delude themselves that they are doing a 'good job'. However, in effect, their interaction with the child may well have been insensitive, based on a mechanistic check of the defined developmental areas rather than a thorough processing of the information and observations. Furthermore, the activity will have been dominated by an adult agenda, failing to draw out the child's feelings and suggestions. Adopting this instrumental approach permits the psychological impact of encounters with children to be ignored, thus feeding the agency's willingness to disregard the emotional threads central to creative social work practice. Children's vulnerabilities, therefore, go unrecognised as workers' efforts are directed towards concealing their own. The Records may be complete, but will only portray a narrow picture of the child's world.

Filling out the Assessment and Action Records turns into an impersonal, lacklustre activity if not undertaken within the context of an established, trusting relationship. Without such a connection, the task assumes potentially abusive connotations, in which the child faces exploitation, being expected to 'give' while receiving nothing. Simultaneously, workers performing as technocrats are robbed of the professional satisfaction vested in witnessing children benefit from direct involvement. Children and young people have clear visions of the qualities they prize in social workers. These attributes include a sense of humour, availability and accessibility, a preparedness to take them out occasionally, understanding, openness and reliability, but above all, good communication and interpersonal skills (Butler and Williamson, 1994; Farnfield, 1998; Hill, 1998; Ince, 1998; Thomas and O'Kane, 1998). Despite these unequivocal guidelines for working with children, plus exhortations about the necessity of spending time together (DHSS, 1976), evidence of unsatisfactory relations between children 'looked after' and their social workers is legion (Fletcher, 1993; Lynes and Goddard, 1995; Butler and Charles, 1996; Smith, G., 1997; Utting, 1997; Morris, 1998a).

As we have highlighted, there are real obstacles to creative practice: external pressures and constraints such as finding the time and space to engage directly with children or completing work within decreed agency timescales are genuine issues. However, these represent only a fraction of the equation. They assume an exalted importance, being offered as the only explanation in arguments as to why relationships between children 'looked after' and their social workers are so difficult to establish, successfully masking the more intangible inhibitors facing practitioners. The secret to liberation from the technical bureaucratic straitjacket and into child centred practice lies in relationship building and effective communication with children. It is to these aspects that we now turn.

Planning and engaging with children

PRACTICE SCENARIO 8.1

Paul is a 10-year-old white boy with a mild learning disability, who is currently living with a foster family. His parents separated when he was five. Paul and his older brother, Daniel, had little contact with their father and lived with their mother, who remarried when Paul was six. Shortly after her marriage, Paul's stepsister, Beth, was born. Six months later, the local authority accommodated Paul at his mother's request. She said the family hated Paul, who had been severely beaten by his stepfather. Paul's total rejection and ill treatment by the family prompted the local authority to apply successfully for a care order.

Although initially he settled well in his foster placement, Paul started to overeat and avoided physical contact. He completely rejected his foster mother, who, unable to live with this, terminated the placement. Two years into his third placement, Paul continues to overeat but has slowly formed relationships with both his foster carers and his foster brother. He is more established at school though still easily distracted. Recent diagnosis of a hearing loss is thought to explain some of his behaviour.

The foster family now has a baby daughter. Since her birth four months ago, Paul's behaviour and progress both at school and at home have deteriorated. His placement is now under severe stress. Paul had usually completed his assessment and action records with his foster mother, who assumed responsibility for writing out the details due to his limited literacy skills and poor concentration span. Paul enjoyed the individual attention accompanying this task and evidently located himself firmly within his foster family. Attempts to introduce his birth family into the discussion

---

seemed to confuse him, so this facet of his life had received scant attention. Paul's records are now due for review, owing to an agency audit of
cases in the social worker's team following criticisms from the Social Services Inspectorate about services generally for 'looked after' children. In the
light of the current tensions in their relationship, it seems inappropriate for
the exercise to be undertaken jointly by Paul and his foster mother.

Practice questions:

- How can this bureaucratic *mezzo* requirement be met, while simul-
  taneously being beneficial to Paul?
- What issues need to be considered before engaging with Paul?
- How can communication with Paul be established?

The agency management audit, a *mezzo* activity, represents a further
bureaucratic device encompassing managerial edicts. These are
designed to ensure that work is completed within specific deadlines,
and, in this instance, to allay the organisational anxiety generated by
the Social Services Inspectorate's remarks. Despite the Inspectorate's
criticisms about the minimalist approach taken towards the completion of the Assessment and Action Records, the audit still potentially
feeds into an accommodating style of practice. The pressure emanating from tight agency timescales, within which more work needs
to be undertaken, adds to the demoralisation engendered by the
Inspectorate's comments on the quality of practice standards. Unable
to voice the impact of this emotional battering, accommodating
workers continue to play 'the organisational game', completing the
documentation with rapidity, and allowing the agency to deliver a
swift response to the concerns raised by the Inspectorate. Reflective
workers, however, resist this approach, refusing to allow resource
constraints and demands for speedy work processing to dictate their
responses. They consciously exploit the criticisms levelled at the
agency as a creative lever to negotiate sufficient time to build relationships, alongside the working space required to complete the
records accurately and sensitively.

In relation to Paul, the worker acknowledges the stress levels inherent in his placement and how he is at potential risk of a further shift
to an alternative setting unless considerable social work effort is
invested immediately. S/he plays on both the Social Services

Inspectorate's disquiet about the number of moves experienced by children 'looked after', and the knowledge of the scarcity of residential and fostering resources. The practitioner emphasises to his/her line manager how timely, thorough intervention, using the Assessment and Action Records as a means of accessing the various aspects of Paul's life, may secure his placement's continuity. In addition, s/he stresses how such activity hooks into the notion of quality standards, portrayed in government initiatives such as *Quality Protects* (DoH, 1998b), and of expectations 'that children are securely attached to carers capable of providing safe and effective care for the duration of childhood' (DoH, 1998c: p. 4). Through this approach, the bureaucratic *mezzo* requirements are addressed whilst simultaneously generating scope for creative engagement with Paul.

Before meeting with Paul, the social worker reflects on the Assessment and Action Records, identifying the interplay between the different developmental areas and locating these within his/her understanding of theories of child development (see Lindon, 1993; Boushel *et al.*, 2000; Bukatko and Daehler, 2001; Keenan, 2002). Reviewing this material enables the practitioner to pinpoint the general developmental task facing children within Paul's age range as being one of gaining comprehension and control of life outside the immediate family setting (Fahlberg, 1994). S/he also recognises how Paul's developmental growth is likely to have been interrupted by five factors: abusive experiences, the loss of his original family, moves between foster families, his learning disability and his sensory impairment. This process allows for the evolution of a range of hypotheses designed to help the worker speculate about the impact of these factors on Paul's overall progress. For instance:

- Has he been able to formulate reasoning skills, moving from 'magical' to 'concrete' thinking? (Piaget, 1959).
- Is he able to devote his energy to learning at school or is he worried about making mistakes? (Erikson, 1977).
- How and in what ways has his hearing impairment affected both his ability to concentrate and learn and his capacity to develop peer relationships?

The practitioner wonders about the connection between Paul's hearing difficulties and his diagnosis of 'learning disabled'. To what degree has his development been impeded by his hearing impairment, preventing him from expressing and having his needs met?

What effect has all this had on his self-esteem and his motivation to learn and interact? Does Paul feel helpless as experience has shown him that no matter what he does, his actions generally fail to produce useful outcomes? (Payne, 1997). These questions provide a launch pad for the areas to be explored with Paul, his carers and other significant people.

Using the Records in this way permits the reflective practitioner to think broadly about Paul's development and the context in which this has taken place, thus avoiding a fixed focus whereby a single factor dominates. Accommodating workers, however, are tempted by this more simplistic approach, choosing, for example, to hone in on Paul's recently determined hearing impairment, and seeing this as the sole root of his current difficulties, which can be remedied through medical intervention.

With the territory for the work mapped out, attention can be turned to ways of engaging with Paul. Mindful of the bureaucratic barriers affecting adult/child interactions, and of Paul's fragile trust in adults, the practitioner recognises that the relationship between the two of them needs to be firmly established or reaffirmed. S/he understands how 'it is all too easy to assume a superiority over children, to disregard their feelings, ignore their needs in our decision making and so reinforce their sense of hopelessness and powerlessness in the face of adult control' (Cattanach, 1993: p. 10). Hence, encounters with Paul must ensure he experiences being taken seriously, with his views given due weight in decision making and planning. The worker appreciates Paul's need to have some choice and control within this process. Paul, therefore, decides when and where they will meet, thus steering clear of their sessions clashing with his favourite television programme and enabling him to decide on a venue where he feels comfortable. The worker also avoids the imposition of an adult-centred communication medium, focused on verbal exchanges, choosing instead to ground his/her interactions with Paul in play. S/he is aware that play, while having an intrinsic value in itself, is children's natural communication medium (Axline, 1964), being essential for their psychological, physical and social development where 'confusions, anxieties and conflicts are often worked through' (Oaklander, 1978: p. 160).

Reflective practitioners make no prior assumptions about the sort of play materials children enjoy nor that their young clients are attracted by activities which were popular in their own childhoods. They hold their options open in respect of specific communication methods, preferring to be flexible and to 'tune in' to verbal cues and activities initiated by individual children (Harper, 1996), who self-select means and materials through which they can express themselves. Paul's worker observes the interest he shows when the local train passes by his foster home. Paul confirms this attraction and readily responds to the suggestion of 'talking' about his life as if he were a train visiting various stations. Using this metaphor, the practitioner learns how Paul views his world and gathers information for inclusion in the Assessment and Action Records, while Paul retains control, deciding which 'stations' are visited, and for how long, and which are out of bounds.

While standing in the school 'station', Paul refers to the fun he enjoys when presented with opportunities to use the class computer. His comment introduces a further communication medium, as the worker identifies how resources available at the *mezzo* level can be harnessed for direct work with children at the *micro* layer. Creative and empowering practice increasingly involves the use of multimedia computer programs in which children acquire greater choice and control over the content and pace of the work, particularly as their skills often outweigh those of practitioners. Computer usage represents a friendly, non-threatening, accessible form of communication (Hapgood, 1988; Resnick, 1994), successfully retaining children's interest, improving their attention spans and facilitating their 'sense of enjoyment and an ability to relax and participate' (Cowan, 1998: p. 56). Use of programs based on the Assessment and Action Records, incorporating child-friendly, appropriate positive images, achieves the objective of the forms being a fun activity (Ward, 1995), which enhances the child's self-esteem. More importantly, rather than detracting from relationship building, the sharing of computer activities aids the development of the child/social worker connection, facilitating additional chances for the individual to divulge his/her perceptions and feelings. Tapping into the child's emotions is an essential component for effective completion of the assessment and action records. While computer based programmes help 'to counterbalance the negative experiences of working through the harder lessons of sadness and loss' (Cowan, 1998: p. 55), practitioners are required to foster skills in being open to and in managing children's feelings.

The reflective practitioner successfully negotiates the tensions between the stated *mezzo* demands and the perceived *micro* needs: first, by demonstrating an appreciation of the theoretical material on which any intervention is founded; second, by purposefully exploiting the *mezzo* concerns to bargain for time and space to build a working relationship with Paul; and third, by showing her/his line manager how s/he intends to use the allocated time actively. However, s/he also understands the need to examine her/his own capacity to deal with emotional pain. The ability to engage with children's pain poses the greatest challenge to creative practice, yet the effectiveness of any intervention hinges upon practitioners' willingness to engage with emotional life of children (Wilson, 2000).

Reflective practitioners use the Assessment and Action Records:

- to ground their professional judgements in child development knowledge and research findings;
- as a flexible means of purposeful questioning and exploration of children's lives;
- as a communication tool;
- as a lever to negotiate time for creative work with children.

Working with emotional pain and distress

Real communication with children holds the potential to expose workers to emotional pain and distress, their own as well as the child's, and, as such, has the capacity to hamper the social worker's ability to engage meaningfully or at all. The experiences endured by 'looked after' children engender powerful feelings in adults to rescue, protect or control them. Practitioners may feel out of their depth (Ruch, 1998), even fearful of children (NSPCC, 1997), as they struggle to appreciate children's perceptions and understanding of their own experiences or are overwhelmed by a pressing desire to avoid any reference to the child's separations and losses (Maluccio *et al.*, 1986). In addition, the universal nature of exposure to loss creates an emotionally charged scenario in which practitioners 'own past experience and memories, including perhaps unresolved and therefore still potentially explosive or poisonous frustrations and angers' (Crompton, 1980: p. 22) percolate to the surface. These feelings of discomfort are then compounded by the directness and behaviour of children themselves, with their ability to induce feelings of incompetence at a glance (Cattanach, 1993), leaving workers feeling foolish and inept once their overtures receive no response or are rejected. Anxious not to add to the emotional damage already sustained by the child, workers question their skills, wondering about the advisability of meddling in areas in which they perceive themselves to possess little expertise (Rose, 1988) or about their ability to handle the emotions aroused. In essence, a vicious circle is created; anxiety fuels attempts to communicate and work directly with children, whose responses further incapacitate workers, who then find that their growing disquiet produces increasing reluctance to engage in future efforts.

The strength of feelings evoked has the potential to provoke inappropriate action. Take, for instance, the behaviour of one of Paul's previous social workers when faced with the devastating distress of a boy who had had no sort of contact with his birth family for many months. A sense of helplessness prompted the worker to purchase a gift, purported to be from Paul's mother, which merely added to his confusion. The practitioner's blinkered thinking, induced by his/her own emotional state, equalled a lesson in deceit for the child whose self-esteem and identity were further dented by the truth. How could Paul learn to trust people and be trustworthy himself when demeaned by such adult deception? (Crompton, 1990).

The inability to tolerate their distress can propel workers into devoting their energies to working around rather than with children. In this way, a degree of self protection is realised, leaving practitioners' difficulties in managing the emotional impact unresolved. Over-reliance on procedures or forms thus facilitates the sidestepping of messy, distressing emotional issues, while focusing on specific techniques, such as ecomaps or flowcharts (DoH, 1988), solely for the purpose of gathering information, neatly circumvents any exploration of the feelings linked with the details. Without the opportunity for a child to express his/her views and feelings about the past, present and future, completing documents such as the assessment and action records becomes merely a *mezzo* fact-finding mission.

Faced simultaneously by these external and internal pressures, how can practitioners work imaginatively with children 'looked after'? First, creative practice is inextricably bound up with the ability to manage the pain involved in interactions with children, and to appreciate the powerful feelings inherent in the work. Second, it concerns workers' needs to be in touch with the joys and hurt of their own childhoods (BAAF, 1984), identifying how their own experiences can block communication with children, pushing them towards mechanistic approaches. Finally, it encompasses perceiving the social work role as a bridge (Horne, 1983; Schofield, 1998) spanning the child's inner and outer worlds. From this vantage point, the social worker acts as a link between the people and external events in the child's life and her/his feelings about these outside influences, recognising the interdependence of the two. In terms of the Assessment and Action Records then, the reflective practitioner becomes the 'glue', holding together all the different developmental dimensions. The various components of the child's exterior world, schools, health professionals, carers, family of origin and other significant figures, and their emotional effects on the child are connected.

Tempting as it may be to concentrate on the external world brimming with tangible issues, bypassing any acknowledgement of the inner emotional dimension merely colludes with the avoidance of pain and diminishes opportunities for reflection and subsequent growth. However, acceptance of the interrelationship between the external and inner domains expedites the flow of creative practice through recognising and appreciating that operating solely at the practical outward level inevitably produces a partial picture. Creativity lies in looking below the surface in order to hold these two worlds together, thus enabling the 'looked after' child to develop a sense of security through understanding and making sense of both events and feelings. The framework tendered by the assessment and action records aids the management of this task. Acting as triggers, the dimensions highlighted and the questions posed guide practitioners' attention towards areas of strength and of concern in the external world which impact on the child's internal emotional life.

Practice questions 8.2

- Bearing in mind what is happening in Paul's life, what theoretical perspectives could usefully inform the worker's practice?
- How can the practitioner enable the foster carers to continue to care for Paul?
- What might the worker's recommendations for future action include?

Employing the Assessment and Action Records as a practice tool, an immediate examination of Paul's current situation reveals that a number of the specified dimensions mirror the present areas of concern. Paul's reactions are affecting his educational progress, damaging his family and social relationships, chipping away at his sense of self-esteem and ultimately jeopardising his placement. While Paul's behaviour is of key concern, a creative response avoids a fixation with this. Prompted by the differences in Paul's conduct and demeanour, the social worker reflects on these changes, placing them within the context of his life history. This analysis identifies how Paul left his family of origin following the birth of his half sister. The practitioner recognises how this pattern, ridden with pain and anxiety for Paul, has been repeated with the advent of his foster sister, resulting in his questioning of his place within the family. Thus a connection is forged between the event in the external world, the arrival of a foster sister, which affects Paul's feelings about himself and his environment, his internal world.

The practitioner understands how Paul's fear of abandonment and rejection by his carers has been activated and how this anxiety about potential loss is communicated through his behaviour (Banks, 1994). This appreciation of Paul's emotional state and the crisis he faces is grounded in the worker's acknowledgement of her/his own experiences. By drawing on her/his own 'childhood agonies; a hint of an old terror of the dark, of being lost in an enormous buzzing store' (Crompton, 1980: p. 22), of going into hospital or starting a new school, s/he is able to empathise with Paul's turmoil and prepare her/himself emotionally for working with him. Simultaneously, the practitioner is influenced by her/his theoretical knowledge of attachment processes and of the impact of separation and losses. Applying this theoretical framework assists the worker at three levels: first, in articulating and understanding what is happening, second, in speculating about individuals' future reactions and finally, in reaching decisions about future interventions and their implementation (Howe, 1996b).

Reviewing Paul's life history, the worker notes how his developmental need for close relationships has been thwarted by his experiences of emotional rebuffs and indifference, affecting the manner in which he handles his present social contacts. Paul's perception of the arrival of his foster sister as a threat has dramatically increased his feelings of uncertainty, activating the insecure, anxious and avoidant attachment pattern (Ainsworth *et al.*, 1978) resulting from his earlier relational experiences. His personal observations suggest adults are both untrustworthy and a potential source of pain. Paul's current attempts to distance himself emotionally and physically from other family members, and to manage without them, are a means of trying to decrease 'the ultimate disaster – having to lose people one has learned to love' (Fahlberg, 1994: p. 302). The practitioner identifies this process, recognising how Paul's efforts to reject the family before they reject him are his way of trying to hang onto a sense of control in a situation within which he feels hopeless and helpless.

His refusal to rely on his carers for anything, his resistance to their overtures and his attempts to parent himself are all indicative of the emotional detachment he is using to protect himself from the psychological distress of yet another separation. Paul's behaviour provides the social worker with valuable information about the true nature of his relationship with his carers. The strength of his reactions, demonstrating the enormity of Paul's potential loss, implies that he has forged a meaningful relationship with them, as generally 'the stronger the relationship, the more traumatic the loss' (Fahlberg, 1994: p. 134). While his carers battle with the rejection of their parenting efforts, Paul is really 'telling' about their significance in his life.

Employing the Assessment and Action Records not only triggers a course of action with Paul, but also highlights his carers' needs. If they are to continue in their struggle to care for Paul, his carers require assistance in comprehending the effects of the additional family member's arrival, in reframing his current behaviour and in appreciating their importance to him. These facets will enable them to understand his attachment patterns (see Howe, 1995, 1996b). In avoiding a sense of parenting failure and any subsequent emotional withdrawal from an unresponsive child, the carers need encouragement to learn about the processes involved in building attachments and to develop strategies to foster attachment behaviour (see Fahlberg, 1994), strengthening Paul's sense of belonging to the family.

As the carers persist in initiating positive interactions and in establishing their relationship with Paul, relationship tensions ease. This relaxation permits the foster mother to resume the task of working with Paul, if he so wishes, on his Assessment and Action Records once he is ready to restart this exercise. The consistent pattern of Paul and his foster carer completing the Records holds importance for his security as well as offering additional opportunities for mutually rewarding interactions, which simultaneously raise his self-esteem and self-worth.

Constructive use of the Assessment and Action Records has enabled the worker to pinpoint areas for future work. Emotional tasks, exploring Paul's feelings, his attachment patterns and how his past experiences are driving his daily behaviour have been clearly identified. The importance of the nature and quality of the relationship with Paul features strongly. S/he is aware of the need to offer a reliable, regular and consistent relationship in which his unhappiness is recognised and his feelings tolerated, so as to help Paul to understand his past, deal with the feelings generated and actively participate in thinking about his future. S/he recognises the key importance of this relationship, without which any emotional work is impossible. The worker has remained 'child focused', avoiding the pull of the adult agenda concerned with Paul's behaviour.

A variety of practice tools, designed to elicit feelings and to encourage children to voice their fears and anxieties, is available to the worker (e.g., see King, 1989; Jewett, 1995; NSPCC, 1997). These may or may not include the dimensions and questions encompassed in the Assessment and Action forms, dependent on Paul's wishes and whether or not he finds these useful. Agreement as to how and by whom these are completed can be negotiated as the work around feelings unfolds. Inevitably, the interaction between Paul and his social worker will generate ideas and wishes about future work. Paul may wish to move onto life story work (Ryan and Walker, 1993) so as to have a coherent narrative of his life, or, having weathered this crisis, aim to enhance his coping abilities when faced with stressful situations (see Smith G., 1997).

In effect, the worker's creative use of the Assessment and Action Records to stimulate and trigger her/his thinking and action has served a range of functions. An opportunity for her/him to establish a relationship with Paul, in which effective communication is possible, has been provided, future interventions with Paul and his carers have been identified, and the formulation of both short- and longer-term action plans facilitated. In line with the requirements of the Assessment and Action Records, these signposts for action are formally recorded, specifying details about proposals for further work and noting who will be involved with which responsibilities. Employing the Records in this way holds a further advantage. If the outcome proves positive and avoids further disruption to Paul's life, the practitioner influences attitudes about the value of long-term planned interventions at the *mezzo* level, which in turn promotes the desirability of focusing resources at the *micro* practice front.

Keeping to the spirit of the Records with their emphasis on positive outcomes to promote children's life chances, the practitioner successfully mediates between the requirements of the bureaucratic *mezzo* level ensuring the Records are completed, while addressing the emotional demands of the practice *micro* level. In essence, effectively negotiating between the two spheres allows the worker to draw on her/his professional knowledge, skills and values, thus avoiding the deskilling impact so frequently associated with bureaucratic and procedural imperatives, and to facilitate the precise completion of the documentation. Such accurate Records provide children with not only a sense of purpose, but also a source of stability and constancy in a world where worker and/or placement continuity is never guaranteed.

Conclusion

Working with children is always difficult and demanding (Axline, 1966; Oaklander, 1978; West, 1992), yet never more so than in the current climate stressing effectiveness, efficiency and economy, where relationships are undervalued and emotions denied. However, despite the constraints facing practitioners, this chapter has demonstrated that creative practice with children is still within their grasp. We have identified the organisational constraints and bureaucratic demands posing limits to and clouding the ideals of child-centred practice. Using the example of the Assessment and Action Records, essentially a bureaucratic device, we have explored how these can be utilised both to meet and transcend procedural requirements, allowing reflective practitioners to retain their practice ideals and work with the emotional threads interwoven throughout direct work with children. We have suggested that the Assessment and Action Records can act as triggers, producing a framework in which workers can organise their thinking, identifying the knowledge, skills and values informing their practice. They provide a lever for negotiating management commitment to spending quality time with children; and ensure that children are seen as individuals with specific wants and needs. Exploiting their creative potential enables the formation of satisfying relationships, in which child-centred, empowering work is undertaken, ensuring that the life chances and opportunities of children 'looked after' are enhanced rather than denied.

9

Social Work with Young Offenders: Practising in a Context of Ambivalence

Rob Canton and Tina Eadie

Introduction

The practice of youth justice has to reconcile society's deep cultural ambivalence towards offending by young people. The need to punish for wrongdoing and to demonstrate disapproval has a strong claim on our collective moral conscience. Moreover, the problem of crime is officially documented as being primarily a problem of young people (Brown, 1998; Muncie, 1999; McLaughlin and Muncie, 2000). In tension with this is a recognition that rule-breaking by young people is not at all uncommon and that the wisest course may be to support young people as they 'grow out of crime' (Rutherford, 1986). An inclination to *help* is made more compelling by a recognition that young people are not always so aware of the consequences of their actions as those who have lived longer – making them less blameworthy (Walker, 1983). There are also well-established associations between offending and various indices of social and emotional disadvantage (Farrington, 1997) which suggest that help may be both more efficacious and fairer. Yet despite this, the socio-political climate has tended to emphasise blame and demand the punishment of young people who transgress the law (Haines and Drakeford, 1998: p. 234).

This chapter focuses on the challenges for youth justice workers[1] arising out of this ambivalence. They are charged with signalling society's disapproval of offending behaviour through appropriate punishment. At the same time, they have to recognise that adolescence is about testing boundaries and help young people address problems so as to find alternative ways of behaving. Located within a *mezzo/micro* analysis, the chapter focuses on the organisational context in which youth justice tasks are undertaken. It examines workers' use of professional discretion at the beginning stage of working with a young offender; as such, it seeks to demonstrate the knowledge, skills and values required in balancing the tension between the prescriptions of the organisation and the exercise of judgement in decision making. An argument is developed which suggests the current managerialist organisational ethos risks constraining reflective practice by attempting, on the pretext of consistency, to prescribe both the what *and* how of practice.

After some initial observations about penal policy and organisations, the chapter advances a model to explore the relationship between agency accountability and practitioner discretion. Drawing on the analyses developed in chapters 2 and 3, a practice scenario will be used to demonstrate how the reflective youth justice worker is both accountable to the organisation *and* retains sufficient (though not unbounded) discretion and judgement. In accounting for her actions, both formally in terms of managerial requirements and substantively in relation to her own decision making (see McWilliams, 1992), the worker in our scenario demonstrates skill in engaging with the 'contradictions and paradoxes' characterising human interactions (Worrall, 1995: p. 41). Overall, our aim is to energise practitioners and stimulate thinking regarding challenges and opportunities to manage these tensions in Youth Offender Teams (YOTs).

Penal policy and organisations

Organisation theories are predicated on the assumption that the organisation has an *objective*, something that it is 'for', but this does

---

[1] Although the authors anticipate that the discussion will be of interest to those working with young offenders in Scotland and Northern Ireland, the chapter addresses youth justice policy in England and Wales specifically.

violence to the development of criminal justice agencies. None of these (with the arguable exception of the Crown Prosecution Service) was created for a set purpose. Rather, they evolved and, in that process, acquired, claimed, or had forced upon them, tasks and responsibilities that cannot be assumed to conduce to a settled objective or function. Conventional histories of youth justice, debating at the *macro* level whether the 'real' purpose of youth justice has been to control the delinquent (justice) or protect the neglected (welfare) (Worrall, 1997: p. 127), often reflect this misunderstanding. However, the development of youth justice policy and practice can only be understood in terms of *both* of these objectives and the dynamic relationship between them.[2]

The ambivalence between punishing or helping, controlling or caring, is a context in which youth justice agencies have always had to function. The agenda, however, has moved from a primary focus on welfare to justice and currently to punishment (Goldson, 1999, 2000). In the 1980s and the early 1990s, agencies worked through a political climate that espoused decarceration for all but the most violent and dangerous young people, to one which announced that 'Prison Works' (Howard, 1993). This was swiftly followed by the Criminal Justice and Public Order Act 1994, which introduced the Secure Training Unit for persistent juvenile offenders aged 12–15 and doubled the amount of time a young person could spend in a Young Offender Institution. The Crime and Disorder Act 1998, alongside the continued expansion of secure and custodial provision for young people, has been criticised for its potential to accelerate young offenders' progress towards custody (Pitts, 1999: p. 17). These political vacillations have been accompanied by debate about the proper locus of community intervention with young offenders, with statutory responsibility being variously assigned to probation services and social services departments, as representing control and care respectively.

The introduction of inter-agency YOTs in the Crime and Disorder Act 1998 took this further. Established throughout England and Wales by April 2000, and comprising social workers, probation officers, police officers and education and health authority staff, these attempted to formalise the co-operation needed between agencies.

---

[2] For that matter, punishment must be understood in cultural and expressive as well as strategic and instrumental terms (Garland, 1990).

Yet it can be anticipated that the coming together of several organisations, each with its distinctive social remit or 'charter' (Harris and Webb, 1987: p. 96), will *add* to the contradictions characterising the work. The range of new sentences also poses challenges for practitioners. As well as the familiar tensions between punishment and welfare, the new measures (quite appropriately) raise difficult questions about the limits of parental responsibility, the relationship between the parents' responsibility and that of the child and, fundamentally, what can be done with or to recalcitrant parents on their children's behalf without making matters very much worse (compare Clarke, 1980).

Accounts of youth justice have often failed to attend sufficiently to the organisational realities which stand between policy and practice. The relationship is never straightforward (Cohen, 1985: p. 115), and among the *mezzo* level influences are occupational culture – by which we mean training, values and practice wisdom – as well as formal lines of control and accountability. Whenever objectives are set for the organisation, they will encounter 'professional', historical and cultural traditions which have developed as practitioners have made sense of their work and responded to its challenges. This occupational culture is neither intractable nor infallible, but is grounded in the requirements of the job and must therefore be taken fully into account and respected in any understanding of the organisation.

An example of the value of retrospective analysis at the *mezzo* level is an understanding of the implementation and consequences of the Children and Young Persons Act 1969. Children in trouble, whether 'depraved' or 'deprived', were to have become the responsibility of social workers. In the event, the next decade saw a retreat from welfare and substantial increases in punitive responses to young offenders (see Morris and Giller, 1987). A *macro* level analysis might suggest that the Act failed to flourish because a new government, already temperamentally unsympathetic to a welfare approach, wanted to respond robustly to the perception of crime increases in the 1970s. A more *mezzo* interpretation stresses the role of the decision makers – including police, social workers, probation officers and magistrates – who effectively abandoned whatever potential for reform the Act contained: 'Quite simply, cumulatively, these disparate bodies of professionals made the wrong decisions about the wrong children at the wrong time' (Thorpe *et al.*, 1980: p. 3). It is, in short, to the *mezzo* no less than the *macro* level that we must turn to understand the character of practice.

Accountability and discretion

Working in the public sector requires an acceptance of agency policies and a willingness to respect the discipline of the organisation. At the same time, qualified social workers receive a professional training that is underpinned by a code of practice-based ethics and values outside of individual organisations (see, e.g., CCETSW, 1995: p. 18). Probation officer training, while separate, requires trainees to obtain a degree from a higher education institution as well as the practice-based National Vocational Qualification (NVQ). As discussed in Chapter 3, this can lead to a conflict for workers between practising in a way which reflects their personal and professional values and accommodating to the managerialist demands of the agency. For youth justice workers, whether from a probation or social services background, this tension has been explicit in *National Standards for the Supervision of Offenders in the Community* (Home Office, 1992, 1995, 2000b) and, for the first time, the separate *National Standards for Youth Justice* introduced in April 2000 (Youth Justice Board, 2000). These have created guidelines for service delivery, detailing expectations for contact, and responsibilities of supervisors when offenders do not meet their obligations.

Analysis at the *mezzo* level in contemporary youth justice practice is addressed in this section by exploring the impact of National Standards on the occupational culture within this setting. We suspect that the proceduralism and bureaucratisation introduced with the Standards could result in workers adopting a more accommodating rather than reflective style of practice with young offenders. As outlined in Chapter 2, social services departments, along with others in the public sector, came under increasing pressure during the latter part of the twentieth century to demonstrate value for money and accountability to the public for services provided. This, in turn, led to questions being asked about the control of employees (Finkelstein, 1996: p. 77) and resulted in the introduction of more explicit standards and measures of performance, increased emphasis on output controls, and a stress on greater discipline and parsimony in resource use (James and Raine, 1998).

As successive versions of the Standards have become 'tougher' in respect of the number of absences tolerated before the instigation of breach action, the language has become more prescriptive. Practitioners were generally happy with the extent to which the 1992 Standards allowed supervisors to exercise professional judgement

(Ellis *et al.*, 1996: p. 23). All stressed that the inclusion of words such as 'reasonable', 'should' or 'may' were helpful since they allowed room for professional interpretation. While the 1995 Standards introduced the explicit notion of 'providing punishment and a disciplined programme for offenders' and reduced the number of warnings about unacceptable absences from three to two (Home Office, 1995: p. 2), the tone set in the general introduction was similar. Of particular importance to our argument here was the acknowledgement of 'practitioners' **professional judgement** to be exercised within a framework of **accountability**' (Home Office, 1995: p. 2, original emphasis) as contributing to the achievement of the overall aim of the Standards in strengthening the supervision of offenders in the community. This does not appear in the revised Standards (Home Office, 2000b; Youth Justice Board, 2000). The requirement that supervision is delivered 'fairly, consistently and without improper discrimination' *has* been retained and, in the *National Standards for Youth Justice*, expanded. Most significantly, however, the language of the *National Standards for Youth Justice* has changed from 'should' to 'must'.

The *National Standards for Youth Justice* set out the principal aim of the youth justice system as being to prevent offending by children and young people. They 'provide a basis for promoting high quality effective work with children, young people, their families, and victims' (Youth Justice Board, 2000: p. 1). While the point has been forcefully made that National Standards represent the government's managerialist attempts to control the activities of local agency managers and practitioners (Haines and Drakeford, 1998: p. 211), we would argue that it is their *interpretation* which determines whether they become a managerialist or professional tool. The Standards are, essentially, a set of procedures for workers to follow and, as such, place limits on their individual discretion. Nevertheless, it is the way in which the accompanying rules are *implemented* that is crucial; if they are drawn too tightly, decreased discretion can lead to discrimination and ineffectiveness. Drawing them too loosely could result in inconsistent and idiosyncratic practice. The model shown in Figure 9.1 offers a framework in which to explore this further.

While the history of youth justice services will not be addressed here (see Harris and Webb, 1987; Pitts, 1988; Newburn, 1997; Muncie, 1999), it is our contention that the youth justice practitioner, until very recently, operated in quadrant B, enjoying wide discretion and low accountability to the organisation. This is represented as 'the bad old days' to acknowledge (but not necessarily agree with) current

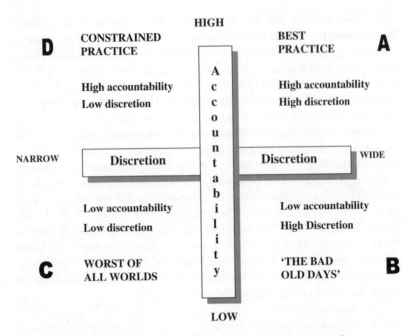

Figure 9.1 Managing accountability and discretion in youth justice practice

interpretations of previous youth policy as having failed[3]. Senior social workers, as the title implies, were experienced practitioners whose role was to advise and to ensure work was being undertaken honestly and conscientiously. Quality standards were the preserve of the practitioner and professional judgement was vindication of a decision. A lack of rigorous monitoring made much of the work undertaken by individual practitioners invisible. The contemporary YOT manager, by contrast, must now ensure that a range of indicators and measurements are met as laid down in the *National Standards for Youth Justice.*

The confluence of a paradigm shift in criminology (Cohen, 1981) and a new conception of management forced change. The 'labelling perspective' affirmed that *nothing* distinguished offenders from non-offenders apart from the societal reaction characterising the action as an offence and the agent as an offender. Formalising and

---

[3] The title and general tenor of the publication *No More Excuses* (Home Office, 1997), illustrates this well.

endorsing the label, the system was intrinsically self-defeating. Within the profession and its academic context, it became near orthodox that young offenders should be kept 'diverted' from the system. The 'nothing works' critique of Martinson (1974) and Brody (1976) further damaged the credibility of social casework, which was also encountering radical political critiques (Bailey and Brake, 1975; Walker and Beaumont, 1981). But all this precipitated a *crisis of method*. Accepting that, in general, the less intrusive the intervention the better, having diverted a young person from formal supervision or from a custodial sentence, what then? The view that there was nothing different about offenders left practitioners with nothing to treat and, in a significant sense, nothing to do.

When the principles of new public management, discussed in Chapter 2, were applied to youth justice, they encountered these crises of purpose and method. *Systems management* was needed, where the processes had to be understood and then manipulated. This in turn entailed targeting and gate-keeping (Thorpe *et al.*, 1980: p. 21), bringing constraints on professional autonomy, together with increased oversight and accountability. There was no room for idiosyncrasy in the new management of systems.

This was the beginning of a relationship change between practitioners and their managers. The first practical manifestations of this were in the monitoring and quality control of social inquiry (now presentence) reports. Proposals had to be appropriate to the strategic management of the penal tariff and some areas even set up advisory panels to oversee this. The 'new' Labour agenda has not only continued down the managerialist path but has extended the processes through an unprecedented emphasis on organisational performance, assessed through measurable and quantifiable outcomes (McLaughlin and Muncie, 2000: p. 182). The *National Standards for Youth Justice* require the YOT manager to be responsible for meeting key measurable objectives and standards, shifting practice more towards a technical process.

In terms of our model, practice began to move from quadrant B to one demanding higher accountability. Whether it came to rest in quadrants A or D (the extent to which it constrained discretion) is debatable: it is dependent upon practitioners' ability to withstand managerial insistence on *sameness* as opposed to professional workers' recognition of *relevant difference*. The Standards serve organisational interests in terms of prioritising working practices, and also offer a guaranteed level of service (Haines and Drakeford, 1998: p. 213).

However, the extent to which this will meet the supervisee's best interests depends upon the *quality* of the contact. A worker operating in quadrant D endorses the rules uncritically, unable or unwilling to acknowledge the unequal opportunities that young offenders experience at personal, cultural and structural levels. This will lead to injustice as well as ineffective work. The professional task is to balance these factors against each person's responsibility for compliance with the rules in order to make informed and accountable decisions.

While standardised prescriptions usually acknowledge there may be cases requiring proper departures (quadrant A), the logic of monitoring militates against this and pushes practitioners towards quadrant D. *Adherence* to standards is inherently acceptable – can be ticked on a monitoring form – while departures have to be recorded and justified, risking criticism, even though adherence itself can generate unfair and ineffective consequences. A reflective practitioner working in quadrant A, the area of high accountability and wide discretion, will adopt a flexible approach to the Standards, recognising that an appropriate shift from them remains possible, whilst expecting the line manager's authority to be used in supporting decisions taken in this way. There is no inconsistency in authorising practitioners to exercise their discretion *and* holding them to account for the manner in which this is done. To be aware of the need to work as a member of an organisation, while also affirming the professional discretion to engage with each young offender on an individual and intuitive basis, is precisely what characterises Schön's (1991) 'reflective practitioner', discussed in Chapter 3.

The ethos of any organisation can and does shift between the quadrants. This is influenced not only by the formal roles and structures of the organisation, but by how this is mediated within the occupational culture (for instance, the extent to which practitioners accept or seek to resist limits on their discretion) and by the economic context. While no one would try to promote practice characterised by low accountability and narrow discretion (quadrant C), quadrant D could degenerate in this way if management systems of scrutiny were indifferent or nonexistent (when, for instance, overwhelmed by the amount of work that has to be monitored).

Acknowledging that the model risks too static a representation of practice reality, our thesis is that practitioners should strive to operate in quadrant A and that managers should endeavour to organise in a manner enabling workers to practise in this way. In particular, we reject the view that there is an intrinsic tension between consistent service of high quality and wide practitioner discretion. No single criterion can determine judgement in complex circumstances and the inherently contested purposes of youth justice work make the retention of discretion essential. The following practice scenario will provide an opportunity to reflect on the knowledge, skills and values required by practitioners to remain in quadrant A, rather than being drawn into quadrant D. We have chosen to focus on assessment at the pre-sentence stage – crucial in shaping the course of a young person's subsequent career – and the practice of enforcement – salient to our discussion and a mode of operating which sharpens the distinctions we wish to highlight.

Assessment and the pre-sentence report

The pre-sentence report (PSR) is intended to provide information to help courts decide on the most suitable sentence for a defendant. Acknowledging the expertise required, previous National Standards for PSRs (Home Office, 1995: pp. 7–16) stated that their purpose is 'to provide a *professional* assessment of the nature and the causes of a person's offending behaviour and the action which can be taken to reduce re-offending' (emphasis added) (Home Office, 1995: p. 7). Although the current Standards have omitted this, youth justice workers are not 'disinterested experts' (Pitts, 1999: p. 71), whose purpose is to provide 'value-free' opinions. They continue to manage the tension between their role as servants of the court and their other role as people who are professionally bound to work in the best interests of the children and young people in trouble, as defined by both the Children Act 1989 and the United Nations Convention on the Rights of the Child as 'children in need' (Pitts, 1999: p. 71). This, we would argue, is a *professional* task.

PRACTICE SCENARIO 9.1

A worker in a Youth Offender Team is allocated a pre-sentence report for the Youth Court. The referral form shows:

Name: Clive **Baker** (aged 15)

Home Circumstances: Clive (dual heritage) living with father (white). Mother (African-Caribbean) left family home last year.

Continued

Offences: 1 Burglary _withdrawn_
                           2 TWOC (milk floats)
                           3 Criminal Damage
Details: On 6 August, entered premises of Mills Dairy
                           and drove a milk float around the yard, playing
                           'dodgems' with co-accused. Damage to value
                           £5,000.
Previous Convictions: Final Warning   Criminal Damage
                           Referral Order   3 months   Theft from Store

Other information: Magistrates considering a community penalty.

On the basis of this information, the worker will undertake a home visit
with a view to formulating an assessment and submitting a report to the
Court.

Section 6.8 Pre-Sentence Reports states (*Youth Justice Board*, 2000:
p. 26):

6.8.1 The YOT Manager must ensure that Pre-Sentence Reports (PSRs)
       are produced using the following standard headings:
–   sources of information;
–   offence analysis;
–   offender assessment
–   assessment of risk to the community, including risk of re-offending
       and risk of harm; and,
–   conclusion.

There is no mention of the requirement on report writers to take
account of welfare considerations such as age, family background and
educational circumstances as previously (Home Office, 1995: p. 13).
The focus is on time limits for allocation and production of reports,
procedures for their quality assurance, and monitoring of the whole
process. This fits with the 'new' Labour emphasis on achieving objectives through continual auditing, setting priorities and targets, monitoring, evaluation and inspection (McLaughlin and Muncie, 2000:
p. 174), further outlined in Chapter 2. Effective work with young
offenders, we would argue, requires more than managing, improving
and accounting for performance levels.

The implementation of the Standards will be influenced at the
mezzo level by the occupational culture – specifically, knowledge, skills

and values about which no account is taken in the Standards. Practitioners need knowledge of:

- Criminological theories (Coleman and Norris, 2000; Maguire *et al.*, 2002; Smith, 1995);
- Criminal justice processes (Ashworth, 1998; Davies *et al.*, 1998);
- The penal system (Cavadino and Dignan, 2002);
- Relevant legislation (Wasik and Taylor, 1995; Leng, Taylor and Wasik, 1998; Birch and Leng, 2000).

They also need to understand the potential for discrimination at different points in the process and how this might be avoided or challenged (see, e.g., FitzGerald, 1993; Denney, 1998; MacPherson, 1999). Also required is an awareness of the availability of resources and of referral systems to specialist agencies: for example, community drug and alcohol teams.

Appropriate skills include interviewing, gathering information, assessing risk, need, and responsivity (see below), avoiding discriminatory or stereotyping language and assumptions and negotiating with other professionals. Good written skills are essential, as is the ability to present the report in court, expressing an opinion to the magistrates or judge confidently and assertively (see Blagg *et al.*, cited in Smith, D., 1996: p. 153).

Most important, the task calls for ethical clarity. In the 1980s, youth justice workers used report writing as an explicit means of diverting young people from custody. Smith (1996: p. 153) argues that this was successful because report writers were not only 'technically competent' but also 'morally engaged'; they had an ethical commitment to reducing the unjust use of care and custody. There have been many attempts to articulate the values that should guide practitioners working with offenders (compare Rutherford, 1993; Nellis, 1995; Williams, B., 1995; Chapman and Hough, 1998). We believe some additional values need further emphasis:

- A recognition of the differential impact of 'the same' penalty;
- An awareness of, and respect for, individual difference;
- A commitment to social and procedural as well as retributive justice;
- An insistence on open and honest procedures for dealing with people.

Without a sense of these informing their work in the criminal justice system, practitioners will use the 'what' of National Standards to write reports that are competent but contribute nothing to the wider remit of social justice.

PRACTICE SCENARIO 9.2

The youth justice worker visits Clive at home. She is greeted on the doorstep by Mr Baker. His barrage of abuse leaves her in no doubt about his view that his son had done nothing wrong – it was all the fault of his co-accused. She explains that she is required to prepare a report outlining the offence and making a proposal to the court. Reluctantly, Mr Baker allows her to enter the house and the interview proceeds. Clive appears wary of his father who sits glowering at him across the living room. He shrugs when asked about the offence, saying he was bored at the time.

The worker later accesses other sources of information. Agency records show that Mr Baker, currently unemployed, had served a sentence of imprisonment for assault on Clive's mother the previous year. Mrs Baker moved out of the home, taking Clive's younger sister with her. Clive was accommodated by the local authority until his father's release. Clive is not attending school regularly and when he does his behaviour is seen to be disruptive.

Practice questions:

- Which key factors need to considered in undertaking an assessment of Clive?
- How relevant is Clive's motivation to change to the sentencing decision?
- In what ways might the worker use her knowledge and understanding of anti-oppressive practice in the assessment?
- To what extent should decisions about these questions rest with the worker or be determined by the organisation?

Many agencies now require practitioners to use structured tools to ensure that an assessment is undertaken systematically and consistently. Assessment should attend to:

- Risk;
- Criminogenic (offending-related) needs;

- Responsivity – matching intervention to offenders' learning styles and engaging their active participation (Chapman and Hough, 1998: p. 6).

Risk assessment and management are now key issues for all practitioners and managers in the field of social care and criminal justice (Kemshall and Pritchard, 1996: p. 1). Workers should know that risk can never be eliminated entirely but, taking information and data from a number of sources and using statistical methods as well as those based on individualised assessments, a 'good guess' can be enhanced to become a judgement with reasonable credibility (Kemshall, 1996: p. 136). These approaches are valuable in guiding practitioners' thinking, but are not intended to replace judgement. In Practice scenario 9.2, for example, if the youth justice worker discovers that Clive has a high risk of reoffending 'score', this is useful information, but it does not tell her which proposal to make to the Court, nor what intervention would make a difference.

Assessment of *need* and *responsivity* is no more straightforward. For example, the favoured contemporary assessment tools emphasise the importance of *motivation*, 'an offender's attitude to changing their behaviour' (Chapman and Hough, 1998: p. 32). Determining motivation is difficult, not least because it is often a function not only of what people want but what they think they can do and their perception of alternative possibilities. In the practice scenario, the worker will appreciate that it is highly unlikely that Clive has a single, uncomplicated attitude towards changing his behaviour. Even if he did, it might be hard for him to be articulate in the presence of his father or, if interviewed on his own, with someone who represents authority (and, in this case, white authority) and in whom, at this stage, he has no reason to trust or confide. The worker must assess other criminogenic needs relevant to both Clive and his social circumstances – for instance, any anti-social attitudes and feelings, evidence of poor decision-making and problem-solving skills, substance misuse, and family factors where linked to offending (Chapman and Hough, 1998: p. 27). Sophisticated judgements are required here, not merely about the quality of the family relationships, but about amenability to change, which the worker is not yet in a position to make.

Reference has already been made to the need for an awareness of the discriminatory *potential* of many decisions in the criminal justice process (see above). There is also compelling evidence of *actual* discrimination at certain points (Hood, 1992; Cook and Hudson, 1993), although the extent and significance of this is disputed (Smith, D. J., 1997). Our worker should anticipate the possibility that Clive has encountered racism, should check out his experiences, and be aware that this, as well as his age, circumstances and ambivalence, will predispose him to reticence and suspicion that could easily be misconstrued as hostility or 'lack of motivation'.

Regarding her own relationship with Clive, the worker will recognise the need for and seek to promote anti-oppressive practice. At the very least, this involves acknowledging that Clive now lives in a household in which there are no Black adults or others to give him strong affirmation of his identity. In exploring the implications of this, the worker might ask Clive about his immediate peer group, or role models in the wider world. She will be interested in his relationship with both parents, asking open, non-threatening questions and using empathy to engage with him, in keeping with the value base outlined earlier. Further, ensuring she uses appropriate language and imagery, she will recognise and work with personal, racial, cultural and social differences between herself and Clive, making responsible use of the power vested in her as a youth justice worker (see Francis Spence, 1995: p. 165).

Having gathered and organised a substantial amount of information, the worker must decide whether to propose a community penalty, as mentioned by the magistrates. The reflective practitioner will not only draw upon her skills and knowledge, but also seek to give expression to the values underpinning her practice. Regardless of whether the offence was undertaken through boredom, or frustration at the lack of structured social activities available in the area, Clive must take responsibility for his actions. In considering her proposal, the worker has mixed feelings about whether a three-month Action Plan Order is appropriate. Combining punishment, rehabilitation and reparation to change offending behaviour and prevent further crime, this Order has been called a 'super' supervision order (Pitts, 1999: p. 62). Yet she is aware that social workers can be too anxious to 'help', tying this to a criminal justice sanction. However, the amount of damage caused increases the seriousness of the offence and, given Clive's recent care experiences and his difficulties at school, agency policy would regard some form of community order as an appropriate proposal, addressing both risk and need. However, if Clive fails to co-operate or re-offends while subject to the Order, he could be at risk of receiving a custodial sentence – something the worker would hope to avoid at all costs. With some misgivings, she decides to propose an Action Plan Order as the strategy most likely to prevent further offending and, hopefully, offer opportunities for change. The magistrates make an Action Plan Order.

In formulating her proposal, the youth justice worker found herself in Schön's 'swampy lowlands' (1991: p. 42), a messy situation familiar to practitioners (see Chapter 3). Ideally, she would have liked time to find out more about Clive's motivation, but the court deadline had to be met. She did, however, remain in quadrant A; her decisions were consistent with agency policy and the organisational culture, ensuring her accountability, but she allowed herself a degree of latitude in reflecting on the most appropriate disposal, and did not *automatically* follow the direction indicated by the magistrates. In contrast, an accommodating worker operating in quadrant D would have focused on whichever checklist and scoring system the agency used, and, if at all possible, would have reflected the magistrates' views in the PSR. Although the outcome was, in this instance, the same, it is the process that is important. The worker's accountability, both to the agency's and her own standards, is therefore better seen as a dynamic process rather than an end state – a point returned to in the next section.

While standardised assessment tools have a real value in promoting consistency and in giving structure to practitioners' judgements, their uncritical application will be unfair and counter-productive. In terms of our model, they are helpful if applied in quadrant A (wide discretion, high accountability), but harmful in quadrant D (narrow discretion, high accountability). As we seek to demonstrate in our discussion of National Standards, quadrant D generates a spurious and seductive sameness which is probably easier to attain than the true consistency which can *only* be achieved in quadrant A.

Responding to needs and enforcing orders

In this section, we argue that the reflective worker, using discretion and judgement while giving account to managers, will be working effectively to reduce the incidence of further offending. The accommodating worker by contrast risks losing sight of the Court's concerns by implementing its Order in a narrowly instrumental way, missing opportunities not only to meet young offenders' needs, but also to address their risk of reoffending.

Any attempt to work with young people and challenge their offending makes assumptions – some more, some less explicit – about reasons for the wrongdoing. Although it is safer to speak of correlations than of causes, a number of factors have been identified that seem associated with the likelihood of offending. These include peer group pressure, a neglectful, inconsistent or abusive parent, poor job prospects, boredom, impulsivity, school absenteeism or exclusion, homelessness, and experimentation with drugs and alcohol (for discussion, see Farrington, 1997). Any purposeful attempt to 'address offending behaviour' within an Action Plan Order must take account of these influences, the reality of young people's lived experiences, and it is these factors, rather than abstract discussions and cognitive-behavioural exercises, that will be most salient in their lives. Indeed, intervention must recognise this. A cognitive-behavioural approach that neglects individuals' lived circumstances is unlikely to succeed (Drakeford and Vanstone, 1996; Crow, 2001).[4]

In order to work with Clive in any of these ways, regular meetings must take place and a working relationship formed. As practice scenario 9.3 demonstrates, this is by no means a straightforward task.

The worker's immediate priority is to engage Clive's motivation at least to the extent of securing his attendance reliably for appointments. To achieve this she must reflect upon what might explain his failure to attend. It could be an expression of pessimism as much as defiance. The worker infers from Clive's engagement in the drawing up of the supervision plan that, at some level, he wants help, both with his offending and with his wider circumstances. Clive's feelings towards formal supervision are likely to be ambivalent. Even if he were clear himself about his wishes and feelings, he has to feel able to express these in the context of a relationship which can emphasise control as much as care. This is not to urge workers to 'look deeper' or to regard clients' own perception of their difficulties as 'the presenting problem'. Practitioners have to find a way of taking with complete seriousness people's expressed preferences and definitions of their needs, while at the same time interpreting what is said with care and sophistication. The worker should draw upon the skills of motivational interviewing (Miller and Rollnick, 1991), which include a serious attempt to understand Clive's own perception of his predicament, avoiding argument and confrontation and encouraging a belief in the possibility of change.

---

[4] Interestingly, it has been suggested (Spiess, cited in Pitts, 1996: p. 283) that, in the case of persistent young offenders, the most effective results have been achieved when formal rehabilitative programmes are ignored for at least the first 12 weeks of an order and practical needs are addressed.

PRACTICE SCENARIO 9.3

Initial contact was made with Clive at Court. He was instructed to report to the worker within five days. This follow-up meeting would be to produce outcomes for supervision and a draft plan for preventing reoffending, in line with National Standards. Clive did not keep this appointment but called in to see the worker the following day. He gave no reason, other than 'I forgot', but showed considerable interest in the supervision plan which was then drawn up between himself and the worker. Clive failed to attend his next appointment. The worker, mindful of the required intensity of the Order over a short period of time, discusses the case with her Manager who insists on Clive's full cooperation with the Order; if this is not taking place, he should be breached. The worker, acknowledging the value of targeting offending behaviour and related needs, argues that the stipulations of the Order (offending behaviour work and reparation) require a degree of personal stability that is simply lacking for Clive. They agree that she will visit Clive the next day and set an appointment that he must keep.

Practice questions:

- How is the worker to appraise Clive's behaviour; do his failures to keep appointments necessarily represent non-compliance with the Order? Alternatively, is this just a manifestation of the difficulties that persuaded the Court to make the original Order in the first place?
- To what extent should the worker involve Clive's father in the management of the Order and how can this be achieved?
- What are the pressures on the manager and practitioner in this situation and are they the same?

Whatever Clive's feelings, there is no real sense in which he is being given a reasonable opportunity (by his family and his life circumstances) to comply. The worker would like to discuss this with Mr Baker. She suspects that Clive is having to organise his affairs well beyond what can fairly be expected of a 15-year-old and believes Mr Baker's co-operation and interest in Clive's progress would be of positive benefit in the management of the Order. She wonders whether a Parenting Order would have helped to secure this, but is not convinced given Mr Baker's attitude to date. She also believes Clive's response when he has attended has to be compared with others on her caseload who merely 'go through the motions'. Here, the issue is not only about welfare, but also of justice, recognising that what is formally the same requirement impacts on individuals differentially.

The tension for the YOT manager is between the agency's responsibility to enforce the Order in strict accordance with National Standards and to undertake effective work with Clive. To 'breach' Clive would be to return to the Court without any serious attempt at finding a solution to the problems which were to be addressed through the Order. Yet the responsibilities under National Standards are clear: 'Breach action must be initiated within 10 working days of the most recent failure to comply, if the offender receives more than two formal warnings during the first 12 weeks of the order (*Youth Justice Board*, 2000: p. 34). There is a collision of principle when the carefully wrought criteria of policy encounter the complexity and vicissitudes of real life – a tension, we suggest, which is entirely characteristic of the *mezzo/micro* interface.

PRACTICE SCENARIO 9.4

Clive misses the crucial appointment but calls in the next day. Exasperated, the worker asks why he did not attend and Clive says he forgot. He seems despondent and tired. She asks him to say more. He tells the worker that he did not get to bed the night before the appointment. His father had come home drunk and had shouted at him, smashing up Clive's things and threatening to throw him out. Angry and frightened, Clive had walked out and spent the night on the streets. Following this disclosure, and the worker's sympathetic response, Clive begins to open up to her. His father has a new partner whose hostility to Clive has racist undertones. She recently moved in and Clive says that she and his father are often out drinking all evening. He is left to fend for himself. Sometimes there is no food in the house and he steals pies and cans of lager from the local supermarket. He is thinking of leaving home. When questioned about where he would go he is vague and says he 'knows of a place where lads like him can stay'. By the end of the session, the worker and Clive have together agreed a family meeting might be of value.

> *Practice questions:*
>
> - What principles should guide the worker's judgement about whether an explanation for missing an appointment is acceptable?
> - Given the 'ultimatum' about this appointment, what action should the worker now take with regard to the Order?
> - How can she develop the trust in her that Clive has begun to demonstrate?

The worker now knows the reasons for Clive's absences and has far more insight into his home circumstances. Her relationship with Clive has been strengthened and his motivation engaged. However, she is no clearer about how to record the forgotten appointment. Would her agency, or the magistrates who sentenced Clive, agree that 'I forgot' – a paradigm case of an unacceptable excuse – is in these circumstances acceptable after all? She decides to record this as an acceptable absence, demonstrating her accountability by first discussing it with her line manager and setting out her reasoning on the written record. Applying this to the model set out in Figure 9.1, the worker located in quadrant A will use her or his judgement to decide how to record the missed appointment. An accommodating worker located in quadrant D would have been less interested in Clive's reasons for forgetting, focusing solely on adherence to the Standards.

Is quadrant A achievable? As implied earlier in this volume, wherever practice is tightly prescribed practitioners will repeatedly discover that an uncritical application of the rules is both oppressive and unfair. In working with Clive, the youth justice worker has been drawing on her knowledge and skills, but is also giving expression to her values. She has been guided by her awareness of the constraints upon Clive and of the differential impact of 'the same' penalty on those whom she supervises. She has continued to offer opportunities to change even when these appear to be rejected. Throughout, she has respected both substantive and procedural justice, working openly and honestly with Clive and with her manager. Had the worker behaved officiously or taken enforcement action prematurely, this would not only have constituted poor social work, but also been reductively ineffective and unjust.

For honourable and principled reasons, then, as in the work with Clive, reflective practitioners will look for ways of legitimately interpreting the prescriptions. Departures from National Standards need not be either whimsical or negligent. Workers are uniquely placed to inform management about the real consequences of the application of policy. For this reason, accountability is better understood as a dynamic process than as an end-state. The youth justice worker makes her decisions and gives a full account of them to her manager. In explaining her judgements, she may adduce considerations that her manager takes to be irrelevant and she can then proceed to work with any instructions given. In this way, practice will be progressively shaped by agency policy, but, in complex cases, as circumstances develop, the need for principled discretion remains – the 'reflection-in-action' outlined in Chapter 3. Ideally, agency policy will be reciprocally influenced by taking intelligence from practice.

Conclusion

In this chapter it is argued that policy makers and managers came to insist on standardisation, which was taken to be a precondition of effective system management. Minimum *procedural* standards for the management of community-based supervision replaced minimum *professional* standards for the supervision of offenders in the community (Haines and Drakeford 1998: p. 214). The endeavour, in terms of our model, was to move practice from quadrant B (wide discretion with low accountability) to quadrant D (narrow discretion and high accountability). Our exposition of the work with Clive, however, suggests that the indefinite number of contingencies in individuals' circumstances requires a confident reaffirmation of the value of discretion, and a commitment to practice in quadrant A (high accountability and wide discretion). Without a principled differentiation of circumstances, standardisation creates sameness but only a spurious consistency. Attention to issues of enforcement and the management of Orders requires principled differentiation and professional judgement.

National Standards, it will be objected, were intended to ensure that courts knew what would happen when they made community sentences. We do not believe, however, that courts would have any difficulty with the proposition that practitioners, in dialogue with managers, should make appropriate judgements within open and principled criteria. Standards were to secure fairness, but fairness involves making relevant distinctions, not treating everyone the same. If quadrant B countenanced too much variation, a move to quadrant D rather than A is possibly more insidious because it conceals injustices beneath a plausible sameness. Research is now giving clear indications about the nature of effective practice (see Chapman and Hough, 1998) and YOT managers are keen to promote this approach. Yet the very idea of a structured programme of intervention implies a level of personal stability that is not present for significant numbers of young offenders (see Eadie and Willis, 1989). Practice in quadrant A acknowledges this, ensuring accountability along with an appropriately individualised response to each young offender.

Whatever the formal constitution of the agencies, it is our contention that youth justice work can only thrive in an organisation that insists on high levels of accountability and empowers its practitioner staff to use their discretion widely and wisely. This approach, like any other, may sometimes lead to difficulties and unfairness, but no more so than a rigid application of rules. It is utterly characteristic of penal policy that it generates unexpected and ironic outcomes. This is part of the reason why increased standardisation is the wrong strategy. Through the *mezzo/micro* interaction, the practice realities of working with damaged and disaffected young men and women needs to be acknowledged at all levels. This will enable practitioners to use their professional judgement in accordance with the demands of each individual offender's situation, avoiding the trap of routinised responses which, whilst satisfying managerialist aspirations, move away from the ideals of both justice and welfare for young offenders.

Part III

Part III

10

The Future of Social Work

Olive Stevenson

Introduction

In considering the future of social work, this chapter links the experience of the past thirty years with current trends. It reflects on the extent to which past and present learning can guide us in the next phases of social work activity. Such an exercise is, of course, limited. Unforeseeable events, political decisions, the impact of European and global influences will introduce new twists in occupational development. Nevertheless, if social work is to remain a significant element in the provision of social services, it must be rebalanced so that the exercise of professional judgement and responsibility interacts effectively with organisational accountability. This chapter attempts to show some of the reasons why the present distortions have arisen and what now needs to be done.

The preceding chapters analyse in considerable detail the complex interaction of *micro*, *mezzo* and *macro* factors in the recent history of social work and develop ideas about the essence of reflective practice in which social work should be rooted. Indeed, one of the important and distinctive features of this book is the attempt to show the relationship between the three levels and the profound effect which the wider social and organisational context has on practice. This is an ambitious endeavour but it is necessary. Too often, these connections are not made in academic and professional literature. As a result, there is a feeling of unreality. Prescriptions and exhortations which are not based on an appreciation of the contexts within which social workers function are largely futile.

Generally, social work is a reactive activity – that is, it is fundamentally a response to the difficulties which individuals, families and groups have in relating satisfactorily to the societal norms in which they are located. Social work would not exist if there were no tension and conflict between the individual and the wider society (and/or its agent, the state), and is one way of dealing with that disequilibrium. This is amply documented both historically and internationally. For example, the rise of voluntary child care agencies in nineteenth-century Britain, many with religious affiliations, was a response to the 'fall out' from industrialisation. In modern China, social work is emerging (with difficulty) as a consequence of economic and social upheaval which has disrupted established patterns of social support. A 'one child' policy, combined with longer life, has shifted the demographic balance so that there are many fewer children to care for elderly relatives. As mobility of labour has been encouraged, families have become geographically separated with consequent broken marriages and associated problems.

A reactive response to this kind of disequilibrium is contentious and accounts for some of the cynicism of social workers, particularly in the 18 years of Conservative administration. Are practitioners simply papering over cracks when basic social structures and institutions need changing? Are they in fact, consciously or unconsciously, colluding with the status quo of established power? The truth is – yes, in part, but not altogether. A profound moral issue is at stake, concerned with the balance between the relief of suffering at the time it occurs and the achievement of societal improvements which will eventually change the circumstances that gave rise to the suffering. There is validity in both objectives, which are in some ways inseparable.

However, even if social work is justifiably described as a 'reactive' activity and has a legitimate function in the 'here and now', there are ethical dilemmas if it seems that social work is in fact distracting attention from efforts to remedy social or community injustice. It has often been suggested that the 'case based' focus of so much social work strengthens the perception of individual failings, as opposed to societal. This is, of course, illogical. To attend to an individual's problems does not necessarily imply that he or she is to blame for them, anymore than someone who has measles is to be blamed for the epidemic. Thus, even if some degree of tension is inherent between reactive and proactive responses to social ills, social workers are subjected to intolerable pressures if the prevailing conditions in the wider society become inimical to the basic values to which they subscribe.

The *macro*

Two powerful influences upon grass roots social work are well known and well rehearsed in these chapters. First, a strong and protracted attack on the idea of a welfare state was made, shaking the consensus which had been broadly maintained since the Second World War. Behind this lay assumptions concerning the need to reduce the state role in ensuring individuals' welfare; a critique of induced 'dependency' followed from this. Consequently, social work's moral base was challenged. Were social workers part of the problem, rather than the solution? The effects of this on those who practised and taught social work should not be underestimated. Social workers' identification with some of the most vulnerable and least attractive societal members has always given rise to public ambivalence to them, but from the end of the 1970s there was more antagonism. Social work was also swept along in the wider political ideology, notably the attack on public services as overcontrolling and bureaucratic. Since most social workers were in state (albeit local) institutions, the ground was prepared for a further criticism of social work as interfering and autocratic.

Into this child abuse fitted all too well. The report of the Maria Colwell Inquiry (DHSS, 1974) began a process, over more than twenty years, of seemingly continuous criticism of failure by agencies and social work in particular to protect children. Paradoxically, there was little evidence of unwarranted 'interfering'; of removal of children from home. On the contrary, most of the stories were about failure to intervene. Although the Cleveland Inquiry (1988) into sexual abuse did expose some professional weaknesses, it was exaggerated by some to confirm a fantasy of widespread authoritarian behaviour, which chimed with the prevailing political antagonism to social work. Despite the fact that the social work role in child protection differs significantly from most other areas of practice, its public impact coloured attitudes to the profession more generally. The convergence of these themes, anti 'state interference' and anti 'bureaucratic', tuned into a political preference for such 'helping' activity as was admissible to be encouraged within the independent sector, voluntary or for-profit.

Changes in the allocation of resources by central to local government were a second, highly significant, factor affecting social work. Wider considerations about the perceived need to control public expenditure and to achieve its more effective use were the background to the difficulties in achieving the maintenance and growth necessary to the health of social services. This is not the place to debate the financial 'facts'. The relevance to this analysis is the widespread perception in social work that such financial stringency was bound up with dislike of social work's fundamental objectives and indifference to its users. Chapter 1 cites a number of examples of wider social policies that confirmed social workers' fears.

However, some of the political rhetoric which fed these attitudes was not matched in reality. Despite the electoral endorsement of the Conservative agenda over the years, many dissenters from all parties held back the excesses of the New Right. Thus, protection of children against abuse was acknowledged (and better resourced) as a major responsibility for social work; other professionals were increasingly drawn into the process as partners. Less recognised but just as important, great strides were made in this era in acknowledging the rights and needs of persons with learning disabilities (see Chapter 6).

The ugly side of this political climate, however, was the reconfiguration of notions of 'deserving and undeserving' (Forsythe and Jordan, 2002). For social workers, this posed intolerable dilemmas. It echoed the futile attempts of the nineteenth-century Charity Organisation Society to make these distinctions in the dispensing of charity. Thus, contemporary values may stress that children and people with learning disabilities are 'deserving'. However, when we are considering the needs of, say, young homeless people, single mothers or young offenders just how 'deserving' are they? The well-being of such groups in recent years is inextricably bound up with prevailing political attitudes, concerning people's 'deserts'.

What can we learn for the future from this analysis? There are three central issues. First, there is no escaping the profound influence of these large scale political and economic factors upon the focus and nature of the social work task. It is illusory to think that the relationship between the two will ever be uncontentious or comfortable. Second, however, the story of the 18 years of Conservative rule shows that this tension can become unbearable to the point when there is a breakdown in shared values between government and those paid by the state to attend to vulnerable people's needs – even disagreement over who may legitimately be described in these ways. The consequences of this can be seen, for example, in the decision to sever the connection between probation officers and social workers in England and Wales (but not Scotland). Chapter 9 of this book deals only with 'juvenile offenders' (not adult) – a sad acknowledgement of the present situation. Although society, through legislation, is entitled to mandate and support certain areas of social work activity and to an extent determine its priorities at particular times, it cannot replace social work's general moral responsibility to all those whose needs and problems may be susceptible to social work intervention.

Third, the implications of such an argument are far reaching. Ironically, they work against a notion of an all-embracing welfare state, if by that we mean one in which social services are predominantly provided or funded by the state. Such an arrangement makes it virtually impossible for alternative views of priorities to flourish, unless the state itself acknowledges that a plurality of perspectives should be welcomed and funded accordingly. There has been some such acknowledgement – it has not been uncommon for central or local government to fund groups one of whose primary purposes was to lobby government for change, thus introducing an element of formalised conflict deemed beneficial to the processes of democratic government. (However, as argued in Chapter 4, there may now be less scope for this.) This depends on the willingness of particular administrations to do business in this way. It is particularly vulnerable to breakdown when real or politically contrived indignation against certain unpopular or 'undeserving' groups is heightened, or certain users or agencies are not in favour yet should claim a share of national resources. Political administrations also vary in their toleration of a 'messy' voluntary sector where a thousand flowers bloom, wither and reseed in different places (see Chapter 4).

Thus, to uphold a definition of the social work enterprise which is not wholly state-controlled, there must be alternative sources of funding. This is well accepted by large charities such as Barnados and Age Concern, many of which have a goal to raise at least half of their income from other sources. It is therefore a matter of concern that the financial position of the major 'service' charities, including long established childrens' organisations, now, in the new millennium, is so precarious. This does not reflect ideological resistance to them in 'new' Labour; on the contrary, the importance of their contribution is stressed. Nonetheless, for reasons too complex to analyse here, they are currently having difficulty in achieving local partnerships which would encourage diversity in provision. It is even more difficult for small local agencies to obtain funding independent of government. Yet these are the very initiatives in which social workers may be valuably located and which offer an opportunity to redress the political preoccupations of a particular time.

The role of the 'for-profit' independent sector in ensuring that services are provided for those whom some deem 'undeserving' is also problematic, even though its value in less controversial service areas such as home care is increasingly accepted. Most of those whom social workers see, or fear will be, neglected are minority groups of marginalised people who are not profitable unless supported by the state or by relatively affluent users who effectively subsidise them. Both voluntary and 'for profit' agencies can and do 'rob Peter to pay Paul', providing services to unpopular groups on the back of more general provision.

How good is social work's record of identifying and working with marginalised groups? Throughout its history social work has shown that such a moral drive is at least part of many individuals' and agencies' motivation, although other motives may cloud the picture. The impetus to reduce suffering, and sometimes to redress inequality, has been a powerful force. Embarrassment and cynicism about the desire to 'do good' is no more realistic than denial of other less worthy motives or of failure to empathise sufficiently with particular groups. Social workers are products of their time and place; they will not always see clearly current and emerging problems at the interface between individuals, groups and society. They will have, as everyone else, their limitations and prejudices. Furthermore, as individuals, there is only so much that workers can 'take on' emotionally. However, they are in a unique position to see at first hand the predicaments and difficulties of many vulnerable groups.

A contemporary example of these thorny issues concerns the position of ethnic and racial minorities in modern Britain. As identified in Chapter 1, to those who lived through social work in the 1980s, there was a certain irony in the heated debates in 1999, engendered by the term 'institutionalised racism' in the report of the Stephen Lawrence Inquiry (MacPherson, 1999). The 1980s were characterised by intense discussion and much anger within social work on these matters. It was accepted that the profession had not grasped the stark facts of racial and ethnic disadvantage and inequality and that neither policy nor practice had adequately addressed these problems. However, despite a stream of allegations of 'political correctness' from the political Right and some harmful applications of the message, social work was in this instance 'ahead of the game'; the agonies of the Metropolitan Police force in the late 1990s clearly mirror those of social work in earlier years.

My argument, then, is that social work should occupy a key position (among others) in identifying and empathising with vulnerable and disadvantaged individuals and groups. Such people cannot depend solely on the political definitions and preoccupations of the moment. However, the nature of the interaction between the state and social work and the extent to which it is predominantly positive or negative, is critical to social work's effectiveness as an occupational entity, and even of its survival.

In reaching that conclusion, one must consider the depressing failure of social work to develop an effective voice through its professional organisation, the British Association of Social Workers. There are complex reasons for this. The lesson, however, to be learned is that confidence in the importance of a relatively new enterprise, as social work is, and in the specialist skills needed to pursue its objectives, must be accompanied by the emergence of influential professional groupings that can counter the excesses or distortions of politicians and the media, which feed, and feed on, the ugly side of popular opinion. The fact that such groupings can be, and sometimes are, used in a narrow, self-interested way does not invalidate their role in bringing together those with a more altruistic motivation and commitment to improved services.

The 'new' Labour administration has been twice elected with a strong mandate for widespread change in fields of direct concern to social work. It is a difficult time to appraise its longer-term impact on social work – one can only, as it were, 'capture the moment' in all its complexities and ambiguities. However, this administration has shown a determination to make changes to improve services and care, highlighting the extent of past state negligence in the spheres of social welfare; two examples are striking but there are many more.

The first concerns the Conservative failure to insist on the regulation of private domiciliary care agencies, despite repeated pleas. Surprisingly, the Conservative government was not hit by major scandals of abuse or exploitation by staff in private agencies for whom it was not even a requirement to take up references. Political arguments at the time against regulation of 'small businesses' were unsustainable in the face of the increasing and vulnerable population served by such agencies. A second example concerns school exclusion and absenteeism of 'looked after children'. The fact that a high proportion of school-age children in this group were not attending school was known for years. In this respect, criticism justly falls on local authorities that were ineffective in addressing the issue. There was an overarching failure by government to ensure that the basic needs or rights of such children were upheld by both education and social services departments. 'New' Labour has set about rectifying this with energy.

These matters, along with many others, are now being seriously tackled with a sense of 'grip' and purpose which is heartening. There are also many new initiatives, with funding attached; most, perhaps all, are welcome in principle. The times are reminiscent of the Labour administration of the 1960s, when the social science world was abuzz with Home Office initiatives for Educational Priority Areas and Community Development Projects (see, e.g., Halsey, 1972; Hatch and Sherrott, 1973). In the twenty-first century, we have Education Action Zones, Health Action Zones, Sure Start, Better Government for Older People and many others, most of which connect with policy development to challenge social exclusion (see Chapter 1 for a more critical perspective on this). It would be perverse to be grudging about these when we have lamented inaction and indifference for disadvantaged groups for so long, although it is too early to pronounce on their effectiveness. However, as the years of the Blair administration roll on, there is a danger of 'project fatigue' and of a flood tide of bureaucracy associated with them. Some of this bureaucracy is justifiable in terms of accountability for public funds, of 'joined-up thinking' and of evaluation of outputs. But there may come a point – and some think it has been reached already – when the pursuit of legitimate subsidiary goals drowns imagination and initiative.

There is one crucial issue which will determine how these initiatives will be judged. This concerns 'time lags' in the experiences and perceptions of hard pressed workers across different agencies, including social services. Present developments are sited in a limited number of localities, chosen on criteria of social disadvantage and from competitive tenders. While this method has much to recommend it, it must follow that their impact on workers' mood and morale nationally will be variable. Many social workers feel left out of the prize-givings. Perhaps they do not work in the localities attracting these resources; perhaps their jobs do not fit the definitions of participants; perhaps their agencies are perceived as less attractive to host the activities. Many statutory social workers feel bowed down by their duties to 'maintain the system' and have little opportunity to engage in the excitement of new work, which, even if exhausting, creates its own energy.

Government activity, however, is by no means limited to projects of the kind discussed above. The White Paper *Modernising Social Services* (DoH, 1998a), and the demanding standards set by the policy document *Quality Protects* for the child welfare services (DoH, 1998b) have received a surprising degree of professional acceptance. There is evidence of a good deal of 'ministerial listening' to professional voices as well as to the wider critique of the social services.

Social services departments are, of course, involved in the debate about the nature of the relationship between central and local government alongside the accusations of 'over centralising' tendencies in the present administration. This is contentious in terms of policy generally, but even those committed to the checks and balances in the present structure of power must admit that the variability in local government provision has in some areas and some aspects of service, gone well beyond the limit, reaching serious 'territorial injustice', as it has been called. This is certainly true of social services departments. The White Paper (DoH, 1998a) lays great emphasis on these issues and on the creation of 'fairer, more consistent services for all'. On the evidence available, it is clear that radical action is necessary.

Underlying these necessary preoccupations, there remains the critical question: how far will this government's approach sit comfortably with the ideals of social work? To most of us, the jury is still out. Only the most cynical would doubt there has been a commitment to challenge social exclusion in a good many spheres of direct relevance to social work. After a nervous start, much affected by a determination not to be seen as economically 'imprudent' or socially 'soft', 'new' Labour, through, for example, taxation, employment and social security policies, is effecting some redistribution by stealth. Of particular interest (and perhaps too little understood by social workers), are the 'New Deal' employment policies which may offer real opportunities to those who have been left out of the job market for many years. However, there is a danger that some within such marginalised groups (lone parents, young unskilled men and women, disabled people, etc.), who do not, or cannot, avail themselves of the support offered may in turn be relegated to the 'undeserving' categories that were earlier described. Through deductions from benefits for 'non compliance', the state creates another category of the socially excluded, whose poverty must be of central concern to social work. Vigilance, rather than weary scepticism, should be the response of social work to 'new' Labour.

The *mezzo*

It is unnecessary to reiterate the detailed discussions in the preceding chapters of the impact on practice of the 'rise of managerialism' and of procedurally driven mechanisms for accountability (see Chapter 2 in particular). Indeed, this book is in part intended to show how it may be possible to rebalance social work within the constraints of such structures. The question now is – what have we learnt for the future? One major theme concerns bureaucracy.

The uses and abuses of bureaucracy

During the 1970s, the radical critique of the oppressive and negative aspects of bureaucracy chimed well with the individualistic attitudes of many social workers, who also distrusted hierarchy. There was a 'literature of dysfunction' about welfare bureaucracies (see, e.g., Heraud, 1970) which was regularly fed to social work students. Although the founding father of bureaucracy, Weber (1947), presented a more dispassionate view of the subject, many workers thought the term inherently pejorative. This is not to deny the validity of many of the criticisms. Insensitivity to the individual, delays, decision making 'up the line' and away from users, excessive 'paper work', all this and much more, remain a source of anger and frustration for social workers.

However, in reality most social workers will work within the context of large 'welfare bureaucracies' (Billis, 1984). Although some practitioners accept this, it often appears to be viewed as necessarily inimical to good practice. Indeed, as has been observed, there is a profound sense of social workers' alienation from 'management', notably in social services departments. Yet rather than rail against bureaucracy it is time for social workers to think about its proper purposes.

One, in particular, stands out as important, and might be described as 'organised equity'. Notions of 'fairness' are inherent in the concept of bureaucracy, which rejects idiosyncratic, unaccountable decision making. What social worker would really want sole power over the allocation of resources for individual users? I first became interested in this subject 30 years ago when I was a social work adviser to the (then) Supplementary Benefits Commission, lodged in the (then) Department of Health and Social Security (Stevenson, 1972). I became acutely conscious of the tension between two different concepts of fairness or social justice. Drawing on the work of the theologian Tillich (1960), I used the terms 'proportional' and 'creative' justice to distinguish between them. (These have, of course, been explored more generally in moral philosophy.)

The attempt to deliver proportional justice represents the best of bureaucracy. To offer the same to people with the same needs or difficulties is a principle widely held in many societal spheres. In terms of state welfare provision it is perceived as fundamental. It is impossible to imagine voluntary or statutory social services organisations without any formalised allocation systems, even though these give rise to much heart searching and tensions between those with overall responsibility for resources and those who are arguing for individuals. More generally, the word 'rationing' often raises hackles. Yet it is idle to imagine that the world we inhabit will ever have sufficient resources to meet unlimited demand.

There are two elements in this rationing which determine whether it is tolerable to field social workers. The first is whether shortage of resources has reached a point when it makes a mockery of the stated principles of the service. When this leads to hypocrisy in political 'speak' about what should be but is not in fact available, it is hard for staff at the sharp end to bear. They are confronted daily with the reality of people's pain. Faced by the suffering and distress of an 85-year-old woman who needs basic services *now* or a carer who desperately needs a break *now,* talk of waiting lists may seem insulting. The second key element in rationing concerns the use of 'eligibility criteria', which are perceived to be fair by all concerned.

When one moves into service delivery, it becomes more difficult to decide when people's needs and difficulties are the same as others, even when there is a legislative framework to work within. What factors should be taken into account? A current, problematic example concerns provision of personal, domiciliary care to older people. Should the existence of a middle-aged woman 'carer', at home or nearby, make a difference to the allocation of resources to a particular case? The question raises issues of principle concerning the role of women as carers, but also the relevance of specific factors in a particular situation.

It is at this point that 'creative' justice comes into play. The moral argument for this rests on the special needs and circumstances of particular individuals. Justice can only be done when these factors are taken into account. Does the carer want to care for her elderly relative? Do we accept this as valid even if she is manifestly exhausted? Do we take into account a history of an ambivalent relationship between the relative and carer? No bureaucratic criteria for eligibility will be able to deal with these refinements.

To a greater or lesser extent then, there is an inevitable tension in which bureaucracy symbolises the ideal of proportional justice and social work of personalised responses in which the exercise of discretion is critical. This is not to suggest that individuals, whether managers who control resources or social workers, see only one or the other. For this tension to be healthy and constructive, each needs some appreciation of each other's preoccupations. However, for social workers, the position may be intolerable when they perceive that the abstract rules (say of eligibility) are so far divorced from the reality of individuals' lives as to create injustice rather than justice. The tension between managers and practitioners can become unbearable and destructive. In the forthcoming decades, it is vital to work analytically and imaginatively on the interface and interactions between these two elements of social justice. Only in that way will social work achieve its proper place and influence within mainstream social services.

Chapter 8 discussed the dominance of 'procedures' over reflective practice in recent child welfare practice. This illustrates a different but related aspect of bureaucratic and professional interaction and conflict which is of such significance to social work. Again, it is a matter of balance rather than of absolutes. 'Procedures' in child protection are a legitimate method of achieving regularity in standards and thus ensuring 'organised equity' in an area of the work highly dependent on individual efficiency and effectiveness. To be explicit about the rules which need to be followed establishes a framework for audit. Sadly, adherence to procedures has been most often (and sometimes only) audited systematically when tragedy has struck – through the mechanism of child deaths or external inspection. This is increasingly recognised to have serious limitations.

While systems to ensure organisational accountability are always necessary, the development of detailed procedures was partly driven by justified anxiety about child abuse. Hence, it became associated in practitioners' minds with negative aspects of authority, processes which enable 'them up there' to blame 'them down there'. Furthermore, they were not adequately balanced by the notion of individual professional responsibility, defined by, and derived from, norms of good practice, set outside the employing organisations. Yet few social workers in child protection would want to dispense with the procedures in such a complex and risk-laden area of work. Rather, they may be seen as a necessary minimum for competent practice, on which to base the subtler framework of reflective practice. At all points in the application of procedures, judgements and skill have to be exercised as to the appropriateness of their use.

Legislation and associated guidance sets the parameters of statutory work. Similarly, inexperienced social workers will take colour from others and from the ethos of the organisation. In recent years, however, there has been a lack of open challenge to authority in relation to the interpretation of current policy and practice, a tendency to go with the flow, albeit often with a deep sense of unease. The present climate of frantic activity at all levels, and consequent exhaustion, makes such debates rare, with an ensuing miserable downward spiral in relationships within the organisation. In work as sensitive, contentious and complex as this, effective intervention is compromised if those with responsibility at field levels are either unconvinced of the merits of the policies they are expected to implement or do not properly understand them. Outward conformity through insecurity, fear, confusion or fatigue masks poor practice (see Chapter 3). Of topical relevance to this crucial issue is the way government initiatives are interpreted and conveyed by senior managers. *Modernising Social Services* (DoH, 1998a) as well as *Quality Protects* (DoH, 1998b) are initiatives illustrating especially well the interaction between the 'three levels' that are the focus of this book. They will fail if those who develop local policies and strategies in response to government requirements do not work well with those implementing them.

Specialisation and location

The preceding discussion, concerning the position of social work within a bureaucracy, attempts to clarify and analyse an area of conflict and tension which has been widely experienced and discussed at all levels in social service organisations. Much less prominent in recent years has been the 'generic/specialisation' argument which raged before and after the reorganisation of 1970 (Seebohm Report, 1968), when new social services departments were created with the intention of providing integrated services for families. With certain important exceptions, statutory social work services, after 1970, were offered by one unified department within local government.

This reorganisation reflected a number of more general trends. In the same year, the British Association of Social Workers was formed from a number of separate associations. During the 1960s, there were many moves towards 'generic' education for social workers, shifting away from training based on the role and function of certain groups (e.g., child care, psychiatric and medical social work). The enthusiasm of British 'movers and shakers' to identify a common basis for social work was considerable and the creation of unified departments was an important element in this. However, the origins of many difficulties facing us today can be seen in those formative years. This is not to deny the force of the 'pro-generic' arguments, both in terms of an analysis of the social work task and of the profound importance of a holistic approach to people's problems. Rather, it was the failure to foresee and deal with adequately the implications of such radical change that led us to the present confused situation.

A serious flaw in post Seebohm social work has been confusion about genericism and specialisation which has never been resolved. The preparation and training before and after 1970 of staff for existing organisational changes were totally inadequate. Existing staff were placed in so called 'generic' teams, lacking the knowledge, confidence, skills (and sometimes the will) to adopt new roles in relation to unfamiliar client groups (see Satyamurti, 1981). The long-term consequences of this, too complex to be analysed here, are still with us. The essence of the generic ideal, the idea of a common base from which specialisation could be developed, was never adequately conceptualised or operationally realised. Difficulties were blamed on 'going generic' and the ideal soon became tarnished, falling into disrepute almost by default. My own efforts to suggest models of specialisation consistent with a common base fell on stony ground (Stevenson, 1981).

These issues remain as important today as 20 years ago. How do we slice the cake of daily work while keeping its overall shape and cohesion? I suggested in 1981 that there were three facets to specialisation:

- the notion of expertise, that is, specialist knowledge needed for particular kinds of work;
- the need to organise work into manageable sections;
- the importance of considering boundaries and connections, within and between agencies, to avoid fragmentation of client need and service provision.

These remain key issues for social work today.

Upon the notion of expertise, it can be argued, the future of social work as a profession must rest. This is pertinent to education and to practice. We now see government acceptance of the need for advanced qualifications, so hotly resisted by unions in the 1980s, when approved social worker qualifications in mental health were forced through. After protracted delays, underpinned by the Conservative administration's hostility to the recognition of social work as a profession, we have at last seen the emergence of post-qualifying courses in child welfare. There is an urgent need to ensure parity of esteem for the other main areas of social work practice, most of all because it signals the right of all users to equally skilled practice. However, this is bound up with the future of social work in health care fields, on which we comment later. Similarly, the organisation of work has preoccupied managers throughout the period under review. Indeed, seemingly endless structural reorganisation has, on occasions, become the problem rather than the solution, partly because work cannot be divided up purely on 'logical' grounds which do not take account of the work satisfactions and dissatisfactions of staff.

With the passage of time, the importance of boundaries and connections has become ever clearer and is now high on the agenda for change. In addition to the issue of their location in health care, a number of local authorities have brought together education and social services and others are planning to do so. With these new configurations, the 'Seebohm dream' has finally been rejected. There are obvious arguments for attempting integration of childrens' services within local government but no one should imagine for one moment that this will resolve the other dilemmas of 'working together' in child welfare, in which, for example, health services for children play such a critical part. Nor can one at present foresee whether these new partners, education and social services, will pay respect to, and achieve a proper balance between, the responsibilities and needs of each.

In the field of child protection specifically, the importance of collaborative working between a range of agencies has long been stressed and its weaknesses exposed in numerous inquiries. The most recent of these is the public inquiry into the death of Victoria Climbié (Laming, 2003). There are many recommendations within this report that call for improvements in multi-agency working, as well as improved processes within each individual agency. However, Laming rejected the idea of establishing a separate national child protection agency, in the awareness that 'it is not possible to separate the protection of children from wider support for families' (Laming, 2003: para. 1.30, p. 61). He therefore stressed the need for close connections between services for child protection and the more widely focussed services for children in need. Furthermore, although 'risk prevention' is of pressing importance on agency agendas, whether regarding dangerous offenders, vulnerable adults or children, there is an underlying acknowledgement, epitomised in the various government initiatives, that 'joined-up thinking' between agencies is essential for successful projects generally. This raises vital questions for the definition of the social work role.

A second flaw in the operation of social services departments concerned size and complexity, which exacerbated the tensions surrounding professionals located within bureaucracies. While there were attractions in the increased power, status and resources which the social services departments had within local authorities, levels of managerial competence were highly variable. Frantic sorties into the world of business studies were not always helpful. The rise of 'managerialism' (documented in Chapter 2) was in part due to the challenge of this unwieldy new structure.

Third, and lastly, in this consideration of the consequences of the 1970 reorganisation, there is the matter of 'locations' from which social workers should operate. At the time of the Seebohm reforms, the case for a social welfare organisation, with a separate identity from other powerful professions and structures seemed strong. Struggling to establish themselves as a profession, with a distinct 'generic identity', there was an understandable resistance among social workers to work in locations in which subservience to other professions was difficult to avoid. Even within local government, a successful war was waged to exclude Medical Officers of Health from appointment as the new directors of social services and at first, social work qualifications for such new appointments were required.

Difficult issues were raised in hospitals, where, from 1974, social workers became employees of the local authority, even though their location was unchanged. As time unfolded, hospital social work was weakened by the lack of knowledge and commitment among managers in social services departments of the health-related social work role. Not surprisingly, medical staff had many complaints about this situation. The decreasing length of stay for most patients in hospital further complicated decisions about the proper location for social workers; hospital discharge arrangements were seen as an overwhelming priority – and remain so.

Now, the creation of Primary Care Trusts and, within them, integrated Primary Health Care Teams (DoH, 1997), raises similar questions regarding the location and employment of health care social workers. Over the years, there have been many experiments with social workers in general practice, at the heart of which are issues of power and influence. One would hope that, moving on from 1970, the assumption of medical *dominance*, of ultimate authority in all decisions, would now be less crude. There is a need to clarify in which areas such authority is essential and in which the professional judgement of others is accepted. As we have seen, however, social workers' status (for both good and bad reasons) remains problematic. We need to be wary about creating new situations in which social workers lack an organisational framework confirming their identity. In this connection, the question of who defines the social work task and how it is defined (say within a Primary Care Team) is critical. It is *reasonable* that the setting should, to an extent, determine the work to be done. It is *unreasonable* that social workers should be subject solely to the wishes of team leaders from other professions.

Although the above discussion has focused on the relationship between health professions and social work, the points being made have wider applicability. Only when social work is strong enough in its sense of professional identity and in the respect it commands can it be secure in agencies led and controlled by other professional groupings. The same analysis would apply, for example, to the role of education social workers, an area in which British social work has been very uneasy. In the present context, it is imperative that the distinction between location and the employer is considered in a more sophisticated way than during the 1970 reorganisation.

The *micro*

The preceding analysis, condensed as it is, shows clearly how the political and organisational context has consumed so much energy in recent years. We should not underestimate the extent to which structural upheavals have created tension and exhaustion amongst social workers and their managers. The cumulative effects of this have been very grave, bearing in mind that they coincided with a period of very rapid expansion in the numbers of social workers recruited and trained, standing on insecure professional foundations. We have seen a dramatic fall in those applying for social work training. This is surely in no small measure due to the effects of the political and organisational pressures which we have earlier described. Figures published in late 2002 (*The Guardian*, 15 October 2002) give a clear indication of these difficulties. During 1995–2001, there was a 59% drop in the number of students applying to take the diploma in social work. Although this downward trend may have been reversed, 'new' Labour has been very slow in addressing the implications of these trends. However, nationally sponsored advertisements and more prominence given to the issue by ministers in public statements suggest that there is now a greater sense of urgency. These difficulties have compounded an already dispiriting situation, since those doing the daily work usually do so in the context of unfilled posts in their teams which places an even greater burden upon them at a time when demands for improved practice have never been higher. If, therefore, we can chart a path for the future of social work, it seems imperative to identify the justification for its existence and the conditions necessary for its survival as an activity, the essence of which is to be found in direct interaction with people who need support or protection.

Whatever the contemporary difficulties, whatever the settings with which social work is best located, can anyone seriously envisage a society, complex and sophisticated, in which something like social work will not be needed? The debate must continue, not only about context but also about its proper roles and tasks, between 'oiling the wheels' and radical or far-reaching 'preventative' activity. The profession does not need to stand in one place; there is room for diversity between settings and individuals. Even the name 'social work' is not sacrosanct, although the alternatives need sceptical scrutiny to see if they have sinister intent and what message they convey about the activity. (See, e.g., the intention behind the decision that qualifying training for the Probation Service should no longer be linked directly to social work.)

At present, the debate is sharpened by doubts about the place of social work in relation to those aspects of social care which are closely allied to health care. The newly emerging Primary Care Trusts may be seen as an alternative employer. The more serious issue, however, is whether the skills of social work are to be valued as are those of health workers or whether the continuing difficulties and uncertainties about their role has undermined their credibility as an important element in social compassion and social justice.

There appear to be three abiding characteristics in any activity which can be called social work. First, as I have already suggested, there is a moral assumption; that it is essential to seek to relieve the suffering and tensions which occur between individuals, groups and the society in which they live. (The drive to reduce inequality between citizens is a necessary consequence of this moral imperative, although its nature and how it is to be achieved remains contentious.) Second, social work is committed to the exercise of 'creative justice', in which individuals' needs and rights are of crucial importance even within a wider framework of 'proportional justice'. This view challenges some aspects of policy. For example, the notion of a 'penal tariff' for juvenile offenders, although it may set broad guidelines, is morally unacceptable if particular individual circumstances cannot officially be taken into account. (This issue is explored in more detail in Chapter 9.)

Third, because social work is focused upon the disequilibrium between its clients and the wider society, its activities must involve movement between the two. The now neglected Barclay Report (1982) grappled with the distinction between 'counselling', in which the term 'social casework' was abandoned and 'social care planning'. Unfortunately, the report was unbalanced in its analysis, leaving an impression that the care planning role was of more significance than counselling. Furthermore, the report did not acknowledge the insep-arability of the two elements in daily social work practice.

There are many situations in which interventions with a 'coun-selling' component are valuable and appropriate. The difficulty for social workers is that the need for such practice skills has been minimised and sometimes denied. 'Counselling' is being perceived as a separate activity. This is misguided and dangerous; unless users' and carers' feelings and views are taken into account, the outcomes will be unsatisfactory. It is in community care of old people that the social care management aspects of the social work role become strikingly dominant to the neglect of 'counselling' (as explored in Chapter 7). For example, older people who are being abused in their own homes by relatives, or who, living alone, are struggling to decide on moving to residential care, may experience deep feelings of anger, grief, fear and, often, profound ambivalence. It is of the utmost importance to their peace of mind that they have an opportunity to explore these emotions. Yet all too often the impression given is of mechanistic, 'system bound' activity. While this approach has been less marked in some other fields of work, it is still a source of grave concern, as we have seen in earlier chapters. It is hard to avoid the conclusion that old people attract less interest as individuals with a full range of human needs and feelings than others (Stevenson, 1989).

Skills (and the associated knowledge) in understanding and relat-ing successfully to a person's feelings and taking these into account in her/his overall welfare are therefore an essential prerequisite of

social work practice (see Seden, 1999). However, unlike most coun-
sellors, social workers are also required to plan and work with, or
sometimes for, individuals in a way which also takes into account
external available or unavailable resources. This, in turn, needs
knowledge and understanding of those resources, be they human or
material. Thus, social workers stand between the person and the
complex environment affecting them; processes of change involve
both, to a greater or lesser degree, according to the circumstances.

An employing agency that does not value both elements of the role
will distort and ultimately destroy the profession. A topical example
concerns the so-called 'Level 3' social worker in local government,
qualified and experienced, who, having reached the top of the salary
scale must move into a managerial role to progress their career and
increase their status. A debate is now opening up in some authorities
about a 'Level 4' worker who would be acknowledged as having specialist expertise in particular fields, backed by an advanced qualification. Such a practitioner could play a key role in consultancy and
inter-agency activity. In child protection, mental health and youth
justice – and very probably in the protection of vulnerable adults –
the need to increase the confidence of the judicial system in the
capacity of social workers to assess and intervene effectively is
pressing.

The essence of progress lies in the improved exercise of discretion
and of judgement in individual situations, necessitating a better
understanding of the person and of her/his context, as the practice
scenarios in this book demonstrate. Practice has to begin with understanding the meaning of the events in which the social worker is asked
to intervene. It is widely recognised that too many so-called 'assessments' describe rather than analyse. This represents a formidable
challenge to those with responsibility for education and staff development, for it inevitably introduces the need for theory-for-
understanding. Drury-Hudson (1999) has tracked the responses of
Australian students to 'theory', from 'I hate theory. I'm not very big
on theory', to 'Theory gives a structure to what you are doing. It
helps you to look at how to deal with things' (pp. 153–54). These
responses also illustrate the confusion around the very concept of
'theory'. As Pilalis (1986) has shown, there are different levels and
types of theory for social work as well as contrasting explanations of
behaviour from which various strategies for intervention are derived.

A neglected aspect of theory concerns the links between past experience and present feelings and behaviour. However controversial the

particular theory, however difficult it may be to *prove* empirically the connections between past and present, it flies in the face of personal and professional experience, and of much sound research, not to make these links. Yet repeatedly, contemporary social work records do not show this awareness, which serves to deny continuities in human experience. Such approaches to understanding the individual also have to be balanced with an analysis of the impact of contemporary influences, forces and events. This type of theory, whether of family systems or of *macro* economic factors, plays a part in an effective assessment of need, and hence, of service provision. It is difficult intellectually for teacher or learner to construct the best ways of using theory for effective practice. Not to develop along these lines, in my view, would mark the end of social work's claim to professional status, and would be an admission of failure to grasp adequately the complexities of the human problems with which social workers are daily confronted. We can encourage debate about the better use of theory and the better exercise of discretion and judgements. Much responsibility for this lies with educational institutions which have, in some crucial ways, failed social work. For these to be successful in achieving more effective and imaginative practice, there has to be a greater agency awareness of social work's proper contribution and a more hospitable environment provided within which it can flourish, especially in opportunities for professional support and development.

Social workers carry very heavy emotional loads, in dealing with some of the most distressed, disturbed and vulnerable members of society (as explored in Chapter 3). In particular, intense conflicts between family members and between the needs and rights of opposing interests bear heavily on practitioners working with *all* user groups. Yet although 'counselling' (*sic.*) may be offered to workers, where an event has been particularly traumatic, there is little ongoing recognition and use of the pain and tension which many situations create in workers (Stevenson, 1992). To reflect on these experiences (not necessarily to be counselled about them) is a valuable component in professional enrichment. It is, to use the old clichés, 'growth through pain' rather than 'burn out'. To foster professional development as well as to ensure bureaucratic competence, it will be necessary to establish suitable arrangements for supervision, consultation and training and to create an atmosphere in which research is utilised and encouraged.

The observations above argue strongly for the inherent importance of the concept of social work in a modern society. Although

I have not insisted on the continuing use of the term social work, recent suggestions from the Institute of Public Policy Research for the fundamental reform of the social care workforce raise more far reaching and contentious possibilities. It 'envisages the creation of a new cadre of social care professionals who will practice a combination of social work, nursing, therapy and teaching. This would mean "social work as we currently know it will cease to exist"' (*The Guardian*, 15 October 2002). Whatever the 'blue skies' merits of such ideas, the implications for education and training of such a new workforce are, frankly, impossible at present to contemplate, especially when the urgency to reform social work education is acknowledged and the impetus to do so is there. However, whatever the next fifty years brings, it would, in my view, be calamitous if we lost the heart of the social work enterprise in a merged social care workforce.

Conclusion

In this chapter it is argued that social work is an essential element in modern industrialised societies. Paradoxically, as it becomes accepted as necessary (rather than peripheral) by the state, moral dilemmas become more acute. Who does it serve, the state or the individual? What governs its values and priorities? There is a necessary tension and conflict in these questions that must be addressed if social work is to achieve a professional identity not totally dominated by external considerations or by the organisational context in which it functions.

I have stressed that social work is an important ingredient in the implementation of social justice because it should, by definition, challenge social exclusion seeking to protect the vulnerable, and it is uniquely placed to pay attention to the element of creative justice in a fair society. There is evidence of a preoccupation with systems and procedures which has not led to effective management, in that it has created a working environment which social workers experience as incongruent with and unsupportive of professional activity. However, social workers must *earn* respect as professionals. Their development should rest upon the better understanding of the relationship between values, knowledge and skills. This has wide implications for 'life long' education and training and for the intelligent utilisation of research. For practice, three key issues must be addressed:

- First, an improved understanding about the social worker's role in holistic assessment and intervention.

- Second, contemporary and flexible approach to the generic/ specialist debate, both in organisational and professional terms.
- Third, a sophisticated appreciation of the nature of evidence, quantitative and qualitative, in evaluating effectiveness.

As this book has so amply demonstrated, the three levels of activity are equally important factors in moving towards the professional improvement so urgently needed. It is counter productive to minimise the impact of national political trends, or of the organisational context, for practice. Yet the third force – a truly independent professional voice – is essential to keep a better balance. We wait to see whether the General Social Care Council (DoH, 1998a) will facilitate or impede the distinctive contribution which social work can make.

Bibliography

Abbott, A. (1988) *The System of Professions*, Chicago, University of Chicago Press.

Adams, R. (1996) *Social Work and Empowerment*, Basingstoke, Macmillan.

Ahmad, A. (1990) *Practice with Care*, London, Race Equality Unit.

Ainsworth, M. D. S., Blehar, M. C., Waters, E. and Wall, S. (1978) *Patterns of Attachment*, Hillsdale, NJ, Erlbaum.

Aldgate, J. and Tunstill, J. (1995) *Making Sense of Section 17*, London, HMSO.

Aldridge, M. (1994) *Making Social Work News*, London, Routledge.

Alibhai-Brown, Y. (1998) *Caring for Ethnic Minority Elders: A Guide*, London, Age Concern.

Alibhai-Brown, Y. (2000) 'Muddled Leaders and the Future of British National Identity', *Political Quarterly*, 71, 1, 26–31.

Allsopp, M. (1995) *Social Workers' Perceptions of Risk in Child Protection*, ESRC Research Project Discussion Paper, Nottingham, University of Nottingham.

Althusser, L. A. (1971) *Lenin and Philosophy and Other Essays*, London, New Left Books.

Amin, A. (ed.) (1994) *Post-Fordism: A Reader*, Oxford, Blackwell.

Amin, K. and Oppenheim, C. (1992) *Poverty in Black and White: Deprivation and Ethnic Minorities*, London, Child Poverty Action Group.

Anderson, J. and Brady, P. (2002) 'Increasing the depth of field: the Voluntary Sector Pathway', *Social Work Education*, 21, 2, 233–245.

Asante, S. (1997) *When Spider Webs Unite: Challenging Articles and Essays on Community, Diversity and Inclusion*, Toronto, Inclusion Press.

Ashworth, A. (1998) *The Criminal Process: An Evaluative Study*, 2nd edn, Oxford, Oxford University Press.

Aspis, S. (1997) 'Self-advocacy for People with Learning Difficulties: Does it Have a Future?', *Disability and Society*, 12, 647–654.

Atkinson, D. and Williams, F. (eds) (1990) *'Know Me As I Am': An Anthology of Prose, Poetry and Art by People with Learning Difficulties*, London, Hodder & Stoughton.

Audit Commission (2000) *The Way to Go Home – Rehabilitation and Remedial Services for Older People*, London, Stationery Office.

Audit Commission/The National Assembly for Wales and Social Services Inspectorate (2000) *People Need People*, Abingdon, Audit Commission.

Axline, V. (1964) *Dibs: In Search of Self. Personality Development in Play Therapy*, Harmondsworth, Penguin.

Bailey, R. and Brake, M. (eds) (1975) *Radical Social Work*, London, Edward Arnold.

Baistow, K. (1994/5) 'Liberation and Regulation? Some Paradoxes of Empowerment', *Critical Social Policy*, 14, 3, 34–46.

Baldwin, M. (1996) 'Is Assessment Working? – Policy and Practice in Care Management', *Practice*, 8, 4, 53–59.

Balloch, S., McLean, J. and Fisher, M. (eds) (1999) *Social Services: Working Under Pressure*, Bristol, Policy Press.

Bamford, T. (1989) 'Discretion and Managerialism', in S. Shardlow (ed.) *The Values of Change in Social Work*, London, Routledge, pp. 135–154.

Bamford, T. (1990) *The Future of Social Work*, Basingstoke, Macmillan.

Banks, N. (1994) 'Issues of Attachment, Separation and Identity in Contested Adoptions', in M. Ryburn (ed.) *Contested Adoptions: Research, Law, Policy and Practice*, Aldershot, Gower/Arena, pp. 105–123.

Bano, A., Crosskill, D., Patel, R., Rashman, L. and Shah, R. (1993) *Improving Practice with People with Learning Disabilities*, Antiracist Social Work Education Series, Leeds, Central Council for Education and Training in Social Work.

Barclay, Sir P. (1995) *Inquiry into Income and Wealth, Volume 1*, York, Joseph Rowntree Foundation.

Barclay Report (1980) *Social Workers: their Role and Tasks*, London, National Institute for Social Work/Bedford Square Press.

Barham, P. and Hayward, R. (1991) *From the Mental Patient to the Person*, London, Routledge.

Barnard, H. and Walker, P. (1994) *Strategies for Success. A Self-Help Guide to Strategic Planning for Voluntary Organisations*, London, NCVO Publications.

Barnes, M. and Bowl, R. (2001) *Taking Over the Asylum: Empowerment and Mental Health*, Basingstoke, Palgrave.

Barnes, M., Harrison, S., Mort, M. and Shardlow, P. (1999) *Unequal Partners: User Groups and Community Care*, Bristol, Policy Press.

Barrett, M. and McIntosh, M. (1982) *The Anti-Social Family*, London, Verso.

Bateman, N. (1999) 'The Best Person for the Job', *Community Care*, 10–16 June, 29.

Bates, F. and Pitkeathley, J. (1996) 'Standing Up to be Counted: Campaigning and Voluntary Agencies', in C. Hanvey and T. Philpot (eds) *Sweet Charity: The Role and Workings of Voluntary Organisations*, London, Routledge, pp. 82–92.

Bates, P. (1996) 'Lessons For Life', *Health Service Journal*, 3 October, 28.

Bates, P. (2000) 'Introducing Circles of Friends', *A Life in the Day*, 4, 4, 20–22.

Bates, P. (2001) *A Real Asset: Developing Support Volunteering Opportunities* Manchester, National Development Team.

Bates, P. (ed.) (2002) *A Resource on Social Inclusion, Citizenship and Mental Health*, London, Sainsbury Centre for Mental Health.

Bates, P. and Pidgeon, J. (1990) 'Intervention: Protection or Control?', *Social Work Today*, 21, 18, 18–19.

Batsleer, J. and Paton, R. (1997) 'Managing voluntary organisations in the contract culture Continuity or change?', in Perri 6 and J. Kendall (eds) *The Contract Culture in Public Services: Studies from Britain, Europe and the USA*, Aldershot, Arena, pp. 47–56.

Bauman, Z. (1999) *Globalization: The Human Consequences*, Cambridge, Polity Press.

Baxter, C., Poonia, K., Ward, L. and Nadirshaw, Z. (1990) *Double Discrimination: Issues and Services for People with Learning Difficulties from Black and Ethnic Minority Communities*, London, The King's Fund/Commission for Racial Equality.

Bebbington, A. and Miles, J. (1989) 'The Background of Children who Enter Local Authority Care' *British Journal of Social Work*, 19, 3, 349–369.

Becker, S. (1997) *Responding to Poverty*, London, Longman.

Bee, H. (1992) *The Developing Child*, London, HarperCollins.

Beeman, P., Ducharme, G. and Mount, B. (1989) *One Candle Power: Building Bridges into Community Life for People with Disabilities*, Manchester CT, Communitas Inc.

Begum, N., Hill, M. and Stevens, S. (1994) *Reflections: Views of Black Disabled People on their Lives and Community Care*, Paper 32, 3, London, CCETSW.

Bennett, G., Kingston, P. and Penhale, B. (1997) *Dimensions of Elder Abuse*, Basingstoke, Macmillan.

Bennett, P., Evans, R. and Tattersall, A. (1993) 'Stress and Coping in Social Workers: A Preliminary Investigation', *British Journal of Social Work*, 23, 1, 31–44.

Beresford, P. and Croft, S. (1993) *Citizen Involvement: A Practical Guide for Change*, Basingstoke, BASW/Macmillan.

Beresford, P. and Turner, M. (1997) *It's Our Welfare: Report of the Citizens Commission on the Future of the Welfare State*, London, National Institute of Social Work.

Beresford, P., Green, D., Lister, R. and Woodard, K. (1999) *Poverty First Hand: Poor People Speak for Themselves*, London, Child Poverty Action Group.

Beveridge, W. (1942) *Social Insurance and Allied Services*, Cmnd. 6404, London, HMSO.

Beveridge, W. (1948) *Voluntary Action: A Report on Methods of Social Advance*, London, Allen & Unwin.

Biggs, S., Phillipson, C. and Kingston, P. (1995) *Elder Abuse in Perspective*, Buckingham, Open University Press.

Billis, D. (1984) *Welfare Bureaucracies*, London, Heninemann.

Bilson, A. and Ross, S. (1999) *Social Work Management and Practice: Systemic Principles*, 2nd edn, London, Jessica Kingsley.

Birch, D. and Leng, R. (2000) Blackstone's Guide to the Youth Justice and Criminal Evidence Act 1999, London, Blackstone Press.

Blair, T. (1998) *The Third Way: New Politics for the New Century*, Fabian Pamphlet 588, London, Fabian Society.

Blair, T. (2000) *Transforming the Welfare State*, Speech to the Institute for Public Policy Research, London, 7 June.

Blakemore, K. and Boneham, M. (1994) *Age, Race and Ethnicity*, Buckingham, Open University Press.

Blaug, R. (1995) 'Distortion of the Face to Face: Communicative Reason and Social Work Practice', *British Journal of Social Work*, 25, 4, 423–439.

Bonnerjea, L. (1990) *Leaving Care in London*, London, London Boroughs Children's Regional Planning Committee.

Boushel, M., Fawcett, M. and Selwyn, J. (eds) (2000) *Focus on Early Childhood: Principles and Realities*, Oxford, Blackwell Science.

Box, S. (1987) *Recession, Crime and Punishment*, London, Macmillan.

Boyne, G. (2000) 'External Regulation and Best Value in Local Government', *Public Money and Management*, July–September, 7–12.

Brandon, D. (1991) *Innovation Without Change? Consumer Power in Psychiatric Services*, London, Macmillan.

Brandon, D., Brandon, A. and Brandon, T. (1995) *Advocacy: Power to People with Disabilities*, Birmingham, Venture Press.

Bray, M. (1997) *The Child's Voice: Poppies on the Rubbish Heap*, London, Jessica Kingsley.

Braye, S. (2000) 'Participation and Involvement in Social Care: An Overview', in H. Kemshall and R. Littlechild (eds) *User Involvement and Participation in Social Care*, London, Jessica Kingsley, pp. 9–28.

Braye, S. and Preston-Shoot, M. (1993) 'Empowerment and Partnership in Mental Health: Towards a Different Relationship', *Journal of Social Work Practice*, 7, 2, 115–28.

Braye, S. and Preston-Shoot, M. (1995) *Empowering Practice in Social Care*, Buckingham, Open University Press.

British Agencies for Adoption and Fostering (BAAF) (ed.) (1984) *In Touch with Children: A Training Pack*, London, BAAF.

British Association of Social Workers (BASW) (1996) *The Code of Ethics for Social Work*, Birmingham, BASW.

Brody, S. (1976) *The Effectiveness of Sentencing: A Review of the Literature*, Home Office Research Study No. 35, London, HMSO.

Brown, C. (1986) *Child Abuse Parents Speaking: Parents' Impressions of Social Workers and the Social Work Process*, Working Paper 63. School for Advanced Urban Studies, Bristol, University of Bristol.

Brown, H. (1994) 'An Ordinary Sexual Life? A Review of the Normalisation Principle as it Applies to the Sexual Options of People with Learning Disabilities', *Disability and Society*, 9, 2, 123–144.

Brown, H. and Craft, A. (eds) (1989) *Thinking the Unthinkable: Papers on Sexual Abuse and People with Learning Difficulties*, London, Family Planning Association.

Brown, H. and Smith, H. (1992a) *Changing Relationships: Shared Action Planning with People with a Mental Handicap*, London, Open University Press.

Brown, H. and Smith, H. (1992b) 'Assertion not Assimilation: A Feminist Perspective on the Normalisation Principle', in H. Brown and H. Smith (eds) *Normalisation: A Reader for the Nineties*, London, Tavistock/Routledge, pp. 149–171.

Brown, H. and Smith, H. (1992c) *Normalisation: A Reader for the Nineties*, London, Routledge.

Brown, H. and Turk, V. (1992) 'Defining Sexual Abuse as it Affects Adults with Learning Disabilities', *Mental Handicap*, 20, 2, 44–55.

Brown, H. and Walmsley, J. (1997) 'When 'Ordinary' Isn't Enough: A Review of the Concept of Normalisation', in J. Bornat, J. Johnson, C. Pereira, D. Pilgrim and F. Williams (eds) *Community Care: A Reader*, 2nd edn, Basingstoke, Macmillan, pp. 227–36.

Brown, H., Egan-Sage, E., Banry, G. and McKay, C. (1996) *Towards Better Interviewing: A Handbook for Police Officers and Social Workers on the Sexual Abuse of Adults with Learning Disabilities*, NAPSAC 'Need to Know' Series, Brighton, Pavilion Publishing.

Brown, H., Skinner, R., Stein, J. and Wilson, B. (1998) *The Investigator's Guide*, Aims for Adult Protection Series, Brighton, Pavilion Publishing.

Brown, H., Stein, J. and Turk, V. (1995) 'The Sexual Abuse of Adults with Learning Disabilities: Report of a Second Two-Year Incidence Survey', *Mental Handicap Research*, 8, 1, 3–24.

Brown, S. (1998) *Understanding Youth and Crime*, Buckingham, Open University Press.

Brugha, T. S. (1991) 'Support and Personal Relationships', in D. H. Bennet and L. Hugh (eds) *Community Psychiatry: The Principles*, Edinburgh, Churchill Livingstone, pp. 115–161.

Bryan, B., Dadzie, S. and Scafe, S. (1985) *The Heart of the Race: Black Women's Lives in Britain*, London, Virago.

Bukatko, D. and Daehler, M. W. (2001) *Child Development: A Thematic Approach*, Boston, Houghton Mifflin.

Bull, R. and Cullen, C. (1992) *Witnesses who Have Mental Handicaps*, Edinburgh, Crown Office.

Bullock, H. F., Wyche, K. F. and Williams, W. R. (2001) 'Media Images of the Poor', *Journal of Social Problems*, 57, 2, 229–246.

Burchard, S. N., Hasazi, J. S., Gordon, L. R. and Yoe, J. (1991) 'An Examination of Lifestyle and Adjustment in Three Community Residential Alternatives', *Research in Developmental Disabilities*, 12, 127–142.

Burghes, L. (1994) *Lone Parenthood and Family Disruption: The Outcomes for Children*, London, Family Policy Studies Centre.

Burgner, T., Russell, P., Whitehead, S., Tinnion, J. and Phipps, L. (1998) *Independent Longcare Inquiry*, Buckinghamshire County Council.

Burke, L. C., Bedard, S. and Ludwig, S. (1998) 'Dealing with the Sexual Abuse of Adults with a Developmental Disability who also Have Impaired Communication: Supportive Procedures for Detection, Disclosure and Follow-up', *The Canadian Journal of Human Sexuality: SIECCAN Newsletter*, 7, 1, 79–91.

Butler, I. and Drakeford, M. (2001) 'Which Blair Project? Communitarianism, Social Authoritarianism and Social Work', *Journal of Social Work*, 1, 1, 7–19.

Butler, I. and Williamson, H. (1994) *Children Speak: Children, Trauma and Social Work*, London, Longman.

Butler, S. and Charles, M. (1996) '"It's A Gimmick!" A Dynamic Analysis of Fostering and Adoption Disruption*, Nottingham, University of Nottingham.

Butler, S. and Wintram, C. (1991) *Feminist Groupwork*, London, Sage.

Butt, J. and Mirza, K. (1997) 'Exploring the Income of Black-Led Organisations', in C. Pharaoh (ed.) *Dimensions of the Voluntary Sector: Key Facts, Figures, Analysis and Trends*, Tunbridge Wells, Charities Aid Foundation, pp. 197–205.

Byrne, P. (1997) *Social Movements in Britain*, London, Routledge.

Bywaters, P. and McLeod, E. (2001) 'The Impact of New Labour Health Policy on Social Services: A New Deal for Service Users' Health?', *British Journal of Social Work*, 31, 4, 579–594.

Cabinet Office (2001) *Action Plan for Neighbourhood Renewal*: <http://www.cabinet-office.gov.uk/seu/2001/Action%20Plan.htm>.

Callender, C. (1996) 'Women and Employment', in C. Hallett (ed.) *Women and Social Policy: An Introduction*, Hemel Hempstead, Harvester Wheatsheaf, pp. 31–51.

Cambridge, P. (1999) 'Building Care Management Competence in Services for People with Learning Disabilities', *British Journal of Social Work*, 29, 3, 393–415.

Cambridge, P., Davies, S., Nichol, J., Thompson, D., Morris, S. and Corbett, A. (1993) *SELHA Needs Assessment Project Report: Men with Learning Difficulties who Have Sex with Men in Public Places*, London, South East London Health Authority.

Campbell, B. (1998) *Goliath*, London, Methuen.

Campbell, J. and Oliver, M. (1996) *Disability Politics: Understanding our Past, Changing our Future*, London, Routledge.

Carling, P. J. (1990) 'Major Mental Illness, Housing and Supports: The Promise of Community Integration', *American Psychologist*, 45, 8, 969–975.

Carling, P. J. (1995) *Return to Community*, New York, Guildford Press.

Carmody, M. (1991) 'Invisible Victims: Sexual Assault of People with Intellectual Disability', *Australia and New Zealand Journal of Developmental Disabilities*, 17, 2, 229–36.

Carson, D. (1992) 'The Law's Contribution to Protecting People with Learning Disabilities from Physical and Sexual Abuse', in J. Harris and A. Craft (eds) *People with Learning Disabilities at Risk of Physical or Sexual Abuse*, Worcestershire: BILD Seminar Papers No. 4, pp. 133–143.

Cattanach, A. (1993) *Play Therapy with Abused Children*, London, Jessica Kingsley.

Cavadino, P. and Dignan, J. (2002) *The Penal System. An Introduction*, 3rd edn, London, Sage.

Central Council for Education and Training in Social Work (CCETSW) (1989) *Requirements and Regulations for the Diploma in Social Work*, London, CCETSW.

Central Council for Education and Training in Social Work (CCETSW) (1991) *Rules and Requirements for the Diploma in Social Work (Second Edition)*, London, CCETSW.

Central Council for Education and Training in Social Work (CCETSW) (1995) *Assuring Quality in the Diploma in Social Work – 1: Rules and Requirements for the Diploma in Social Work*, London, CCETSW.

Chadda, D. (1998) 'Staff Damn Government Unit as "Middle Class"', *Community Care*, 26 November–2 December, 1.

Challis, D. (1994) 'Care Management', in N. Malin (ed.) *Implementing Community Care*, Buckingham, Open University Press, pp. 59–82.

Challis, D. and Davies, B. (1986) *Case Management in Community Care*, Aldershot, Gower.

Challis, D., Darton, R., Johnson, L., Stone, K. and Traske, L. (1995) *Care Management and Health Care of Older People*, Aldershot, Arena.

Challis, D., Weiner, K., Darton, R., Hughes, J. and Stewart, K. (2001) 'Emerging Patterns of Care Management: Arrangements for Older People in England', *Social Policy and Administration*, 35, 6, 672–687.

Chapman, T. and Hough, M. (1998) *Evidence Based Practice: A Guide to Effective Practice*, London, Home Office.

Chappell, A. L. (1992) 'Towards a Sociological Critique of the Normalisation Principle', *Disability, Handicap and Society*, 7, 1, 35–51.

Chappell, A. L., Goodley, D. and Lawthorn, R. (2001) 'Making connections: the relevance of the social model of disability for people with learning difficulties', *British Journal of Learning Disabilities*, 29, 2, 45–50.

Charles, M., Kingaby, D. and Thorn, J. (1996) *Fun and Families*, Report of Nottingham Area Child Protection Committee. Available from: M. Charles, Centre for Social Work, University of Nottingham.

Churchill, J., Brown, H., Craft, A. and Horrocks, C. (eds) (1997) *There Are No Easy Answers*, Chesterfield and Nottingham, ARC and NAPSAC.

Churchill, J., Craft, A., Holding, A. and Horrocks, C. (eds) (1996) *It Could Never Happen Here!*, revised edn, Chesterfield and Nottingham, ARC and NAPSAC.

Clare, I. C. H. and Gudjonsson, G. H. (1993) 'Interrogative Suggestibility, Confabulation, and Acquiescence in People with Mild Learning Disabilities: Implications for Reliability During Police Interrogations', *British Journal of Clinical Psychology*, 32, 295–301.

Clarke, J. (1980) 'Social Democratic Delinquents and Fabian Families', in National Deviancy Conference (Sheffield, 1977) *Permissiveness and Control*, London, Macmillan, pp. 72–95.

Clarke, J. (1998) 'Thriving on Chaos? Managerialisation and Social Welfare', in J. Carter (ed.) *Postmodernity and the Fragmentation of Welfare*, London, Routledge, pp. 171–186.

Clarke, J., Gewirtz, S. and McClaughlin, E. (eds) (2000) *New Managerialism, New Welfare?*, London, Sage/Open University.

Clarke, J. and Glendinning, C. (2002) 'Partnership and the remaking of welfare governance', in C. Glendinning, M. Powell and K. Rummery (eds) *Partnerships, New Labour and the Governance of Welfare*, Bristol, Policy Press, pp. 33–50.

Clarke, J. and Newman, J. (1997) *The Managerial State*, London, Sage.

Clegg, S. (1989) *Frameworks of Power*, London and Newbury Park, CA, Sage.

The Cleveland Inquiry (1988) *Report of the Inquiry into Child Abuse in Cleveland 1987*, London, HMSO.

Clifford, B. (1997) 'A Commentary on Ebbesen and Koneci's "Eyewitness Memory Research: Probative v. Prejudicial Value"', *Expert Evidence*, 5, 4, 140–143.

Coates, D. (1996) 'Labour Governments: Old Constraints and New Parameters', *New Left Review*, 219, 62–78.

Cohen, R. and Tarpey, M. (1988) *Single Payments: The Disappearing Safety Net*, London, Child Poverty Action Group.

Cohen, R., Coxall, J., Craig, G. and Sadiq-Sangster, A. (1992) *Hardship Britain: Being Poor in the 1990s*, London, Child Poverty Action Group.

Cohen, S. (1975) 'It's All Right for You to Talk: Political and Sociological Manifestos for Social Work Action', in R. Bailey and M. Brake (eds) *Radical Social Work*, London, Edward Arnold, pp. 76–95.

Cohen, S. (1981) 'Footprints in the Sand: A Further Report on Criminology and the Sociology of Deviance in Britain', in M. Fitzgerald, G. McLennan and J. Pawson (eds) *Crime and Society: Readings in History and Theory*, London, Routledge, pp. 220–267.

Cohen, S. (1985) *Visions of Social Control: Crime, Punishment and Classification*, Cambridge, Polity Press.

Cohen, S., Humphries, B. and Mynott, E. (2002) *From Immigration Controls to Welfare Controls*, London, Routledge.

Coleman, C. and Norris, C. (2000) *Introducing Criminology*, Cullompton, Willan Publishing.

Collings, J. and Murray, P. (1996) 'Predictors of Stress Amongst Social Workers: An Empirical Study', *British Journal of Social Work*, 26, 3, 375–388.

Collins, J., Holman, A., Aspis, S. and Amor, Y. (1997) *Funding Freedom*, London, Values into Action.

Collins, P. H. (1991) *Black Feminist Thought. Knowledge, Consciousness and the Politics of Empowerment*, London, Routledge.

Colton, M., Sanders, R. and Williams, M. (2001) *An Introduction to Working with Children: A Guide for Social Workers*, Basingstoke, Palgrave.

Cook, D. and Hudson, B. (eds) (1993) *Racism and Criminology*, London, Sage.

Cooke, P. and Davies, G. (2001) 'Achieving best evidence from people with learning disabilities: new guidance', *British Journal of Learning Disabilities*, 29, 3, 84–87.

Cooper, J. (1983) *The Creation of the British Social Services*, London, Heinemann Educational Books.

Corbett, J. (1994) 'A Proud Label: Exploring the Relationship between Disability Politics and Gay Pride', *Disability and Society*, 9, 3, 343–357.

Cornwell, N. (1992) 'Assessment and accountability in community care', *Critical Social Policy*, 36, 40–52.

Coulshed, V. and Orme, J. (1998) *Social Work Practice: An Introduction*, 3rd edn, Basingstoke, Macmillan.

Cowan, L. (1998) 'Computers in Child Care: New Resources, New Opportunities', *Adoption and Fostering*, 22, 3, 53–57.

Cowie, H. (1991) *Understanding Children's Development*, Oxford, Blackwell.

Craft, A. (1987) *Mental Handicap and Sexuality: Issues and Perspectives*, Tunbridge Wells, Costello.

Craft, A. (1991) 'The Living Your Life Programme', *British Journal of Education*, 18, 4, 157–160.

Craft, A. (1992) 'Guest Editorial: Special Issue on Sexuality', *Mental Handicap*, 20, 2, 42–43.

Craft, A. and Hitching, M. (1989). 'Keeping Safe: Sex Education and Assertiveness Skills', in H. Brown and A. Craft (eds) *Thinking the Unthinkable: Papers on Sexual Abuse and People with Learning Difficulties*, London, Family Planning Association, pp. 29–38.

Craft, A. (ed.) (1994) *Practice Issues in Sexuality and Learning Disabilities*, London, Routledge.

Craig, G. (ed.) (1989) *Your Flexible Friend: Voluntary Organisations, Claimants and the Social Fund*, London, Child Poverty Action Group.

Craig, G. (2002) 'Poverty, Social Work and Social Justice', *British Journal of Social Work*, 32, 6, 669–682.

Craig, G. and Manthorpe, J. (1998) 'Small is beautiful?: local government reorganization and social services departments', *Policy and Politics*, 26, 2, 189–207.

Craig, G. and Taylor, M. (2002) 'Willing partners?', in C. Glendinning, M. Powell and K. Rummery (eds) *Perspectives on Partnership*, Bristol, Policy Press, pp. 131–148.

Croft, S. and Beresford, P. (1990) *From Paternalism to Participation: Involving People in Social Services*, York, Joseph Rowntree Foundation/Open Services Project.

Croft, S. and Beresford, P. (1998) 'Postmodernity and the future of welfare: Whose critiques, whose welfare?', in J. Carter (ed.) *Postmodernity and the Fragmentation of Welfare*, London, Routledge, pp. 103–117.

Crompton, M. (1980) *Respecting Children: Social Work with Young People*, London, Edward Arnold.

Crompton, M. (1990) *Attending to Children: Direct Work in Social and Health Care*, London, Edward Arnold.

Crow, I. (2001) *The Treatment and Rehabilitation of Offenders*, London, Sage.

Crown Prosecution Service (CPS) and Association for Chief Police Officers (ACPO) (2000) *Speaking up for justice, recommendations 26 and 27: special measures for vulnerable or intimidated witnesses to give evidence. Draft guidance*, York, Crown Prosecution Service and Association for Chief Police Officers.

Crowther, M. A. (1981) *The Workhouse System 1834–1929: the history of an English social institution*, London, Batsford.

Dalley, G. (1989) 'Professional Ideology and Organisational Tribalism? The Health Service – Social Work Divide', in R. Taylor and J. Ford (eds) *Social Work and Health Care*, London, Jessica Kingsley, pp. 102–117.

Dalley, G. (1996) *Ideologies of Caring*, 2nd edn, Basingstoke, Macmillan.

Dalrymple, J. and Burke, B. (1995) *Anti-Oppressive Practice*, Buckingham, Open University Press.

Davey, B. (1998) *Strategies for Outsiders: Helping the Last to Come First in the Ecological Transformation of Society*, Nottingham, Nottingham Advocacy Group.

Davidson, M. J. (1997) *The Black and Ethnic Minority Women Manager: Cracking the Concrete Ceiling*, London, Paul Chapman/Sage.

Davies, M. (1994) *The Essential Social Worker*, 3rd edn, Aldershot, Arena.

Davies, M., Croall, H. and Tyrer, J. (1998) *Criminal Justice. An Introduction to the Criminal Justice System in England and Wales*, Harlow, Addison Wesley Longman.

Davies, N. (1995) 'Poverty: The Untold Story', *Professional Social Work*, July, 4.

Davies, R. (ed.) (1998) *Stress in Social Work*, London, Jessica Kingsley.

Davis, A. (1991) 'A Structural Approach to Social Work', in J. Lishman (ed.) *Handbook of Theory for Practice Teachers in Social Work*, London, Jessica Kingsley, pp. 64–74.

Davis, A. (1992) 'Men's Imprisonment: The Financial Cost to Women and Children', in R. Shaw (ed.) *Prisoners' Children: What are the Issues?*, London, Routledge, pp. 74–85.

Davis, A. (1996) 'Risk Work and Mental Health', in H. Kemshall and J. Pritchard (eds) *Good Practice in Risk Assessment and Risk Management*, London, Jessica Kingsley, pp. 109–120.

Davis, A. and Hill, P. (2000) *Poverty, Social Exclusion and Mental Health: A Resource Pack*, London, Mental Health Foundation.

Davis, A., Ellis, K. and Rummery, K. (1997) *Access to Assessment: Disabled People's Experiences of Assessment for Community Care Services*, York, Policy Press.

Davis, M. (1990) *City of Quartz: Excavating the Future in Los Angeles*, London, Vintage.

Davis Smith, J. (1995) 'The Voluntary Tradition. Philanthropy and Self-Help in Britain 1500–1945', in J. Davis Smith, C. Rochester and R. Hedley (eds) *An Introduction to the Voluntary Sector*, London, Routledge, pp. 9–39.

Deakin, N. (1994) *The Politics of Welfare*, 2nd edn, Hemel Hempstead, Harvester Wheatsheaf.

Deakin, N. (1995) 'The perils of partnership: The voluntary sector and the state 1945–1992', in J. Davis-Smith, C. Rochester and R. Hedley (eds) *An Introduction to the Voluntary Sector*, London, Routledge, pp. 40–65.

Deakin, N. (1996a) *Meeting the Challenge of Change: Voluntary Action into the 21st Century. Report of the Commission on the Future of the Voluntary Sector*, London, NCVO Publications.

Deakin, N. (1996b) 'What does Contracting do to Users?', in D. Billis and M. Harris (eds) *Voluntary Agencies: Challenges of Organisation and Management*, Basingstoke, Macmillan, pp. 113–129.

Dean, H. (2001) 'Welfare Rights and the "Workfare" State', *Benefits*, January–February, 1–5.

Dean, H. and Melrose, M. (1999) *Poverty, Riches and Social Citizenship*, Basingstoke, Macmillan.

Deegan, P. (1996) 'Recovery as a Journey of the Heart', *Psychiatric Rehabilitation Journal*, 19, 3, 91–7.

Deitchman, W. S. (1980) 'How Many Case Managers Does it Take to Screw in a Light Bulb?', *Hospital and Community*, 31, 11, 788–789.

Denney, D. (1998) 'Anti Racism and the Limits of Equal Opportunities Policy in the Criminal Justice System', in C. Jones Finer and M. Nellis (eds) *Crime and Social Exclusion*, Oxford, Blackwell.

Department of Health (DoH) (1988) *Protecting Children, A Guide for Social Workers Undertaking a Comprehensive Assessment*, London, HMSO.

Department of Health (DoH) (1989). *Caring for People: Community Care in the Next Decade and Beyond*, Cmnd. 849, London, HMSO.

Department of Health (DoH) (1990) *Community Care in the Next Decade and Beyond: Policy Guidance*, London, HMSO.

Department of Health (DoH) (1991a) *Working Together: A Guide to Arrangements for Inter-Agency Co-operation for the Protection of Children from Abuse*, London, HMSO.

Department of Health (DoH) (1991b) *Patterns and Outcomes in Child Placement: Messages from Current Research and their Implications*, London, HMSO.

Department of Health (DoH) (1991c) *Looking After Children: Guidelines for Users of the Assessment and Action Records*, London, HMSO.

Department of Health (DoH) (1995a) *Looking After Children: Good Parenting, Good Outcomes*, London, HMSO.

Department of Health (DoH) (1995b) *Child Protection: Messages from Research*, London, HMSO.

Department of Health (DoH) (1997) *The New NHS: Modern – Dependable*, Cmnd. 3807, London, Stationery Office.

Department of Health (DoH) (1998a) *Modernising Social Services: Promoting Independence, Improving Protection, Raising Standards*, Cmnd. 4169, London, Stationery Office.

Department of Health (DoH) (1998b) *Quality Protects: Framework for Action*, London, Stationery Office.

Department of Health (DoH) (1998c) *Objectives for Social Services for Children*, London, Stationery Office.

Department of Health (DoH) (1999a) *Convention on the Rights of the Child. Second Report to the U.N. Committee on the Rights of the Child by the United Kingdom 1999*, London, Stationery Office.

Department of Health (DoH) (1999b) *National Service Frameworks for Mental Health: modern standards and service models*, London, Stationery Office.

Department of Health (DoH) (1999c) *Working Together to Safeguard Children: New Government Guidance on Inter-agency Co-operation*, London, Stationery Office.

Department of Health (DoH) (2000a) *A Quality Strategy for Social Care*, London, Stationery Office.

Department of Health (DoH) (2000b) *The NHS Plan*, London, Stationery Office.

Department of Health (DoH) (2000c) *Looking beyond labels: Widening the employment opportunities for disabled people in the new NHS*, London, Department of Health.

Department of Health (DoH) (2000d) *No Secrets: The Protection of Vulnerable Adults.* London, Department of Health.

Department of Health (DoH) (2001a) *Valuing People: A New Strategy for Learning Disability for the 21st Century*, Cmnd. 5806, London, Stationery Office.

Department of Health (DoH) (2001b) *The National Service Framework for Older People*, London, Stationery Office.

Department of Health (DoH) (2002a) *Requirements for Social Work Training*, London, Department of Health.

Department of Health (DoH) (2002b) *Guidance on the Single Assessment Process for Older People*, HSC2002/001: LAC (2002)1, London, Department of Health.

Department of Health (DoH) (2002c) *The Single Assessment Process: Guidance for Local Implementation*, London, Department of Health.

Department of Health and Social Security (DHSS) (1974) *Report of the Committee of Inquiry into the Care and Supervision Provided in Relation to Maria Colwell*, London, HMSO.

Department of Health and Social Security (DHSS) (1976) *Foster Care: A Guide to Practice*, London, HMSO.

Department of Health and Social Security (DHSS) (1985) *Social Work Decisions in Child Care: Recent Findings and their Implications*, London, HMSO.

Department of Health, Department for Education and Employment and Home Office (DoH *et al.*) (2000) *Framework for the Assessment of Children in Need and their Families*, London, Stationery Office.

Department of Health/Social Services Inspectorate (DoH/SSI) (1991a) *Purchase of Service*, London, HMSO.

Department of Health/Social Services Inspectorate (DoH/SSI) (1991b) *Care Management and Assessment: Practitioners' Guide*, London, HMSO.

Department of Health/Social Services Inspectorate (DoH/SSI) (1991c) *Care Management and Assessment: Managers' Guide*, London, HMSO.

Department of Social Security (DSS) (2001) *Households Below Average Income, 1999–2000*, London, Department of Social Security.

Department of the Environment, Transport and the Regions (DETR) (1998) *Modernising Local Government: In Touch with the People*, Cmnd. 4014, London, DETR.

Dickenson, D., Johnson, M. and Katz, J. S. (eds) (2000) *Death, Dying and Bereavement*, 2nd edn, London, Sage/Open University Press.

Dingwall, R. (1982) 'Problems of Teamwork in Primary Care', in A. W. Clare and R. H. Corney (eds) *Social Work and Primary Health Care*, London, Academic Press, pp. 83–98.

Dodd, J. and Sandell, R. (2001) *Including Museums: perspectives on museums, galleries and social inclusion*, Leicester, Research Centre for Museums and Galleries, University of Leicester.

Dominelli, L. (1997) *Anti-Racist Practice*, 2nd edn, Basingstoke, Macmillan.

Dominelli, L. (1998) 'Anti-oppressive Practice in Context', in R. Adams, L. Dominelli and M. Payne (eds) *Social Work: Themes, Issues and Critical Debates*, Basingstoke, Macmillan, pp. 3–23.

Dominelli, L. (1999) 'CCETSW and Anti-Oppressive Practice: Strengths and Limitations of the Policy'. Unpublished paper presented to 'Anti-Racism and Anti-Oppressive Practice Conference', University of Leeds, 9 June.

Dominelli, L. and Hoogvelt, A. (1996) 'Globalization and the Technocratization of Social Work', *Critical Social Policy*, 16, 2, 45–62.

Donzelot, J. (1979) *The Policing of Families*, London, Hutchinson.

Dooley, B. (1998) *Black and Green: The Fight for Civil Rights in Northern Ireland and Black America*, London, Pluto Press.

Douglas, A. and Philpot, T. (1998) *Caring and Coping. A Guide to Social Services*, London, Routledge.

Drakeford, M. and Vanstone, M. eds. (1996) Beyond Offending Behaviour, Aldershot, Arena.

Drury-Hudson, J. (1999) 'Decision Making in Child Protection', *British Journal of Social Work*, 29, 1, 147–170.

Duffy, S. (1996) *Unlocking the Imagination – Strategies for Purchasing Services for People with Learning Disabilities*, London, Choice Press.

Duncan, G. and Worrall, J. (2000) 'Social policy and social work in New Zealand', *European Journal of Social Work*, 3, 3, 283–296.

Dunn, S. (1999) *Creating Accepting Communities: Report of the MIND Inquiry into Social Exclusion and Mental Health Problems*, London, Mind Publications.

Eadie, T. and Lymbery, M. (2002) 'Understanding and Working in Welfare Organisations: Helping Students Survive the Workplace', *Social Work Education*, 21, 5, 515–527.

Eadie, T. and Willis, A. (1989) 'National Standards for Discipline and Breach Proceedings in Community Service: An Exercise In Penal Rhetoric?', *Criminal Law Review*, June, 412–419.

Eichenbaum, L. and Orbach, S. (1985) *Understanding Women*, Harmondsworth: Penguin.

Ellis, J. W. (1990) 'Presidential Address: Mental Retardation at the Close of the 20th Century: New Realism', *Mental Retardation*, 28, 1, 263–267.

Ellis, T., Hedderman, C. and Mortimer, E. (1996) *Enforcing Community Sentences: Supervisors' Perspectives on Ensuring Compliance and Dealing with Breach*, Home Office Research Study 158, London, Home Office.

England, H. (1986) *Social Work as Art: Making Sense of Good Practice*, London, Allen & Unwin.

Erikson, E. H. (1977) *Childhood and Society*, Harmondsworth, Penguin.

Ernst, S. and Goodison, L. (1981) *In Our Own Hands. A Book of Self-Help Therapy*, London, Women's Press.

Estroff, S. (1989) 'Self, Identity and Subjective Experiences of Schizophrenia: In Search of the Subject', *Schizophrenia Bulletin*, 15, 2, 189–196.

Evans, D. and Kearney, J. (1996) *Social Care: A Systemic Approach*, Aldershot, Arena.

Evans, G., Felce, D., de Paiva, S. and Todd, S. (1992) 'Observing the Delivery of a Domiciliary Support Service', *Disability, Handicap and Society*, 7, 1, 19–34.

Evans, M. (1998) 'Social Security: Dismantling the Pyramids?' in H. Glennerster and J. Hills (eds) *The State of Welfare: The Economics of Social Spending*, 2nd edn, Oxford, Oxford University Press, pp. 257–307.

Evers, A. (1993) 'The Welfare Mix Approach: Understanding the Pluralism of Welfare Systems', in A. Evers and I. Svetlik (eds) *Balancing Pluralism: New Welfare Mixes in Care for the Elderly*, Aldershot, Avebury, pp. 3–31.

Evers, H., Cameron, E. and Badger, F. (1994) 'Inter-professional Work with Old and Disabled People', in A. Leathard (ed.) *Going Inter-Professional*, London, Routledge, pp. 143–157.

Fahlberg, V. I. (1994) *A Child's Journey through Placement*, London, BAAF.

Faludi, S. (1992) *Backlash: The Undeclared War on Women*, London, Vintage.

Farmer, E. and Owen, M. (1995) *Child Protection Practice: Private Risks and Public Remedies – Decision Making, Intervention and Outcomes in Child Protection Work*, London, HMSO.

Farnfield, S. (1998) 'The Rights and Wrongs of Social Work with Children and Young People', in J. Cheetham and M. A. F. Kazi, *The Working of Social Work*, London, Jessica Kingsley, pp. 53–68.

Farnham, D. and Horton, S. (1996) 'Public Service Managerialism: A Review and Evaluation', in D. Farnham and S. Horton (eds) *Managing the New Public Services*, 2nd edn, Basingstoke, Macmillan, pp. 259–276.

Farrington, D. (1997) 'Human Development and Criminal Careers', in M. Maguire, R. Morgan and R. Reiner (eds) *The Oxford Handbook of Criminology*, 2nd edn, Oxford, Oxford University Press, pp. 361–408.

Fawcett, B. and Featherstone, B. (1996) ' "Carers" and "Caring": New Thoughts on Old Questions', in B. Humphries (ed.) *Critical Perspectives on Empowerment*, Birmingham, Venture Press, pp. 53–68.

Ferguson, I. and Lavalette, M. (1999) 'Social Work, Postmodernism and Marxism', *European Journal of Social Work*, 2, 1, 27–40.

Field, D., Hockey, J. and Small, N. (eds) (1997) *Death, Gender and Ethnicity*, London, Routledge.

Finch, J. (1990) *Family Obligations and Social Change*, Oxford, Polity Press.

Finkelstein, E. (1996) 'Values in Context: Quality Assurance, Autonomy and Accountability', in T. May and A. A. Vass (eds) *Working with Offenders: Issues, Contexts and Outcomes*, London, Sage, pp. 76–95.

Finlay, M. and Lyons, E. (1998) 'Social Identity and People with Learning Difficulties: Implications for Self-advocacy Groups', *Disability and Society*, 13, 37–51.

Firth, H. and Short, D. (1987) 'A Move From Hospital to Community: Evaluation of Community Contacts', *Child: Care, Health and Development*, 13, 341–354.

Fisher, M., Marsh, P. and Phillips, D. with Sainsbury, E. (1986) *In and Out of Care: the Experiences of Children, Parents and Social Workers*, London, Batsford/BAAF.

Fisher, R. and Geiselman, R. (1992) *Memory Enhancing Techniques for Investigative Interviewing – The Cognitive Interview*, New York, Charles C. Thomas.

Fitzgerald, M. (1993) *Ethnic Minorities and the Criminal Justice System*, Royal Commission on Criminal Justice Research Study No. 20, London, HMSO.

Fletcher, B. (1993) *Not Just A Name*, London, Who Cares? Trust/National Consumer Council.

Flynn, M. C. (1989) *Independent Living for Adults with Mental Handicap: 'A Place of My Own'*, London, Cassell.

Ford, J. (1991) *Consuming Credit: Debt and Poverty in the U.K.*, London, Child Poverty Action Group.

Forsythe, B. (1995) 'Discrimination in Social Work', *British Journal of Social Work*, 25, 1, 1–17.

Forsythe, B. and Jordan, B. (2002) 'The Victorian Ethical Foundation of Social Work in England – Continuity and Contradiction', *British Journal of Social Work*, 32, 7, 847–862.

Foster, P. and Wilding, P. (2000) 'Whither Welfare Professionalism?', *Social Policy and Administration*, 34, 2, 143–159.

Foucault, M. (1977) *Discipline and Punish*, Harmondsworth, London.

Foulds, J., Hall, G. and Lockton, D. (1996) 'Contact Issues in Cases of Child Sexual Abuse', *Contemporary Issues in Law*, 2, 3, 19–32.

Francis Spence, M. (1995) 'Justice: Do They Mean For Us? Black Probation Officers and Black Clients in the Probation Service', in D. Ward and M. Lacey (eds) *Probation Working for Justice*, London, Whiting & Birch, pp. 154–169.

Franklin, B. (1998) *Hard Pressed: National Newspaper Reporting of Social Work and Social Services*, Sutton, Community Care.

Freidson, E. (1986) *Professional Powers*, Chicago, University of Chicago Press.

Freire, P. (1972) *The Pedagogy of the Oppressed*, Harmondsworth, Penguin.

Frude, N. (1994) 'Marital Violence: An Interactional Perspective', in J. Archer (ed.) *Male Violence*, London, Routledge, pp. 153–169.

Fuller, R. and Petch, A. (1995) *Practitioner Research: The Reflexive Social Worker*, Buckingham, Open University Press.

Gaje, J. (1998) 'Learning Disability: Dimensions of Professional Empowerment', *Journal of Learning Disabilities for Nursing, Health and Social Care*, 2, 110–115.

Gamble, A. (1994) *The Free Economy and the Strong State: The Politics of Thatcherism*, 2nd edn, Basingstoke, Macmillan.

Gann, N. (1996) *Managing Change in Voluntary Organisations*, Buckingham, Open University Press.

Garland, D. (1990) *Punishment and Modern Society: A Study in Social Theory*, Oxford, Oxford University Press.

Garnett, L. (1992) *Leaving Care and After*, London, National Children's Bureau.

Garrett, P. M. (1998) 'Notes from the Diaspora: Anti-discriminatory Social Work Practice, Irish People and the Practice Curriculum', *Social Work Education*, 17, 4, 435–449.

Garrett, P. M. (1999a) 'Questioning the New Orthodoxy: The "Looking After Children (LAC)" System and its Discourse on Parenting', *Practice*, 11, 1, 53–65.

Garrett, P. M. (1999b) 'Mapping Child Care Social Work in the Final Years of the Twentieth Century: A Critical Response to the 'Looking After Children' System', *British Journal of Social Work*, 29, 1, 27–47.

Garrett, P. M. (2000a) 'The abnormal flight: The migration and repatriation of Irish unmarried mothers', *Social History*, 25, 3, 330–344.

Garrett, P. M. (2000b) 'The hidden history of the PFIs: The repatriation of unmarried mothers and their children from England to Ireland in the 1950s and 1960s', *Immigrants & Minorities*, 19, 3, 25–44.

Garrett, P. M. (2000c) 'Responding to Irish "invisibility": Anti-discriminatory social work practice and the placement of Irish children in Britain', *Adoption and Fostering*, 24, 1, 23–34.

Garrett, P. M. (2002a) ' "No Irish Need Apply": Social Work in Britain and the History and Politics of Exclusionary Paradigms and Practices', *British Journal of Social Work*, 32, 4, 477–494.

Garrett, P. M. (2002b) 'Getting a grip: New Labour and the reform of the law on child adoption', *Critical Social Policy*, 22, 2, 174–202.

Garrett, P. M. (2002c) 'Encounters in the new welfare domains of the Third Way: Social Work, the Connexions Agency and Personal Advisers', *Critical Social Policy*, 22, 4, 592–615.

Garrett, P. M. (2002d) 'Social Work and the Just Society: Diversity, Difference and the Sequestration of Poverty', *Journal of Social Work*, 2, 2, 187–210.

Garrett, P. M. (2002e) 'Yes Minister: Reviewing the 'Looking After Children' Experience and Identifying the Messages for Social Work Research', *British Journal of Social Work*, 32, 7, 831–846.

Garrett, P. M. (2003) 'The "Daring Experiment": The London County Council and the discharge from care of children to Ireland in the 1950s and 1960s', *Journal of Social Policy*, 32, 1, 1–18.

Gates, B. (1997) 'Editorial: Value of Learning Disabled People and the Never Ending Appeal of Eugenics', *Journal of Learning Disabilities for Nursing, Health and Social Care*, 1, 159–161.

Gates, B. (2001) 'Editorial: Valuing People: Long awaited strategy for people with learning disabilities for the twenty-first century in England', *Journal of Learning Disabilities*, 5, 3, 203–207.

Geddes, M. and Martin, S. (2000) 'The policy and politics of Best Value: currents, crosscurrents and undercurrents in the new regime', *Policy and Politics*, 28, 3, 379–395.

Gelsthorpe, L. and Morris, A. (1994) 'Juvenile Justice 1945–1992', in M. Maguire, R. Morgan and R. Reiner (eds) *The Oxford Handbook of Criminology*, Oxford, Oxford University Press, pp. 949–993.

General Social Care Council (GSCC) (2002) 'About Us', *General Social Care Council Website*. <http://www.gscc.org.uk/about.htm>.

George, M. (1998) 'Social Worker or Big Brother?', *Community Care*, 5–11 November, 22–24.

George, V. and Miller, S. (1994a) 'Squaring the welfare circle', in V. George and S. Miller (eds) *Social Policy Towards 2000: Squaring the Welfare Circle*, London, Routledge, pp. 6–21.

George, V. and Miller, S. (1994b) 'The Thatcherite attempt to square the circle', in V. George and S. Miller (eds) *Social Policy Towards 2000: Squaring the Welfare Circle*, London, Routledge, pp. 22–48.

George, V. and Wilding, P. (1994) *Welfare and Ideology*, Hemel Hempstead, Harvester Wheatsheaf.

Gibbons, J. (1997) 'Relating Outcomes to Objectives in Child Protection Policy', in N. Parton (ed.) *Child Protection and Family Support: Tensions, Contradictions and Possibilities*, London, Routledge, pp. 78–91.

Gibson, F., McGrath, A. and Reid, N. (1989) 'Occupational Stress in Social Work', *British Journal of Social Work*, 19, 1–16.

Giddens, A. (1998) *The Third Way: The Renewal of Social Democracy*, Cambridge, Polity.

Gilroy, P. (1987) 'The Myth of Black Criminality', in P. Scraton (ed.) *Law, Order and the Authoritarian State*, Milton Keynes, Open University Press, pp. 107–121.

Gledhill, A. (1989) *Who Cares?*, London, Centre for Policy Studies.

Glendinning, C. and Millar, J. (1992) *Women and Poverty in Britain: The 1990s*, Hemel Hempstead, Harvester Wheatsheaf.

Glendinning, C., Powell, M. and Rummery, K. (eds) (2002) *Partnerships, New Labour and the Governance of Welfare*, Bristol, Policy Press.

Goffman, E. (1961) *Asylums: Essays on the Social Situation of Mental Patients and Other Inmates*, Harmondsworth, Penguin.

Gold, M. (1976) 'Task Analysis of a Complex Assembly Task by the Retarded Blind', *Exceptional Child*, 43, 20, 78–84.

Golding, P. (1991) 'Do-gooders on display: social workers, public attitudes and the mass media', in B. Franklin and N. Parton (eds) *Social Work, the Media and Public Relations*, London, Routledge, pp. 88–104.

Goldsmith, M. (1996) *Hearing the Voice of People with Dementia*, London, Jessica Kingsley.

Goldson, B. (ed.) (1999) *Youth Justice: Contemporary Policy and Practice*, Aldershot, Ashgate.

Goldson, B. (ed.) (2000) *The New Youth Justice*, Lyme Regis, Russell House Publishing.

Goldstein, H. (1990) 'The Knowledge Base of Social Work Practice: Theory, Wisdom, Analogue or Art?', *Families in Society: The Journal of Contemporary Human Services*, 73, 48–55.

Graddol, D. and Swann, J. (1989) *Gender Voices*, Oxford, Blackwell.

Grant, G. (2001) 'User involvement, empowerment and research', *Journal of Learning Disabilities*, 5, 2, 91–95.

Green, G. (2001) 'Vulnerability of witnesses with learning disabilities: preparing to give evidence against a perpetrator of sexual abuse', *British Journal of Learning Disabilities*, 29, 3, 103–109.

Gregory, S., Brown, J. and Johnson, S. (1998) *Sexual Exploitation of Children*, Nottingham, Nottinghamshire County Council.

Griffiths, R. (1988) *Community Care: Agenda for Action*, London, HMSO.

Gunn, M. J. (1996) *Sex and the Law: A Brief Guide for Staff Working with People with Learning Difficulties*, 4th edn, London, Family Planning Association.

Gutch, R., Kung, C. and Spencer, K. (1990) *Partners or Agents*, London, National Coalition of Voluntary Organisations.

H. M. Government (1999) *Youth Justice and Criminal Evidence Act*, London, Stationery Office.

Hadley, R. and Clough, R. (1996) *Care in Chaos: Frustration and Challenge in Community Care*, London, Cassell.

Hahn, H. (1988) 'The Politics of Physical Differences: Disability and Discrimination', *Journal of Social Issues*, 44, 1, 39–47.

Haines, K. and Drakeford, M. (1998) *Young People and Youth Justice*, Basingstoke, Macmillan.

Hakim, C. (1993) 'The Myth of Rising Female Employment', *Work, Employment and Society*, 7, 1, 97–120.

Halford, S. and Leonard, P. (2001) *Gender and Power in Organisations*, Basingstoke, Palgrave.

Hall, S. (1991) 'The Local and the Global: Globalization and Ethnicity', in A. D. King (ed.) *Culture, Globalization and the World-System*, London, MacMillan, pp. 41–68.

Hall, S. (1994) 'Son of Margaret?', *New Statesman and Society*, 6 October, 23–27.

Hall, S. and Jacques, M. (eds) (1983) *The Politics of Thatcherism*, London, Lawrence and Wishart.

Hall, S. and Jacques, M. (eds) (1989) *New Times: The Changing Face of Politics in the 1990s*, London, Lawrence & Wishart.

Hall, S., Critcher, C., Jefferson, T., Clarke, J. and Roberts, B. (1979) *Policing the Crisis: Mugging, the State and Law and Order*, London, Macmillan.

Hallett, C. (1982) *The Personal Social Services in Local Government*, London, Allen & Unwin.

Halsey A. H. (ed.) (1972) *Educational Priority No 1, EDA Problems and Policies*, London, HMSO.

Hanvey, C. and Philpot, T. (1996) 'Introduction', in C. Hanvey and T. Philpot (eds) *Sweet Charity: The Role and Workings of Voluntary Organisations*, London, Routledge, pp. 1–6.

Hapgood, M. (1988) 'Creative Direct Work with Adolescents: The Story of Craig Brooks', in J. Aldgate and J. Simmonds (eds) *Direct Work with Children: A Guide for Practitioners*, London, Batsford/BAAF, pp. 87–100.

Hardy, B., Leedham, I. and Wistow, G. (1996) 'Care Manager Co-Location in GP Practices', in R. Bland (ed.) *Developing Services for Older People and their Families*, London, Jessica Kingsley, pp. 161–178.

Harman, C. (1988) *The Fire Next Time: 1968 and After*, London, Bookmarks.

Harper, J. (1996) 'Recapturing the Past: Alternative Methods of Life Story Work in Adoption and Fostering', *Adoption and Fostering*, 20, 3, 21–28.

Harris, J. (1998) 'Scientific Management, Bureau-Professionalism, New Managerialism: The Labour Process of State Social Work', *British Journal of Social Work*, 28, 6, 839–862.

Harris, J. (2002) *The Social Work Business*, London, Routledge.

Harris, J., Froggett, L. and Paylor, I. (eds) (2000) *Reclaiming Social Work: The Southport Papers Volume 1*, Birmingham, BASW/Venture Press.

Harris, N. (1987) 'Defensive Social Work', *British Journal of Social Work*, 17, 1, 61–69.

Harris, R. (1997) 'Power', in M. Davies (ed.) *The Blackwell Companion to Social Work*, Oxford, Blackwell, pp. 28–33.

Harris, R. and Webb, D. (1987) *Welfare, Power, and Juvenile Justice*, London, Tavistock Publications.

Hart, J. (1980) 'It's Just a Stage We're Going Through: The Sexual Politics of Casework', in M. Brake and R. Bailey (eds) *Radical Social Work and Practice*, London, Edward Arnold, pp. 43–63.

Hatch S. and Sherrott P. (1973) 'Positive Discrimination and the Distribution of Discriminations', *Policy and Politics*, 1, 3, 223–240.

Hawkins, J. M. (ed.) (1987) *The Oxford Reference Dictionary*, London, Guild Publishing.

Hawkins, L., Fook, J. and Ryan, M. (2001) 'Social Workers' Use of the Language of Social Justice', *British Journal of Social Work*, 31, 1, 1–13.

Hawkins, P. and Shohet, R. (2000) *Supervision in the Helping Professions*, 2nd edn, Buckingham, Open University Press.

Healy, K. (2000) *Social Work Practices: Contemporary Perspectives on Change*, London, Sage.

Hearn, J. (1996) 'Men's Violence to Known Women: Historical, Everyday and Theoretical Constructions by Men', in B. Fawcett, B. Featherstone, J. Hearn and C. Toft (eds) *Violence and Gender Relations: Theories and Interventions*, London, Sage, pp. 22–37.

Hedley, R. (1995) 'Inside the Voluntary Sector', in J. Davis Smith, C. Rochester and R. Hedley (eds) (1995) *An Introduction to the Voluntary Sector*, London, Routledge, pp. 96–113.

Heidensohn, F. (1985) *Women and Crime*, London, Macmillan.

Henderson, R. and Pochin, M. (2001) *A Right Result? Advocacy, justice and empowerment*, Bristol, Policy Press.

Hendey, N. and Pascall, G. (1998) 'Independent Living: Gender, Violence and the Threat of Violence', *Disability and Society*, 13, 415–427.

Hendrix, E. (1981) 'The Fallacies in the Concept of Normalisation', *Mental Retardation*, 19, 6, 295–296.

Her Majesty's Treasury (1997) *Employment Opportunity in a Changing Labour Market: Pre-Budget Report Publications: The Modernisation of Britain's Tax and Benefit System No. 1*, London, HM Treasury.

Heraud B. (1970) *Sociology and Social Work*, London, Pergamon Press.

Herbert, M. (1989) *Discipline: A Positive Guide for Parents*, Oxford, Blackwell.

Herod, J. and Lymbery, M. (2002) 'The Social Work Role in Multi-disciplinary Teams', *Practice*, 14, 4, 17–27.

Heron, J. (1996) *Co-operative Inquiry: Research into the Human Condition*, London, Sage.

Hickman, M. J. and Walter, B. (1997) *Discrimination and the Irish Community in Britain*, London, Commission for Racial Equality.

Hill, M. (1990) 'The Manifest and Latent Lessons of Child Abuse Inquiries', *British Journal of Social Work*, 20, 2, 197–213.

Hill, M. (1993) *The Welfare State in Britain*, Aldershot, Edward Elgar.

Hill, M. (1998) 'What Children and Young People Say they Want from Social Services', *Research, Policy and Planning*, 15, 3, 17–27.

Hills, J. (1995) *Joseph Rowntree Inquiry into Income and Wealth*, Volume 2, York, Joseph Rowntree Foundation.

Hills, J. (1998) 'Housing: A Decent Home within the Reach of Every Family?', in H. Glennerster and J. Hills (eds) *The State of Welfare: The Economics of Social Spending*, 2nd edn, Oxford, Oxford University Press, pp. 122–188.

Hillyard, P. (1993) *Suspect Community*, London, Pluto.

Hillyard, P. and Percy-Smith, J. (1988) *The Coercive State*, London, Pinter.

Hockey, J., Katz, J. and Small, N. (eds) (2001) *Grief, Mourning and Death Ritual*, Buckingham, Open University Press.

Hodgkin, C. (1993) 'Policy and Paper Clips: Rejecting the Lure of the Corporate Model', *Nonprofit Management and Leadership*, 3, 4, 415–428.

Hohmann, M. and Weikart, D. P. (1995) *Educating Young Children: Active Learning Practices for Preschool and Child Care Programs*, Michigan, Yspilanti, MI, High Scope Press.

Hollingshead, A. B. and Redlich, F. C. (1958) *Social Class and Mental Illness*, New York, John Wiley.

Holloway, F. (1988) 'Day Care and Community Support', in A. Lavender and F. Holloway (eds) *Community Care in Practice*, Chichester, Wiley, pp. 161–186.

Holman, B. (1993) *A New Deal for Social Welfare*, Oxford, Lion Publishing.

Holman, B. (1998) 'Neighbourhoods and Exclusion', in C. Hallett and M. Barry (eds) *Social Exclusion and Social Work*, Lyme Regis, Russell House Publishing, pp. 62–73.

Home Office (1992) *National Standards for the Supervision of Offenders in the Community*, London, Home Office.

Home Office (1995) *National Standards for the Supervision of Offenders in the Community*, London, Home Office.

Home Office (1997) *No More Excuses: A New Approach to Tackling Youth Crime in England and Wales*, London, Home Office.

Home Office (1998a) *Getting it Right Together: Compact on Relations between Government and the Voluntary and Community Sector in England*, London, Stationery Office.

Home Office (1998b) *Speaking Up for Justice: Report of the Interdepartmental Working Group on the Treatment of Vulnerable or Intimidated Witnesses in the Criminal Justice System*, London, Home Office.

Home Office (2000a) *Achieving Best Evidence in Criminal Proceedings: guidance for vulnerable or intimidated witnesses, including children*, London, Home Office.

Home Office (2000b) *National Standards for the Supervision of Offenders in the Community*, London, Home Office.

Home Office (2001) *Getting it Right Together: Compact on Funding: a Code of Good Practice*, London, Stationery Office.

Home Office and Department of Health (DoH) (1992) *Memorandum of Good Practice on Video Recorded Interviews with Child Witnesses for Criminal Proceedings*, London, HMSO.

Hood, C. (1991) 'A public management for all seasons?', *Public Administration*, 69, 1, 3–19.

Hood, R. (1992) *Race and Sentencing: A Study in the Crown Court*, Oxford, Clarendon Press.

Hood, S. (1997) 'The purchaser/provider separation in child and family social work: Implications for service delivery and for the role of social worker', *Child and Family Social Work*, 2, 25–35.

hooks, b. (1982) *Ain't I A Woman: Black Women and Feminism*, London, Pluto.

Hopton, J. (1997) 'Anti-discriminatory Practice and Anti-oppressive Practice', *Critical Social Policy*, 17, 3, 47–61.

Horne, J. (1983) 'When the Social Worker is a Bridge', in P. Sawbridge (ed.) *Parents for Children*, London, BAAF, pp. 26–30.

Horton, B. T. (1996) 'Supporting Diversity: What Will It Take?', *Impact*, 9, 3, Summer, 2–3.

House, J. S., Umberson, D. and Landis, K. R. (1988) 'Structures and Processes of Social Support', *Annual Review of Sociology*, 14, 293–318.

Howard, M. (1993) Speech by the Rt. Hon. Michael Howard QC MP, the Home Secretary, to the 110th Conservative Party Conference, 6 October, London, Conservative Party Central Office.

Howe, D. (1986) *Social Workers and their Practice in Welfare Bureaucracies*, Aldershot, Gower.

Howe, D. (1991) 'Knowledge, Power and the Shape of Social Work Practice', in M. Davies (ed.) *The Sociology of Social Work*, London, Routledge, pp. 147–162.

Howe, D. (1992) 'Child Abuse and the Bureaucratization of Social Work', *Sociological Review*, 40, 3, 491–508.

Howe, D. (1994) 'Modernity, Postmodernity and Social Work', *British Journal of Social Work*, 24, 5, 513–532.

Howe, D. (1995) *Attachment Theory for Social Work Practice*, Basingstoke, Macmillan.

Howe, D. (1996a) 'Surface and depth in social work practice', in N. Parton (ed.) *Social Theory, Social Change and Social Work*, London, Routledge, pp. 77–97.

Howe, D. (ed.) (1996b) *Attachment and Loss in Child and Family Social Work*, Aldershot, Avebury.

Howe, D. (1998) 'Relationship-Based Thinking and Practice in Social Work', *Journal of Social Work Practice*, 12, 1, May, pp. 45–56.

Hudson, B. (2002) 'Interprofessionality in health and social care: the Achilles' heel of partnership', *Journal of Interprofessional Care* 16, 1, 7–17.

Hudson, B., Hardy, B., Henwood, M. and Wistow, G. (1997) 'Working Across Professional Boundaries: Primary Health Care and Social Care', *Public Money and Management*, October–December, 25–30.

Hughes, B. (1995) *Community Care and Older People*, Buckingham, Open University Press.

Hughes, M. and Gove, W. R. (1981) 'Living Alone, Social Integration and Mental Health', *American Journal of Sociology*, 87, 1, 48–74.

Hugman, R. (1998a) *Social Welfare and Social Value: The Role of the Caring Professions*, Basingstoke, Macmillan.

Hugman, R. (1998b) 'Social work and de-professionalization', in P. Abbott and L. Meerabeau (eds) *The Sociology of the Caring Professions*, 2nd edn, London, UCL Press, pp. 178–198.

Humphries, B. (ed.) (1996a) *Critical Perspectives on Empowerment*, Birmingham, Venture Press.

Humphries, B. (1996b) 'Contradictions in the Culture of Empowerment', in B. Humphries (ed.) *Critical Perspectives on Empowerment*, Birmingham, Venture Press, pp. 1–16.

Humphries, B. (1997) 'Reading Social Work: Competing Discourses in the Rules and Requirements for the Diploma in Social Work', *British Journal of Social Work*, 27, 5, 641–658.

Huxley, P. (1993) 'Case Management and Care Management in Community Care', *British Journal of Social Work*, 23, 4, 365–381.

Ince, L. (1998) *Making it Alone: A Study of the Care Experiences of Young Black People*, London, BAAF.

Itzin, C. and Newman, J. (eds) (1995) *Gender, Culture and Organizational Change*, London, Routledge.

Jackson, M. and Jackson, E. (1998) 'Choice-Making for People with a Learning Disability', *Learning Disability Practice*, 1, 3, 22–25.

Jackson, S. (1987) *The Education of Children in Care*, Bristol Papers No 1, Bristol, School of Applied Social Studies, University of Bristol.

Jackson, S. (1998) 'Looking After Children; A New Approach or Just an Exercise in Formfilling? A Response to Knight and Caveney', *British Journal of Social Work*, 28, 1, 45–56.

James, A. and Raine, J. (1998) *The New Politics of Criminal Justice*, Harlow, Longman.

Jamous, H. and Peloille, B. (1970) 'Professions or Self-Perpetuating Systems? Changes in the French University Hospital System', in J. A. Jackson (ed.) *Professions and Professionalization*, Cambridge, Cambridge University Press, pp. 111–152.

Jewett, C. (1995) *Helping Children Cope with Separation and Loss*, 2nd edn, London, BAAF/Batsford.

Johnson, J. (2002) 'Taking Care of Later Life: A Matter of Justice?', *British Journal of Social Work*, 32, 6, 139–150.

Johnson, N. (1999) *Mixed Economies of Welfare*, Hemel Hempstead, Prentice-Hall.

Johnson, N. (2001) 'The Personal Social Services', in S. P. Savage and R. Atkinson (eds) *Public Policy Under Blair*, Basingstoke, Palgrave, pp. 174–191.

Johnson, T. (1972) *Professions and Power*, Basingstoke, Macmillan Education.

Jones, C. (1983) *State Social Work and the Working Class*, Basingstoke, Macmillan.

Jones, C. (1996a) 'Regulating Social Work: A Review of the Review', in M. Preston-Shoot and S. Jackson (eds) *Educating Social Workers in a Changing Policy Context*, London, Whiting & Birch, pp. 10–25.

Jones, C. (1996b) 'Anti-intellectualism and the peculiarities of British social work education', in N. Parton (ed.) *Social Theory, Social Change and Social Work*, London, Routledge.

Jones, C. (1997) 'British Social Work and the Classless Society: The Failure of a Profession', in H. Jones (ed.) *Towards a Classless Society*, London, Routledge, pp. 179–200.

Jones, C. (1998) 'Social Work and Society', in R. Adams, L. Dominelli and M. Payne (eds) *Social Work: Themes, Issues and Critical Debates*, Basingstoke, Macmillan, pp. 34–43.

Jones, C. (2001) 'Voices from the Frontline: State Social Workers and New Labour', *British Journal of Social Work*, 31, 4, 547–562.

Jones, C. and Novak, T. (1999) *Poverty, Welfare and the Disciplinary State*, London, Routledge.

Jones, F., Fletcher, B. and Ibbetson, K. (1991) 'Stressors and Strains Amongst Social Workers: Demands, Supports, Constraints and Psychological Health', *British Journal of Social Work*, 21, 4, 443–469.

Jones, R. (1996) 'Swimming Together: the Tidal Change for Statutory Agencies and the Voluntary Sector', in C. Hanvey and T. Philpot (eds) *Sweet Charity: The Role and Workings of Voluntary Organisations*, London, Routledge, pp. 39–57.

Jordan, B. (1984) *Invitation to Social Work*, Oxford, Martin Robertson.

Jordan, B. (1990) *Social Work in an Unjust Society*, Hemel Hempstead, Harvester Wheatsheaf.

Jordan, B. (2001) 'Tough Love: Social Work, Social Exclusion and the Third Way', *British Journal of Social Work*, 31, 4, 527–546.

Jordan, B. with Jordan, C. (2000) *Social Work and the Third Way: Tough Love as Social Policy*, London, Sage.

Joseph Rowntree Foundation (1996) *The Future of the Voluntary Sector*, Social Policy Summary 9, July, York, Joseph Rowntree Foundation.

Keenan, T. (2002) *An Introduction to Child Development*, London: Sage.

Kelly, L. (1988) *Surviving Sexual Violence*, Cambridge, Polity Press.

Kempson, E. (1996) *Life on a Low Income*, York, Joseph Rowntree Foundation.

Kempson, E., Bryson, A. and Rowlingson, K. (1994) *Hard Times? How Poor Families Make Ends Meet*, London, Policy Studies Institute.

Kemshall, H. (1996) 'Offender Risk and Probation Practice', in H. Kemshall and J. Pritchard (eds) *Good Practice in Risk Assessment and Risk Management*, London, Jessica Kingsley, pp. 133–145.

Kemshall, H. and Pritchard, J. (eds) (1996) *Good Practice in Risk Assessment and Risk Management*, London, Jessica Kingsley.

Kendall, J. and Knapp, M. (1995) 'A Loose and Baggy Monster: Boundaries, Definitions and Typologies', in J. Davis Smith, C. Rochester and R. Hedley (eds) (1995) *An Introduction to the Voluntary Sector*, London, Routledge, pp. 66–95.

Kilewer, C. and Drake, S. (1998) 'Disability, Eugenics and the Current Ideology of Segregation: A Modern Moral Tale', *Disability and Society*, 13, pp. 95–111.

King, P. (1989) *Talking Pictures: Trigger Pictures to Help Children Talk About Themselves*, London, BAAF.

Kingston, P. and Penhale, B. (eds) (1995) *Family Violence and the Caring Professions*, Basingstoke, Macmillan.

Kitchin, R. (1998) ' "Out of Place", "Knowing One's Place": Space, Power and the Exclusion of Disabled People', *Disability and Society*, 13, 343–356.

Knapp, M., Bryson, D. and Lewis, J. (1985) *The Objectives of Child Care and Their Attainment Over a 12 Month Period for a Cohort of New Admissions*, Suffolk Cohort Study, Discussion Paper 373, PSSRU, University of Kent.

Knapp, M., Cambridge, P., Thomason, C., Beecham, J., Allen, C. and Darton, R. (1992) *Care in the Community: Challenge and Demonstration*, Aldershot, Arena.

Knight, B. (1993) *Voluntary Action*, London, Centris.

Knight, T. and Caveney, S. (1998) 'Assessment and Action Records: Will they Promote Good Parenting?', *British Journal of Social Work*, 28, 1, 29–43.

Kolb, D. A. (1984) *Experiential Learning*, Englewood Cliffs, NJ, Prentice-Hall.

Laming, H. (1998) *Social Services: Facing the Future*, London, Stationery Office.

Laming, Lord (2003) *The Victoria Climbié Inquiry*, London, Stationery Office.

Langan, M. (2000) 'Social Services: Managing the Third Way', in J. Clarke, S. Gewirtz and E. McClaughlin (eds) *New Managerialism, New Welfare?*, London, Sage/Open University, pp. 152–168.

Langan, M. and Clarke, J. (1994) 'Managing in the Mixed Economy of Care', in J. Clarke, A. Cochrane and E. McClaughlin (eds) *Managing Social Policy*, London, Sage/Open University, pp. 73–92.

Langan, M. and Day, L. (1992) *Women, Oppression and Social Work: Issues in Anti-Discriminatory Practice*, London, Routledge.

Larson, M. S. (1977) *The Rise of Professionalism: A Sociological Analysis*, Berkeley, CA, University of California Press.

Le Grand, J. and Bartlett, W. (eds) (1993) *Quasi-Markets and Social Policy*, Basingstoke, Macmillan.

Leat, D. (1993) *The Development of Community Care by the Independent Sector*, London, Policy Studies Institute.

Leathard, A. (1994) *Going Inter-professional: Working Together for Health and Welfare*, London, Routledge.

Leff, J. and Vaughn, C. (1985) *Expressed Emotion in Families*, New York, Guildford Press.

Leicester, M. and Cooke, P. (2002) 'Rights not Restrictions for Learning Disabled Adults: a response to Spiecker and Steutel', *Journal of Moral Education*, 31, 2, pp. 181–188.

Leng, R., Taylor, R. D. and Wasik, M. (1998) Blackstone's Guide to the Crime and Disorder Act 1998, London, Blackstone Press.

Leonard, P. (1997) *Postmodern Welfare: Reconstructing an Emancipatory Project*, London, Sage.

Lewis, J. (1993) 'Developing the Mixed Economy of Care: Emerging Issues for Voluntary Organisations', *Journal of Social Policy*, 22, 2, 173–192.

Lewis, J. (1995) *The Voluntary Sector, the State and Social Work in Britain*, Aldershot, Edward Elgar.

Lewis, J. (1996a) 'What does contracting do to voluntary organisations?', in D. Billis and M. Harris (eds) *Voluntary Agencies: Challenges of Management and Organisation*, Basingstoke, Macmillan, pp. 98–112.

Lewis, J. (1996b) *Give Us A Voice*, London, Choice Press.

Lewis, J. (2001) 'Older People and the Health-Social Care Boundary in the UK: Half a Century of Hidden Policy Conflict', *Social Policy and Administration*, 35, 4, 343–359.

Lewis, J. and Glennerster, H. (1996) *Implementing the New Community Care*, Buckingham, Open University Press.

Lewis, J. with Bernstock, P., Bovell, V. and Wookey, F. (1997) 'Implementing Care Management: Issues in Relation to the New Community Care', *British Journal of Social Work*, 27, 1, 5–24.

Lightman, E. S. and Riches, G. (2000) 'From modest rights to commodification in Canada's welfare state', *European Journal of Social Work*, 3, 2, 179–190.

Lilley, R., Lambden, P. and Newdick, C. (2001) *Understanding the Human Rights Act: a tool kit for the health service*, Abingdon, Radcliffe Medical Press.

Lindon, J. (1993) *Child Development from Birth to Eight*, London, National Children's Bureau.

Lipsky, M. (1980) *Street Level Bureaucracy: Dilemmas of the Individual in Public Services*, New York, Russell Sage Foundation.

Lishman, J. (1994) *Communication in Social Work*, Basingstoke, Macmillan.

Lister, R. (1998) 'In From the Margins: Citizenship, Inclusion and Exclusion', in M. Barry and C. Hallett (eds) *Social Exclusion and Social Work: Issues of Theory, Policy and Practice*, Dorset, Russell House Publishing, pp. 26–38.

Lister, R. and Beresford, P. (1991) *Working Together Against Poverty*, London, Open Services Project.

Lloyd, M. (1997) 'Dying and Bereavement, Spirituality and Social Work in a Market Economy of Welfare', *British Journal of Social Work*, 27, 2, 175–190.

Lomley, J. and Calpin-Davies, P. (1998) 'Sexual Health and the Learning Disabled Client: A Policy Gap?', *Learning Disability Practice*, 1, 3, 10–12.

Lord Chancellor's Department (1997) *Who Decides? Making Decisions on Behalf of Mentally Incapacitated Adults*, London, Lord Chancellor's Department.

Lovett, H. (1996) *Learning to Listen*, London, Jessica Kingsley.

Lowe, K. and de Paiva, S. (1991) 'Clients' Community and Social Contacts: Results of a 5 Year Longitudinal Study', *Journal of Mental Deficiency Research*, 35, 308–323.

Ludlum, C. D. (1993) *Tending the Candle: A Booklet for Circle Facilitators*, Manchester, CT, Communitas Inc.

Lymbery, M. (1998a) 'Care Management and Professional Autonomy: the Impact of Community Care Legislation on Social Work with Older People', *British Journal of Social Work*, 28, 6, 863–878.

Lymbery, M. (1998b) 'Social Work in General Practice: Dilemmas and Possible Solutions', *Journal of Interprofessional Care*, 12, 2, 199–208.

Lymbery, M. (2000) 'The Retreat from Professionalism: from Social Worker to Care Manager', in N. Malin (ed.) *Professionalism, Boundaries and the Workplace*, London, Routledge, pp. 123–138.

Lymbery, M. (2001) 'Social Work at the Crossroads', *British Journal of Social Work*, 31, 3, 369–384.

Lymbery, M. (2003a) 'Negotiating the Contradictions between Competence and Creativity in Social Work Education', *Journal of Social Work*, 3, 1, 99–117.

Lymbery, M. (2003b) 'Collaborating for the social and health care of older people', in C. Whittington, J. Weinstein and T. Leiba (eds) *Collaboration in Social Work Practice*, London, Jessica Kingsley, pp. 219–238.

Lymbery, M. and Millward, A. (2000) 'The Primary Care Interface', in G. Bradley and J. Manthorpe (eds) *Working on the Faultline: Social Work and Health Care*, Birmingham, Venture Press, pp. 11–44.

Lymbery, M. and Millward, A. (2001) 'Community Care in Practice: Social Work in Primary Health Care', *Social Work in Health Care*, 34, 3/4, 241–259.

Lynes, D. and Goddard, J. (1995) *The View from the Front: The User View of Childcare in Norfolk*, Norwich, Norfolk County Council, Norfolk In Care Group, Norfolk Social Services Department.

Lyon, C. (1994) *Legal Issues Arising from the Care, Control and Safety of Children with Learning Disabilities who also Present Severe Challenging Behaviour*, London, Mental Health Foundation.

Macdonald, G. M. and Sheldon, B. (1992) 'Contemporary Studies of the Effectiveness of Social Work', *British Journal of Social Work*, 22, 6, 615–643.

MacPherson, Sir William, of Cluny (1999) *The Stephen Lawrence Inquiry*, London, Stationery Office.

Maguire, M., Morgan, R. and Reiner, R. (eds) (2002) *The Oxford Handbook of Criminology*, 3rd edn, Oxford, Oxford University Press.

Magura, S., Moses, B. S. and Jones, M. A. (1987) *Assessing Risk and Measuring Change in Families: The Family Risk Scales*, Washington, DC, Child Welfare League of America.

Maluccio, A. N., Fein, E. and Olmstead, K. A. (1986) *Permanency Planning for Children*, London, Tavistock.

Mandelstam, M. (1998) *An A–Z of Community Care Law*, London, Jessica Kingsley.

Mandelstam, M. (1999) *Community Care Practice and the Law*, 2nd edn, London, Jessica Kingsley.

Mann, M. (2001) 'Globalization after September 11', *New Left Review*, 12, 51–73.

Marchant, R. and Page, M. (1993) *Bridging the Gap: Child Protection Work with Children with Multiple Disabilities*, London, National Society for the Prevention of Cruelty to Children.

Marris, P. (1986) *Loss and Change*, revised edn, London, Routledge.

Marsh, P. and Triseliotis, J. (1996) *Ready to Practise? Social Workers and Probation Officers: Their Training and First Year in Work*, Aldershot, Avebury.

Marshall, M. and Dixon, M. (1996) *Social Work with Older People*, 3rd edn, Basingstoke, Macmillan.

Marshall, M. (ed.) (1990) *Working with Dementia*, Birmingham, Venture Press.

Marshall, T. F. (1996) 'Can We Define the Voluntary Sector?', in D. Billis and M. Harris (eds) *Voluntary Agencies: Challenges of Organisation & Management*, Basingstoke, Macmillan, pp. 45–60.

Martinez-Brawley, E. E. and Mendez-Bonito Zorita, P. (1998) 'At the Edge of the Frame: Beyond Science and Art in Social Work', *British Journal of Social Work*, 28, 2, 197–212.

Martinson, R. (1974) 'What Works? Questions and Answers about Prison Reform', *The Public Interest*, Spring, 35, 22–54.

Massey, A. (1993) *Managing the Public Sector*, Aldershot, Edward Elgar.

Matza, D. (1969) *Becoming Deviant*, Englewood Cliffs, NJ, Prentice-Hall.

May, T. (1991) *Probation: Politics, Policy and Practice*, Buckingham, Open University Press.

May, T. and Buck, M. (2000) 'Social Work, Professionalism and the Rationality of Organisational Change', in N. Malin (ed.) *Professionalism, Boundaries and the Workplace*, London, Routledge, pp. 139–157.

Mayo, M. (1975) 'Community Development: A Radical Alternative?', in R. Bailey and M. Brake (eds) *Radical Social Work*, London, Edward Arnold, pp. 129–143.

Mayo, M. (1980) 'Beyond CDP: Reaction and Community Action', in M. Brake and R. Bailey (eds) *Radical Social Work and Practice*, London, Edward Arnold, pp. 182–196.

McBeath, G. B. and Webb, S. A. (1991) 'Social Work, Modernity and Post-Modernity', *Sociological Review*, 39, 4, 745–762.

McCarthy, M. (1993) 'Sexual Experiences of Women with Learning Difficulties in Long-Stay Hospitals', *Sexuality and Disability*, 11, 4, 277–286.

McCarthy, M. and Thompson, D. (1992) *Sex and the 3 R's: Rights, Responsibilities and Risks. A Sex Education Resource Package for People with Learning Difficulties*, Brighton, Pavilion Publishing and Aids Awareness/Sex Education Project.

McCarthy, M. and Thompson, D. (1994) *Sex and Staff Training: Sexuality, Sexual Abuse and Safer Sex: A Training Manual for Staff Working with People with Learning Difficulties*, Brighton, Pavilion Publishing.

McCarthy, M. and Thompson, D. (1996) 'Sexual Abuse by Design: An Examination of the Issues in Learning Disability Services', *Disability and Society*, 11, 2, 205–217.

McDonald, P. and Coleman, M. (1999) 'Deconstructing Hierarchies of Oppression and Adopting a 'Multiple Model' Approach to Anti-oppressive Practice', *Social Work Education*, 18, 1, 19–34.

McGovern, D. and Hemmings, P. (1994) 'A Follow-up of Second Generation Afro-Caribbeans and White British with a First Admission Diagnosis of Schizophrenia: Attitudes to Mental Illness and Psychiatric Services of Patients and Relatives', *Social Science and Medicine*, 38, 1, 117–127.

McGrath, M., Ramcharan, P., Grant, G., Parry-Jones, B., Caldock, K. and Robinson, C. (1996) 'The Roles and Tasks of Care Managers in Wales', *Community Care Management and Planning Review*, 4, 6, 185–194.

McGuire, J. (ed.) (1995) *What Works? Reducing Re-offending*, Chichester, Wiley.

McIntosh, B. and Whittaker, A. (1999) *Days of Change*, London, King's Fund/National Development Team.

McKnight, J. L., in O'Brien, J. and O'Brien, C. L. (1996) *Members of Each Other: Building Community in Company with People with Developmental Disabilities*, Toronto, CA, Inclusion Press, pp. 42–44.

McLaughlin, E. and Muncie, J. (2000) 'The Criminal Justice System: New Labour's New Partnerships', in J. Clarke, S. Gewirtz and E. McLaughlin (eds) *New Managerialism New Welfare?*, London, Sage.

McWilliams, W. (1992) 'The Rise and Development of Management Thought in the English Probation System', in R. Statham and P. Whitehead (eds) *Managing the Probation Service: Issues for the 1990s*, Harlow, Longman, pp. 3–29.

Means, R. and Smith, R. (1996) *Community Care, Housing and Homelessness*, Bristol, Polity Press.

Means, R. and Smith, R. (1998) *Community Care: Policy and Practice*, 2nd edn, Basingstoke, Macmillan.

Means, R., Hoyes, M., Lart, R. and Taylor, M. (1994) 'Quasi-markets and community care: towards user empowerment?', in W. Bartlett, C. Propper, D. Wilson and J. Le Grand (eds) *Quasi-Markets in the Welfare State*, Bristol, SAUS, pp. 158–183.

Meiksins Wood, E. (1995) 'A Chronology of the New Left and Its Successors, Or: Who's Old-Fashioned Now?', in L. Panitch (ed.) *Socialist Register 1995*, London, Merlin Press, pp. 22–50.

Mental Health Foundation (2000) *In Good Faith*, London, Mental Health Foundation Strategies for Living Project.

Menzies, I. (1970) *The Functioning of Social Systems as a Defence Against Anxiety*, London, Tavistock Institute of Human Relations.

Meyer, C. H. (1993) *Assessment in Social Work Practice*, New York, Columbia University Press.

Middleton, L. (1997) *The Art of Assessment*, Birmingham, Venture Press.

Middleton, S., Ashworth, K. and Walker, R. (1994) *Family Fortunes: Pressures on Parents and Children in the 1990s*, London, Child Poverty Action Group.

Midwinter, E. (1994) *The Development of Social Welfare in Britain*, Buckingham, Open University Press.

Millar, J. (1996) 'Women, Poverty and Social Security', in C. Hallett (ed.) *Women and Social Policy: An Introduction*, Hemel Hempstead, Harvester Wheatsheaf, pp. 52–64.

Millar, J. (1998) 'Social Policy and Family Policy', in P. Alcock, A. Erskine and M. May (eds) *The Student's Companion to Social Policy*, Oxford, Blackwell, pp. 121–127.

Miller, W. R. and Rollnick, S. (1991) *Motivational Interviewing*, New York, Guilford.

Millham, S., Bullock, R., Hosie, K. and Haak, M. (1986) *Lost in Care: the Problem of Maintaining Links between Children in Care and their Families*, Aldershot, Gower.

Millward, A. (2001) personal communication.

Milne, R. and Bull, R. (1999) *Investigative Interviewing: Psychology and Practice*, London, Wiley.

Milne, R., Clare, I. and Bull, R. (1997) *Using the Cognitive Interview with Adults with Mild Learning Disabilities*, manuscript.

Milner, J. and O'Byrne, P. (1998) *Assessment in Social Work*, Basingstoke, Macmillan.

Modood, T. and Berthoud, R. with Lakey, J., Nazroo, J., Smith, P., Virdee, S. and Beishon, S. (1997) *Ethnic Minorities in Britain: diversity and disadvantage*, London, Policy Studies Institute.

Morgan, G. (1997) *Images of Organization*, 2nd edn, London, Sage.

Morley, R. (1993) 'Recent Responses to "Domestic Violence" against Women: A Feminist Critique', in R. Page and J. Baldock (eds) *Social Policy Review 5*, Social Policy Association, University of Kent at Canterbury, pp. 177–206.

Morris, A. and Giller, H. (1987) *Understanding Juvenile Justice*, London, Croom Helm.

Morris, J. (1998a) *Still Missing? Volume 1. The Experience of Disabled Children and Young People Living Away From Their Families*, London, The Who Cares? Trust.

Morris, J. (1998b) *Still Missing? Volume 2. Disabled Children and the Children Act*, London, The Who Cares? Trust.

Morris, J. (1998c) *Don't Leave Us Out: Involving Disabled Children and Young People with Communication Impairments*, York, Joseph Rowntree Foundation.

Morris, L. (1993) *Dangerous Classes, the Underclass and Social Citizenship*, London, Routledge.

Morrison, T. (1996) *Staff Supervision in Social Care: An Action Learning Approach*, Brighton, Pavilion Publishing.

Morton, H. (1998) *Report to the Disability and Mental Health Services Development Committee, 9th September 1998: The Enquiry into Woodfold Day Services*, unpublished, Sheffield Family and Community Services Department.

Mount, B. and Zwernik, K. (1989) *It's Never Too Early, It's Never Too Late: A Booklet About Personal Futures Planning*, St Paul, MN, Governor's Planning Council on Developmental Disabilities.

Mount, B., Beeman, P. and Ducharme, G. (1988) *What Are We Learning about Bridge Building?*, Manchester, CT, Communitas Inc.

Moxley, D. P. (1989) *The Practice of Case Management*, Beverly Hills, CA, Sage.

Mullaly, R. (1997) *Structural Social Work: Ideology, Theory and Practice*, 2nd edn, Oxford, Oxford University Press.

Mullender, A. (1996) *Rethinking Domestic Violence: The Social Work and Probation Response*, London, Routledge.

Mullender, A. and Ward, D. (1991) *Self-Directed Groupwork. Users Take Action for Empowerment*, London, Whiting & Birch.

Muncie, J. (1999) *Youth and Crime: a critical introduction*, London, Sage.

Munro, E. (1998a) 'Improving Social Workers' Knowledge Base in Child Protection Work', *British Journal of Social Work*, 28, 1, 89–105.

Munro, E. (1998b) *Understanding Social Work: An Empirical Approach*, London, Athlone Press.

Munro, E. (2000) 'Defending Professional Social Work Practice', in J. Harris, L. Froggett and I. Paylor (eds) (2000) *Reclaiming Social Work: The Southport Papers Volume 1*, Birmingham, BASW/Venture Press, pp. 1–10.

Murie, A. (1998) 'Housing', in P. Alcock, A. Erskine and M. May (eds) *The Student's Companion to Social Policy*, Oxford, Blackwell, pp. 299–305.

Murray, C. (1990) *The Emerging British Underclass*, London, Institute of Economic Affairs.

Myers, F., Ager, A., Kerr, P. and Myles, S. (1998) 'Outside Looking In? Studies of the Community Integration of People with Learning Disabilities', *Disability and Society*, 13, 389–413.

National Society for the Prevention of Cruelty to Children (NSPCC) (1997) *Turning Points – A Resource Pack for Communicating with Children*, London, NSPCC.

Nellis, M. (1995) 'Probation Values for the 1990s', The Howard Journal of Criminal Justice, 34, 1, 19–44.

Nelson, G., Hall, G. B., Squire, D. and Walsh-Bowers, R. T. (1992) 'Social Network Transactions of Psychiatric Patients', *Social Science and Medicine*, 34, 4, 433–455.

Netten, A., Darton, R., Bebbington, A. and Brown, P. (2001) 'Residential or nursing home care? The appropriateness of placement decisions', *Ageing and Society*, 21, 3–23.

Newburn, T. (1997) 'Youth, Crime and Justice', in M. Maguire, R. Morgan and R. Reiner (eds) *The Oxford Handbook of Criminology*, 2nd edn, Oxford, Oxford University Press.

Newman, J. (1998) 'Managerialism and Social Welfare', in G. Hughes and G. Lewis (eds) *Unsettling Welfare: The Reconstruction of Social Policy*, London, Routledge, pp. 333–374.

Newman, J. and Clarke, J. (1994) 'Going about our Business? The Managerialization of Public Services', in J. Clarke, A. Cochrane and E. McLaughlin (eds) *Managing Social Policy*, London, Sage/Open University, pp. 13–31.

Norris, M. (1984) *Integration of Special Hospital Patients into the Community*, Aldershot, Gower.

O'Brien, J. (1981) *The Principle of Normalisation: a foundation for effective services*, London, CMH.

O'Brien, J. (1987) 'A Guide to Lifestyle Planning Using the Activities Catalogue to Integrate Services and National Support Systems', in B. Wilcox and G. T. Bellamy (eds) *A Comprehensive Guide to the Activities Catalog*, Baltimore, Paul H. Brookes, pp. 175–189.

O'Brien, J. and O'Brien, C. L. (1992) *Remembering the Soul of Our Work*, Madison WI, Options in Community Living.

O'Brien, M. and Penna, S. (1998) *Theorising Welfare: Enlightenment and Modern Society*, London, Sage.

O'Connor, S. (1992) 'Culture, Disability and Family Policy', *Disability and Family Policy Bulletin*, Center of Human Policy, Syracuse University, 2, Spring, 4–5.

O'Connor, S. (1993) *Multiculturalism and Disability: A Collection of Resources and Issues*, Center of Human Policy, Syracuse, NY, Syracuse University.

Oaklander, V. (1978) *Windows to Our Children: A Gestalt Approach to Children and Adolescents*, Moab, UT, Real People Press.

Office for National Statistics (1998) *Social Trends 28: 1998 Edition*, London, Stationery Office.

Office of the Deputy Prime Minister (ODPM) (2002) *Draft Circular on Best Value and Performance Improvement*, London, ODPM.

Oliver, M. (1983) *Social Work with Disabled People*, London, Macmillan.

Oliver, M. (1996) *Understanding Disability: From Theory to Practice*, Basingstoke, Macmillan.

Oliver, M. and Sapey, B. (1999) *Social Work with Disabled People*, 2nd edn, Basingstoke, Macmillan.

Oliver, P. (1984) 'The Politics of Disability', *Critical Social Policy*, 11, 21–33.

Olson, D., Cioffi, A., Yovanoff, P. and Mank, D. (2000) 'Gender differences in supported employment', *Mental Retardation*, 38, 2, 89–96.

Oppenheim, C. (1997) 'The growth of poverty and inequality', in A. Walker and C. Walker (eds) *Britain Divided: The Growth of Social Exclusion in the 1980s and 1990s*, London, Child Poverty Action Group, pp. 17–31.

Orme, J. (2001) 'Regulation or fragmentation? Directions for Social Work under New Labour', *British Journal of Social Work*, 31, 4, 611–624.

Orme, J. and Glastonbury, B. (1993) *Care Management*, Basingstoke, Macmillan.

Osborne, S. P. and McLaughlin, K. (2002) 'Trends and Issues in the Implementation of Local "Voluntary Sector Compacts" in England', *Public Money and Management*, 22, 1, January–March, 55–63.

Øvretveit, J. (1993) *Coordinating Community Care*, Basingstoke, Macmillan.

Owen, D. (1964) *English Philanthropy 1660–1960*, London, Oxford University Press.

Owens, P., Carrier, J. and Horder, J. (eds) (1995) *Interprofessional Issues in Community and Primary Health Care*, Basingstoke, Macmillan.

Packman, J., Randall, J. and Jacques, N. (1986) *Who Needs Care? Social Work Decisions about Children*, Oxford, Blackwell.

Padbury, P. and Frost, N. (2001) *Problem Solving in Foster Care. Research Report*, London, The Children's Society.

Page, R. (1992) 'Empowerment, Oppression and Beyond: A Coherent Strategy? A Reply to Ward and Mullender (CSP Issue 32)', *Critical Social Policy*, 35, 89–92.

Pahl, J. (1994) ' "Like the Job – But Hate the Organisation": Social Workers and Managers in Social Services', in R. Page and J. Baldock (eds) *Social Policy Review*, 6, Social Policy Association, University of Kent at Canterbury, 190–211.

Park, D. C. and Radford, J. P. (1998) 'From the Case Files: Reconstructing a History of Involuntary Sterilisation', *Disability and Society*, 13, 316–342.

Parker, R., Ward, H., Jackson, S., Aldgate, J. and Wedge, P. (eds) (1991) *Looking After Children: Assessing Outcomes in Child Care*, London, HMSO.

Parkes, C. M. (1986) *Bereavement: Studies of Grief in Adult Life*, 2nd edn, London, Tavistock.

Parsloe, P. (ed.) (1999) *Risk Assessment in Social Care and Social Work*, London, Jessica Kingsley.

Parton, N. (1991) *Governing the Family: Child Care, Child Protection and the State*, London, Macmillan.

Parton, N. (1994) 'Problematics of Governance: (Post) Modernity and Social Work', *British Journal of Social Work*, 24, 1, 9–32.

Parton, N. (1996a) 'Social Theory, Social Change and Social Work: An Introduction', in N. Parton (ed.) *Social Theory, Social Change and Social Work*, London, Routledge, pp. 4–18.

Parton, N. (1996b) 'Social Work, Risk and the "Blaming System"', in N. Parton (ed.) *Social Theory, Social Change and Social Work*, London, Routledge, pp. 98–114.

Parton, N. (ed.) (1997) *Child Protection and Family Support: Tensions, Contradictions and Possibilities*, London, Routledge.

Parton, N. (1998) 'Risk, Advanced Liberalism and Child Welfare: The Need to Rediscover Uncertainty and Ambiguity', *British Journal of Social Work*, 28, 1, 5–27.

Parton, N. (2000) 'Some Thoughts on the Relationship between Theory and Practice in and for Social Work', *British Journal of Social Work*, 30, 4, 449–463.

Parton, N. and Marshall, W. (1998) 'Postmodernism and Discourse Approaches to Social Work', in R. Adams, L. Dominelli and M. Payne (eds) *Social Work, Themes, Issues and Critical Debates*, London, Macmillan, pp. 240–249.

Parton, N. and O'Byrne, P. (2000) *Constructive Social Work: towards a new practice*, Basingstoke, Palgrave.

Parton, N., Thorpe, D. and Wattam, C. (1997) Child Protection: Risk and the Moral Order, Basingstoke, Macmillan – now Palgrave Macmillan.

Patel, N. (1999) 'Endemic Racism? Lessons from the Campaign Against CCETSW', unpublished paper presented to 'Anti-Racism and Anti-Oppressive Practice Conference', University of Leeds, 9 June.

Paton, R. (1996) 'How are Values Handled in Voluntary Agencies?', in D. Billis and M. Harris (eds) *Voluntary Agencies: Challenges of Organisation & Management*, Basingstoke, Macmillan, pp. 29–44.

Patterson, T. (2001) 'Welfare Rights Advice and the New Managerialism', *Benefits*, January–February, 5–11.

Paylor, I., Froggett, L. and Harris, J. (eds) (2000) *Reclaiming Social Work: The Southport Papers Volume 2*, Birmingham, BASW/Venture Press.

Payne, M. (1995) *Social Work and Community Care*, Basingstoke, Macmillan.

Payne, M. (1997) *Modern Social Work Theory: A Critical Introduction*, 2nd edn, Basingstoke, Macmillan.

Payne, M. (2000a) *Teamwork in Multiprofessional Care*, Basingstoke, Macmillan.

Payne, M. (2000b) 'The Politics of Case Management and Social Work', *International Journal of Social Welfare*, 9, 2, 82–91.

Payne, M. (2001) 'Knowledge *Bases* and Knowledge *Biases* in Social Work', *Journal of Social Work*, 1, 2, 133–146.

Payne, M. (2002) 'The Role and Achievements of a Professional Association in the Late Twentieth Century: the British Association of Social Workers 1970–2000', *British Journal of Social Work*, 32, 8, 969–995.

Peile, C. and McCouat, M. (1997) 'The Rise of Relativism: The Future of Theory and Knowledge Development in Social Work', *British Journal of Social Work*, 27, 3, 343–360.

Perri 6 and Fieldgrass, J. (1992) *Snapshots of the Voluntary Sector Today*, London, NCVO Publications.

Perske, R. (1988) *Circles of friends: people with disabilities and their friends enrich the lives of one another*, Nashville, TN, Abingdon Press.

Phillips, M. (1997) 'Death of Dad', *The Observer*, 2 November.

Philpot, T. (ed.) (1999) *Political Correctness and Social Work*, London, Institute of Economic Affairs.

Piachaud, D. and Sutherland, H. (2001) 'Child Poverty in Britain and the New Labour Government', *Journal of Social Policy*, 30, 1, 95–118.

Piaget, J. (1959) *The Language and Thought of the Child*, London, Routledge & Kegan Paul.

Pierson, J. (2002) *Tackling social exclusion*, London, Routledge.

Pilalis, J. (1986) ' "The Integration of Theory and Practice": A Re-examination of a Paradoxical Expectation', *British Journal of Social Work*, 16, 1, 79–96.

Pilger, J. (1995) 'Hail to the New Tories', *New Statesman and Society*, 5 May, 17–18.

Pithouse, A. (1998) *Social Work: The Social Organisation of an Invisible Trade*, 2nd edn, Aldershot, Ashgate.

Pitts, J. (1988) *The Politics of Juvenile Crime*, London, Sage.

Pitts, J. (1996) 'The Politics and Practice of Youth Justice', in E. McLaughlin and J. Muncie (eds) *Controlling Crime*, London, Sage, pp. 249–291.

Pitts, J. (1999) *Working with Young Offenders*, 2nd edn, Basingstoke, Macmillan – now Palgrave Macmillan.

Platt, D. (1998) 'Report on NISW Conference. News Section', *Community Care*, 1–7 October, 2.

Pollitt, C. (1993) *Managerialism and the Public Services*, 2nd edn, Oxford, Blackwell.

Postle, K. (1999) 'Deconstructing and Reconstructing Social Work for Older People in the 21st Century', *Issues in Social Work Education*, 19, 2, 23–38.

Postle, K. (2001) 'The social work side is disappearing. I guess it started with us being called care managers', *Practice*, 13, 1, 13–26.

Postle, K. (2002) 'Working "Between the Idea and the Reality": Ambiguities and Tensions in Care Managers' Work', *British Journal of Social Work*, 32, 3, 335–351.

Powell, M. (2000) 'New Labour and the third way in the British welfare state; a new and distinctive approach?', *Critical Social Policy*, 20, 1, 39–60.

Power, M. (1997) *The Audit Society*, Oxford, Oxford University Press.

Pratt, L. (2002) *Parallel Lives? Poverty among ethnic minority groups in Britain*, London, Child Poverty Action Group.

Priestley, P. and McGuire, J. (1985) *Offending Behaviour: Skills and Stratagems for Going Straight*, London, Sage.

Puddifoot, J. E. (1995) 'Dimensions of Community Identity', *Journal of Community and Applied Social Psychology*, 5, 357–370.

Pugh, G., De'Ath, E. and Smith, C. (1994) *Confident Parents, Confident Children: Policy and Practice in Parent Education and Support*, London, National Children's Bureau.

Pugh, R. and Gould, I. (2000) 'Globalization, social work and social welfare', *European Journal of Social Work*, 3, 2, 123–138.

Putnam, R. D. (2000) *Bowling Alone*, New York, Touchstone.

Racino, J. A. (1994) 'Creating Change in States, Agencies and Communities', in V. J. Bradley, J. W. Ashbugh and B. C. Blaney (eds) *Creating Individual Supports for People with Developmental Disabilities: A Mandate for Change at Many Levels*, Baltimore, Paul H. Brookes, pp. 171–196.

Radia, K. (1996) *Ignored, Silenced, Neglected: Housing and Mental Health Care Needs of Asian People*, York, Joseph Rowntree Foundation.

Raine, J. and Willson, M. (1993) *Managing Criminal Justice*, Hemel Hempstead, Harvester Wheatsheaf.

Rainford, L., Mason, V. and Hickman, M. (eds) (2000) *Health in England 1998: Investigating the links between social inequalities and health*, London, Office for National Statistics.

Ramcharan, P., Grant, G., Parry-Jones, B. and Robinson, C. (1999) 'The Roles and Tasks of Care Management Practitioners in Wales – Revisited', *Managing Community Care*, 7, 3, 29–37.

Ramon, S. (ed.) (1991) *Beyond Care: Normalisation and Integration Work*, Basingstoke, Macmillan.

Ransom, S. and Stewart, J. (1994) *Management for the Public Domain*, Basingstoke, Macmillan.

Rapp, C. A. and Wintersteen, R. (1989) 'The Strengths Model of Case Management: Results from Demonstrations', *Psycho-Social Rehabilitation*, 13, 1, 23–32.

Raynor, P., Smith, D. and Vanstone, M. (1994) *Effective Probation Practice*, Basingstoke, Macmillan.

Reason, P. and Bradbury, H. (eds) (2000) *Handbook of Action Research: Participative Inquiry and Practice*, London, Sage.

Reder, P., Duncan, S. and Gray, M. (1993) *Beyond Blame: Child Abuse Tragedies Revisited*, London, Routledge.

Rees, S. (1999) 'Managerialism in social welfare: proposals for a humanitarian alternative – an Australian perspective', *European Journal of Social Work*, 2, 2, 193–202.

Rees, S. and Wallace, A. (1982) *Verdicts on Social Work*, London, Edward Arnold.

Reiser, R. (ed.) (1995) *Invisible Children. Report of the Joint Conference On Children, Images and Disability*, London, Save the Children.

Reiter, S. and Levi, A. M. (1980) 'Factors Affecting Social integration of Non-institutionalised Mentally Retarded Adults', *American Journal of Mental Deficiency*, 85, 1, 25–30.

Resnick, H. (ed.) (1994) *Electronic Tools for Social Work Practice and Education*, New York, Haworth Press.

Revans, L. (2001) 'Party Politics', *Community Care*, 27 September–3 October, 34–35.

Rhodes, D. and McNeill, S. (eds) (1985) *Women Against Violence Against Women*, London, Only Women Press.

Richards, S. (2000) 'Bridging the Divide: Elders and the Assessment Process', *British Journal of Social Work*, 30, 1, 37–49.

Richardson, A. and Ritchie, J. (1989) *Developing Friendships: Enabling People with Learning Difficulties to Make and Maintain Friends*, London, Policy Studies Institute in association with Social and Community Planning Research.

Richardson, M. (1997) 'Reflection and Celebration – Neal (1960–1987): Narrative of a Young Man with Profound and Multiple Disabilities', *Journal of Learning Disabilities for Nursing, Health and Social Care*, 1, 191–195.

Roberts, C. (1989) *Women and Rape*, Hemel Hempstead, Harvester Wheatsheaf.

Rodger, J. J. (1991) 'Discourse Analysis and Social Relationships in Social Work', *British Journal of Social Work*, 21, 1, 63–79.

Roediger, D. R. (1994) *Towards the Abolition of Whiteness*, London, Verso.

Rogers, A. and Pilgrim, D. (1989) 'Mental Health and Citizenship', *Critical Social Policy*, 26, 44–56.

Rojek, C. (1986) 'The "Subject" in Social Work', *British Journal of Social Work*, 16, 1, 65–77.

Rooney, B. (1987) *Racism and Resistance to Change*, Liverpool, Merseyside Area Profile Group.

Rose, E. (1988) 'Art Therapy: A Brief Guide', *Adoption and Fostering*, 12, 1, 48–50.

Rose, N. (1985) *The Psychological Complex: Psychology, Politics and Society in England 1869–1939*, London, Routledge & Kegan Paul.

Rossiter, A. (1996) 'Finding Meaning in Social Work in Transitional Times', in N. Gould and I. Taylor (eds) *Reflexive Learning for Social Work*, Aldershot, Arena, pp. 141–151.

Rowe, J. and Lambert, L. (1973) *Children Who Wait: A Study of Children Needing Substitute Families*, London, Association of British Adoption Agencies.

Ruch, G. (1998) 'Direct Work with Children – The Practitioner's Perspective', *Practice*, 10, 1, 37–44.

Rusch, F. R. and Hughes, C. (1989) 'Overview of Supported Employment', *Journal of Applied Behavior Analysis*, 22, 4, 351–363.

Russell, D. E. H. (1984) *Sexual Exploitation: Rape, Child Sexual Abuse and Workplace Harassment*, Sage Library of Social Research, 155, London, Sage.

Russell, L., Scott, D. and Wilding, P. (1995) *Mixed Fortunes – The Funding of the Voluntary Sector*, Manchester, University of Manchester.

Rutherford, A. (1986) *Growing Out of Crime*, Harmondsworth, Penguin.

Rutherford, A. (1993) *Criminal Justice and the Pursuit of Decency*, Oxford, Oxford University Press.

Ryan, W. (1971) *Blaming the Victim*, London, Orbach and Chambers

Ryan, T. (1996) 'Risk Management and People with Mental Health Problems', in H. Kemshall and J. Pritchard (eds) *Good Practice in Risk Assessment and Risk Management*, London, Jessica Kingsley, pp. 93–108.

Ryan, T. and Walker, R. (1993) *Making Life Story Books*, 2nd edn, London, BAAF.

Sanders, A., Creaton, J., Bird, S. and Weber, L. (1997) *Victims with Learning Disabilities – Negotiating the Criminal Justice System*, Occasional Paper No. 17, Oxford, Centre for Criminological Research.

Sanderson, I. (2001) 'Performance management, evaluation and learning in 'modern' local government', *Public Administration*, 79, 2, 297–313.

Sanderson, I. (2002) 'Evaluation, policy learning and evidence-based policy making', *Public Administration*, 80, 1, 1–22.

Sassoon, M. and Lindow, V. (1995) 'Consulting and Empowering Black Mental Health System Users', in Femando, S. (ed.) *Mental Health in a Multi-Ethnic Society: A Multi-Disciplinary Handbook*, London, Routledge, pp. 90–106.

Satyamurti, C. (1981) *Occupational Survival*, Oxford, Blackwell.

Savage, S. P. and Atkinson, R. (eds) (2001) *Public Policy Under Blair*, Basingstoke, Palgrave,

Saxby, H., Thomas, M., Felce, D. and de Kock, U. (1986) 'The Use of Shops, Cafes and Public Houses by Severely and Profoundly Mentally Handicapped Adults', *British Journal of Mental Subnormality*, 32, 69–81.

Sayce, L. (2000) *From Psychiatric Patient to Citizen: Overcoming Discrimination and Social Exclusion*, Basingstoke, Macmillan.

Schalock, R. L. and Lilley, M. A. (1986) 'Placement from Community-based Mental Retardation Programmes: How Well do Clients do After 8 to 10 Years?', *American Journal of Mental Deficiency*, 90, 6, 669–676.

Schofield, G. (1998) 'Inner and Outer Worlds: A Psychosocial Framework for Child and Family Social Work', *Child and Family Social Work*, 3, 57–67.

Schön, D. A. (1987) *Educating the Reflective Practitioner: Toward a New Design for Teaching and Learning in the Professions*, San Francisco, Jossey-Bass.

Schön, D. A. (1991) *The Reflective Practitioner*, Aldershot, Arena (first published 1983).

Schorr, A. L. (1992) *The Personal Social Services: An Outside View*, York, Joseph Rowntree Foundation.

Schur, E. (1973) *Radical Non-Intervention*, New York, Prentice-Hall.

Scraton, P. (ed.) (1987a) *Law, Order and the Authoritarian State*, Milton Keynes, Open University Press.

Scraton, P. (1987b) 'Unreasonable Force: Policing, Punishment and Marginalisation', in P. Scraton (ed.) *Law, Order and the Authoritarian State*, Milton Keynes, Open University Press, pp. 145–190.

Seden, J. (1999) *Counselling Skills in Social Work Practice*, Buckingham, Open University Press.

Seebohm Report (1968) *Report of the Committee on Local Authority and Allied Personal Services*, Cmnd. 3703, London, HMSO.

Seed, P. (1973) *The Expansion of Social Work in Britain*, London, Routledge & Kegan Paul.

Segal, L. (1987) *Is the Future Female? Troubled Thoughts on Contemporary Feminism*, London, Virago.

Seiter, M. (1992) *Mental Retardation: Definition, Classification and Systems of Support*, Washington, American Association of Mental Retardation.

Shakespeare, T. (1998) 'Choices and Rights: Eugenics, Genetics and Disability Equality', *Disability and Society*, 13, 5, 665–681.

Sharp, H. (2001) 'Steps towards justice for people with learning disabilities as victims of crime: the important role of the police', *British Journal of Learning Disabilities*, 29, 88–92.

Shaw, I. (1997) 'Engaging the User: Participation, Empowerment and the Rhetoric of Quality', in A. Pithouse and H. Williamson (eds) *Engaging the User in Welfare Services*, Birmingham, Venture Press, pp. 1–20.

Shaw, I. and Shaw, A. (1997) 'Keeping Social Work Honest', *British Journal of Social Work*, 27, 6, 847–869.

Shaw, J. and Perrons, D. (eds) (1995) *Making Gender Work: Managing Equal Opportunities*, Buckingham, Open University Press.

Shearer, A. (1980) *Handicapped Children in Residential Care. A Study in Policy Failure*, London, Bedford Square Press.

Sheldon, B. (2001) 'Research Note. The Validity of Evidence-Based Practice in Social Work: A Reply to Stephen Webb', *British Journal of Social Work*, 31, 5, 801–809.

Sheldon, B. and Chilvers, R. (2000) *Evidence-Based Social Care*, Lyme Regis, Russell House Publishing.

Sheppard, M. (1990) *Mental Health: The Role of the Approved Social Worker*, Social Services Monographs: Research in Practice. Sheffield, Community Care/University of Sheffield.

Sheppard, M. (1995a) *Care Management and the New Social Work: A Critical Analysis*, London, Whiting & Birch.

Sheppard, M. (1995b) 'Social Work, Social Science and Practice Wisdom', *British Journal of Social Work*, 25, 2, 265–293.

Sherman Heyl, B. (1998) 'Parents, Politics and the Public Press', *Disability and Society*, 13, 5, 683–707.

Sidell, M. (1993) 'Death, Dying and Bereavement', in J. Bond, P. Coleman and S. Peace (eds) *Ageing in Society*, London, Sage, pp. 151–179.

Silberfeld, M. (1978) 'Psychological Symptoms and Social Supports', *Social Psychiatry*, 13, 11–17.

Silvestri, F. and Jue, K. (2002) 'Defining inclusive mental health services', in P. Bates (ed.) *A Resource on Social Inclusion, Citizenship and Mental Health*, London, Sainsbury Centre for Mental Health, pp. 29–33.

Sim, A. and Mackay, R. (1997) 'Advocacy in the U.K.', *Practice*, 9, 2, pp. 5–12.

Simms, M. (1988) 'The Health Surveillance of Children in Care – Are There Serious Problems?', *Adoption and Fostering*, 12, 4, 20–23.

Simons, K. (1997) *A Foot in the Door*, Manchester, National Development Team.

Simpkin, M. (1983) *Trapped Within Welfare*, 2nd edn, Basingstoke, Macmillan.

Singh, G. (1997) 'Developing Critical Perspectives in Anti-Racist and Anti-Oppressive Theory and Practice – Into the New Millennium', paper delivered at the National Organisation of Practice Teachers (NOPT) Annual Conference, University of Manchester Institute of Science and Technology, 9–11 July.

Siporin, J. (1988) 'Clinical Social Work as an Art Form', *Social Casework: The Journal of Contemporary Social Work*, 69, 177–184.

Sivanandan, A. (1982) 'From Resistance to Rebellion: Asian and Afro-Caribbean Struggles in Britain', *Race and Class*, 23, 111–152.

Sivanandan, A. (1990) *Communities of Resistance: Black Struggles for Socialism*, London, Verso.

Sivanandan, A. (1998/99) 'Globalism and the Left', *Race and Class*, 44, 2/3, 5–20.

Smale, G. and Tuson, G., with Biehal, N. and Marsh, P. (1993) *Empowerment, Assessment, Care Management and the Skilled Worker*, London, National Institute for Social Work.

Smith, C. and White, S. (1997) 'Parton, Howe and Postmodernity: A Critical Comment on Mistaken Identity', *British Journal of Social Work*, 27, 2, 275–295.

Smith, D. (1995) *Criminology for Social Work*, Basingstoke, Macmillan.

Smith, D. (1996) 'Pre-Sentence Reports', in T. May and A. A. Vass (eds) *Working With Offenders. Issues, Contexts and Outcomes*, London, Sage, pp. 134–156.

Smith, D. J. (1997) 'Ethnic Origins, Crime and Criminal Justice', in M. Maguire, R. Morgan and R. Reiner (eds) *The Oxford Handbook of Criminology*, 2nd edn, Oxford, Oxford University Press, pp. 703–760.

Smith, G. (1997) 'Psychological Resilience', in *Turning Points – A Resource Pack for Communicating with Children. Module 3 – Key Theories*, London, NSPCC, pp. 49–52.

Smith, G., Smith, T. and Wright, G. (1996) 'Poverty and Schooling: Choice, Diversity or Division?', in A. Walker and C. Walker (eds) *Britain Divided: The Growth of Social Exclusion in the 1980s and 1990s*, London, Child Poverty Action Group, pp. 123–140.

Smith, P. (1996) 'A Social Work Perspective', in R. Davie, G. Upton and V. Varma (eds) *The Voice of the Child: A Handbook for Professionals*, London, Falmer, pp. 49–60.

Smith, R. (1993) *Working Together for Better Community Care*, Bristol, School of Advanced Urban Studies.

Smith, S. R. (1999) 'Arguing against cuts in lone parent benefits: reclaiming desert ground in the UK', *Critical Social Policy* 19, 3, 313–335.

Smith, T. and Noble, M. (1995) *Poverty and Schooling in the 1990s*, London, Child Poverty Action Group.

Smith, T., Noble, M. with Barlow, J., Sharland, E. and Smith, G. (1995) *Education Divides: Poverty and Schooling in the 1990s*, London: Child Poverty Action Group.

Sobsey, D. (1994) *Violence and Abuse in the Lives of People with Disabilities: The End of Silent Acceptance?*, Baltimore, Paul H. Brookes.

Sobsey, D. and Varnhagen, C. (1989) 'Sexual Abuse and Exploitation of People with Disabilities: Towards Prevention and Treatment', in M. Csapo and L. Gougen (eds) *Special Education Across Canada: Challenges for the '90s*. Vancouver, Centre for Human Development and Research, pp. 199–218.

Social Care Institute for Excellence (SCIE) (2002) 'About SCIE', *Social Care Institute for Excellence Website*. <http://www.scie.org.uk/aboutscie/about.htm>.

Social Exclusion Unit (1999) 'What's it all about?', *Cabinet Office Website*. <http://www.cabinet-office.gov.uk/seu/index/faqs.html>.

Social Services Inspectorate (SSI) (1997) *Issues Emerging From Children and Families Overview Reports*, London, HMSO.

Social Services Inspectorate (SSI) (1998) *Report of an Inspection of the London Borough of Ealing*, London, Stationery Office.

Social Services Inspectorate (SSI) (2001) *Making it work: Inspection of welfare to work for disabled people*, London, Department of Health.

Soler, M. I., Shotton, A. C. and Bell, J. R. (1993) *Glass Walls: Confidentiality Provisions and Inter-Agency Collaboration*, The Youth Law Center, 114, Sansome St., Suite 950, San Francisco, CA 94104, USA.

Solomon, B. (1976) *Black Empowerment: Social Work in Oppressed Communities*, New York, Columbia University Press.

Spender, D. (1985) *Man Made Language*, 2nd edn, London, Routledge & Kegan Paul.

Spicer, D. (1995) *A Hard Act to Follow?*, Nottinghamshire County Council, Unpublished.

Stanley, N. (1999) 'User-Practitioner Transactions in the New Culture of Community Care', *British Journal of Social Work*, 29, 3, 417–435.

Staples, L. H. (1990) 'Powerful Ideas About Empowerment', *Administration in Social Work*, 14, 2, 29–41.

Statham, D. (1996) *The Future of Social and Personal Care*, London, National Institute of Social Work.

Stein, M. and Carey, K. (1986) *Leaving Care*, Oxford, Blackwell.

Stevenson O. (1972) *Claimant or Client?*, London, Allen & Unwin.

Stevenson O. (1981) *Specialisation in Social Service Teams*, London, Allen & Unwin.

Stevenson O. (1989) *Ageing and Vulnerability: A Guide to Better Care*, London, Edward Arnold.

Stevenson O. (1992) 'Social Work Intervention', *Child Abuse Review*, 1, 19–32.

Stevenson, O. (1995) 'Care Management: Does Social Work Have a Future?', *Issues in Social Work Education*, 15, 1, 48–59.

Stevenson, O. (1996) 'Emotional Abuse and Neglect: A Time for Reappraisal', *Child and Family Social Work*, 1, 1, 13–18.

Stevenson, O. and Parsloe, P. (1993) *Community Care and Empowerment*, York, Joseph Rowntree Foundation.

Stewart, G. and Stewart, J. (1986) *Boundary Changes: Social Work and Social Security*, London, Child Poverty Action Group.

Stowe, K. (1998) 'Compact on relations between government and the voluntary and community sector in England and Wales', *Public Administration and Development*, 18, 5, 519–522.

Sturges, P. (1996) 'Care Management Practice: Lessons from the USA', in C. Clark and I. Lapsley (eds) *Planning and Costing Care in the Community*, London, Jessica Kingsley, pp. 33–53.

Summit, R. C. (1983) 'The Child Sexual Abuse Accommodation Syndrome', *Child Abuse and Neglect*, 7, 177–193.

Swain, J., Heyman, B. and Gillman, M. (1998) 'Public Research, Private Concerns: Ethical Issues in the Use of Open-ended Interviews with People who have Learning Difficulties', *Disability and Society*, 13, 21–36.

Sykes, G. and Matza, D. (1957) 'Techniques of Neutralization: a Theory of Delinquency', *American Sociological Review*, 22, 664–670.

Szivos, S. (1992) 'The Limits to Normalisation', in H. Brown and H. Smith (eds) *Normalisation: A Reader for the Nineties*, London, Tavistock/Routledge, pp. 114–131.

Taylor, B. and Devine, T. (1994) *Assessing Needs and Planning Care in Social Work*, Aldershot, Arena.

Taylor, C. and White, S. (2000) *Practising Reflexivity in Health and Welfare Making Knowledge*, Buckingham, Open University Press.

Taylor, C. and White, S. (2001) 'Knowledge, Truth and Reflexivity: The Problem of Judgement in Social Work', *Journal of Social Work*, 1, 1, 37–59.

Taylor, G. (1993) 'Challenges from the Margins', in J. Clarke (ed.) *A Crisis in Care: Challenges to Social Work*, London, Sage/Open University, pp. 103–146.

Taylor, I. (1996) 'Reflective Learning, Social Work Education and Practice in the 21st Century', in N. Gould and I. Taylor (ed.) *Reflective Learning for Social Work*, Aldershot, Arena, pp. 153–161.

Taylor, I. (1999) *Crime in Context: A Critical Criminology of Market Societies*, Cambridge, Polity Press.

Taylor, I. (2000) 'New Labour and the enabling state', *Health and Social Care in the Community*, 8, 6, 372–379.

Taylor, M. and Langan, J. (1996) 'Map of the New Country: What is the Voluntary Sector?', in C. Hanvey and T. Philpot (eds) *Sweet Charity: The Role and Workings of Voluntary Organisations*, London, Routledge, pp. 22–38.

Taylor, M. and Lewis, J. (1997) 'Contracting: What does it do to voluntary and non-profit organisations?', in Perri 6 and J. Kendall (eds) *The Contract Culture in Public Services*, Aldershot, Arena, pp. 27–45.

Taylor, M., Hoyes, L., Lart, R. and Means, R. (1992) *User Empowerment in Community Care: Unravelling the Issues*, Studies in De-Centralisation and Quasi-Markets No. 11, SAUS Publications, University of Bristol.

Taylor, M., Langan, J. and Hoggett, P. (1995) *Encouraging Diversity: Voluntary and Private Organisations in Community Care*, Aldershot, Arena.

Taylor, R. D. W. and Huxley, P. J. (1984) 'Social Networks and Support in Social Work', *Social Work Education*, 3, 2, 25–29.

Thoburn, J., Lewis, A. and Shemmings, D. (1995) *Paternalism or Partnership? Family Involvement in the Child Protection Process*, London: HMSO.

Thomas, N. and O'Kane, C. (1998) *Children and Decision Making*, Swansea, International Centre for Childhood Studies, University of Wales.

Thompson, N. (1995) *Age and Dignity: Working with Older People*, Aldershot, Arena.

Thompson, N. (1997) *Anti-Discriminatory Practice*, 2nd edn, Basingstoke, Macmillan.

Thompson, N. (1998) 'The Ontology of Ageing', *British Journal of Social Work*, 28, 5, 695–707.

Thompson, N. (2001) *Anti-Discriminatory Practice*, 3rd edn, Basingstoke, Palgrave.

Thompson, N. (2002) 'Social Movements, Social Justice and Social Work', *British Journal of Social Work*, 32, 6, 711–722.

Thompson, N., Stradling, S., Murphy, M. and O'Neill, P. (1996) 'Stress and Organisational Culture', *British Journal of Social Work*, 26, 5, 647–666.

Thompson, N. and Thompson, S. (2001) 'Empowering Older People: Beyond the Care Model', *Journal of Social Work*, 1, 1, 61–76.

Thorpe, D. H., Smith, D., Green, C. J. and Paley, J. H. (1980) *Out of Care: The Community Support of Juvenile Offenders*, London, Allen & Unwin.

Tillich, P. (1960) *Love, Power and Justice*, Oxford, Oxford University Press.

Tinker, A. (1997) *Older People in Modern Society*, 4th edn, Harlow, Longman.

Tolsdorf, C. (1976) 'Social Networks, Support and Coping: An Exploratory Study', *Family Process* 15, 407–417.

Townsend, P. and Davidson, N. (1982) *Inequalities in Health: The Black Report*, Harmondsworth, Penguin.

Traustadottir, R., Lutfiyya, Z. M. and Shoultz. B. (1994) 'Community living: A multicultural perspective', in M. Hayden and B. Abery (eds) (1994) *Challenges for a service system in transition: Ensuring quality community experiences for persons with developmental disabilities*, Baltimore, Paul H. Brookes.

Trinder, L. (1996) 'Social Work Research: the State of the Art (or Science)', *Child and Family Social Work*, 1, 233–242.

Triseliotis, J., Borland, M. and Hill, M. (1998) 'Foster Carers Who Cease to Foster', *Adoption and Fostering*, 22, 2, 54–61.

Tully, B. and Cahill, D. (1984) *Police Interviewing of the Mentally Handicapped. An Experimental Study*, London, Police Foundation.

Tully, B. and Fritzon, K. (eds) (1996) *Resource Manual of Specialised Investigative Interviewing*, London, London Psychologists in Law Group.

Turk, V. and Brown, H. (1993). 'The Sexual Abuse of Adults with Learning Disabilities: Results of a Two Year Survey', *Mental Handicap Research*, 6, 193–216.

Twigg, J. and Atkin, K. (1994) *Carers Perceived*, Buckingham, Open University Press.

United Kingdom Central Council for Nursing, Midwifery and Health Visiting (1996) *Guidelines for Professional Practice*, London, UKCC.

Utting, W. (1997) *People Like Us: The Report of the Review of the Safeguards For Children Living Away From Home*, London, Department of Health/Welsh Office.

Vernon, J. and Fruin, D. (1986) *In Care: A Study of Social Work Decision Making*, London, National Children's Bureau.

Vernon, S. (1993) *Social Work and the Law*, London, Butterworth.

Walker, A. (1993) 'Poverty and Inequality in Old Age', in J. Bond, P. Coleman and S. Peace (eds) *Ageing in Society*, 2nd edn, London, Sage, pp. 280–303.

Walker, A. and Walker, C. (eds) (1997) *Britain Divided: The Growth of Social Exclusion in the 1980s and 1990s*, London, Child Poverty Action Group.

Walker, C. (1994) *Managing Poverty: The Limits of Social Assistance*, London, Routledge.

Walker, C. and Walker, A. (1998) 'Social Policy and Social Work', in R. Adams, L. Dominelli and M. Payne (eds) *Social Work: Themes, Issues and Critical Debates*, Basingstoke, Macmillan, pp. 44–55.

Walker, H. and Beaumont, B. (1981) *Probation Work. Critical Theory and Socialist Practice*, Oxford, Blackwell.

Walker, N. (1983) 'Childhood and Madness: History and Theory', in A. Morris and H. Giller (eds) *Providing Criminal Justice for Children*, London, Edward Arnold, pp. 19–35.

Walker, R. with Howard, M. (2000) *The Making of a Welfare Class? Benefit Receipt in Britain*, Bristol, Policy Press.

Walker, S. (1998) 'People with Learning Disabilities from Minority Ethnic Communities: The Identification of Cultural Issues That May Prove Relevant When Identifying, Reporting and Investigating Abuse', *NAPSAC Bulletin*, 22, 4–11.

Wallis, L. and Frost, N. (1998) *Cause for Complaint: The Complaints Procedure for Young People in Care*, London, Children's Society.

Walmsley, J. (1996) *Working Together for Change*, Workbook 3, K503 Equal People Course, Milton Keynes, Open University.

Ward, D. and Mullender, A. (1991) 'Empowerment and Oppression: An Indissoluble Pairing for Contemporary Social Work', *Critical Social Policy*, 32, 21–30.

Ward, H. (1995) *Looking After Children: Research into Practice*, London, HMSO.

Washington, J. and Paylor, I. (1998) 'Europe, Social Exclusion and the Identity of Social Work' *European Journal of Social Work*, 1, 3, 327–338.

Wasik, M. and Taylor, R. D. (1995) *Blackstone's Guide to the Criminal Justice and Public Order Act 1994*, London, Blackstone Press.

Waterhouse, L. and Carnie, J. (1992) 'Assessing Child Protection Risk', *British Journal of Social Work*, 22, 1, 47–60.

Watson, D. (2002) 'A Critical Perspective on Quality within the Personal Social Services: Prospects and Concerns', *British Journal of Social Work*, 32, 7, 877–891.

Waxman, B. F. (1991) 'Hatred: The Unacknowledged Dimension in Violence Against Disabled People', *Sexuality and Disability*, 9, 3, 185–199.

Webb, S. A. (2001) 'Some Considerations on the Validity of Evidence-based Practice in Social Work', *British Journal of Social Work*, 31, 1, 57–79.

Webb, S. A. and McBeath, G. B. (1989) 'A Political Critique of Kantian Ethics in Social Work', *British Journal of Social Work*, 19, 4, 491–506.

Weber M. (1947) *The Theory of Social and Economic Organisation*, New York, Free Press.

Weeks, J. (1985) *Sexuality and its Discontents: Meanings, Myths and Modern Sexualities*, London, Routledge.

Wenger, G. C. (1993) *Support Network Variation and Informal Partipation in Community Care*, Bangor, Centre for Social Policy Research and Development, University of Wales.

Wertheimer, A. (1992) *Changing Lives*, Manchester, National Development Team.

West, J. (1992) *Child-Centred Play Therapy*, London, Edward Arnold.

Westcott, H. and Cross, M. (1996) *This Far and No Further. Towards Ending the Abuse of Disabled Children*, Birmingham, Venture Press.

Whelan, R. (1996) *The Corrosion of Charity – From Moral Renewal to Contract Culture*, London, Institute of Economic Affairs.

Wilcox, B. and Bellamy, G. T. (1987) *A Comprehensive Guide to the Activities Catalog*, Baltimore, Paul H. Brookes.

Wilcox, D. (1994) *The Guide to Effective Participation*, London, Partnership Books.

Wilding, P. (1982) *Professional Power and Social Welfare*, London, Routledge & Kegan Paul.

Wilensky, H. (1964) 'The Professionalization of Everyone?', *American Journal of Sociology*, 70, 137–158.

Wilkinson, R. G. (1996) *Unhealthy Societies: The Afflictions of Inequality*, London, Routledge.

Williams, B. (ed.) (1995) *Probation Values*, Birmingham, Venture Press.

Williams, C. (1993) 'Vulnerable Victims? A Current Awareness of the Victimisation of People with Learning Disabilities', *Disability, Handicap and Society*, 8, 2, 161–172.

Williams, C. (1995) *Invisible Victims: Crime and Abuse Against People with Learning Disabilities*, London, Jessica Kingsley.

Williams, C. (1999) 'Connecting Anti-racist and Anti-oppressive Theory and Practice: Retrenchment or Reappraisal?', *British Journal of Social Work*, 29, 2, 211–230.

Williams, F. (1996) 'Postmodernism, Feminism and Difference', in N. Parton (ed.) *Social Theory, Social Change and Social Work*, London, Routledge, pp. 61–76.

Willmott, P. (1986) *Social Networks, Informal Care and Public Policy*, London, Policy Studies Institute.

Willow, C. (2001) *It's Not Fair! Young People's Reflections on Children's Rights*, London, Children's Society.

Willow, C. (2002) *Participation in Practice: Children and Young People as Partners in Change*, London, Children's Society.

Wilson, C. and Brewer, N. (1992) 'The Incidence of Criminal Victimisation of Individuals with an Intellectual Disability', *Australian Psychologist*, 27, 114–117.

Wilson, C., Seaman, L. and Nettelbeck, T. (1996) 'Vulnerability to Criminal Exploitation: Influence and Interpersonal Competence Differences Among People with Mental Retardation', *Journal of Intellectual Disability Research*, 40, 1, 8–16.

Wilson, E. (1977) *Women and the Welfare State*, London, Tavistock.

Wilson, G. and Dockrell, J. (1995) 'Elderly Care', in P. Owens, J. Carrier and J. Horder (eds) *Interprofessional Issues in Community and Primary Health Care*, Basingstoke, Macmillan, pp. 95–110.

Wilson, G. (ed.) (1995) *Community Care: Asking the Users*, London, Chapman & Hall.

Wilson, K. (2000) 'Commentary from an academic perspective', in H. Martyn (ed.) *Developing Reflective Practice: Making sense of social work in a world of change*, Bristol: Policy Press, pp. 75–85.

Wistow, G. and Barnes, M. (1993) 'User Involvement in Community Care: Origins, Purposes and Applications', *Public Administration*, 71, 279–299.

Wistow, G., Knapp, M., Hardy, B. and Allen, C. (1994) *Social Care in a Mixed Economy*, Buckingham, Open University Press.

Wistow, G., Knapp, M., Hardy, B., Forder, J., Kendall, J. and Manning, R. (1996) *Social Care Markets: Progress and Prospects*, Buckingham, Open University Press.

Wolfensberger, W. (1972) *Normalisation: The Principles of Normalisation in Human Services*, Toronto, National Institute of Mental Retardation.

Wolfensberger, W. (1980) 'The Definition of Normalisation: Update, Problems, Disagreements and Misunderstandings', in R. J. Flynn and K. E. Nitch (eds) *Normalisation, Social Integration and Community Services*, Baltimore, University Park Press.

Wolfensberger, W. (1983) 'Social Role Valorization: A Proposed New Term for the Principle of Normalisation', *Journal of Mental Retardation*, December, 234–239.

Woodroofe, K. (1962) *From Charity to Social Work*, London, Routledge & Kegan Paul.

Worden, W. J. (1991) *Grief Counselling and Grief Therapy*, 2nd edn, London.

Worrall, A. (1995) 'Equal Opportunities', in B. Williams (ed.) *Probation Values*, Birmingham, Venture Press, pp. 29–46.

Worrall, A. (1997) *Punishment in the Community. The Future of Criminal Justice*, Harlow, Addison Wesley Longman.

Worth, A. (2001) 'Assessment of the needs of older people by district nurses and social workers: a changing culture', *Journal of Interprofessional Care*, 15, 3, 257–266.

Yee, L. and Mussenden, B. (1998) 'Come in From the Cold', *Community Care*, 5–11 March, 26.

Yelloly, M. and Henkel, M. (eds) (1995) *Learning and Teaching in Social Work: Towards Reflective Practice*, London, Jessica Kingsley.

Young, A. and Ashton, E. (1956) *British Social Work in the Nineteenth Century*, London, Routledge & Kegan Paul.

Younghusband, E. (1978) *Social Work in Britain: 1950–1975*, vol. 1, London, George Allen & Unwin.

Youth Justice Board (2000) *National Standards for Youth Justice*, London, Youth Justice Board.

Yuval-Davis, N. (1994) 'Women, Ethnicity and Empowerment', in K. K. Bhavnani and A. Phoenix (eds) *Shifting Identities, Shifting Racisms*, London, Sage, pp. 179–197.

Name Index

Subject Index